The Child in the Family

JAY BELSKY
Pennsylvania State University

RICHARD M. LERNER
Pennsylvania State University

GRAHAM B. SPANIER
State University of New York at Stony Brook

 ADDISON-WESLEY PUBLISHING COMPANY
Reading, Massachusetts
Menlo Park, California
London
Amsterdam
Don Mills, Ontario
Sydney

D1475525

This book is in the Addison-Wesley Series
Topics in Developmental Psychology

Consulting Editor: Claire B. Kopp

Library of Congress Cataloging in Publication Data

Belsky, Jay, 1952–
    The child in the family

    1. Children—United States—Social conditions—
Case studies. 2. Children—Family relationships.
3. Parent and child. 4. Child development. 5. Family.
I. Lerner, Richard M.   II. Spanier, Graham B.
III. Title.
HQ792.U5B44   1984   306.8'74   83-12255

ISBN: 0-201-10147-5
BCDEFGHIJK-MA-8987654

To the children in our families

Daniel and Jesse Belsky
Justin and Blair Lerner
Brian Spanier

Preface

The 1970s were a time of great change in the social and the behavioral sciences dealing with human development. Time-honored approaches to studying child and adolescent development, the family, and socialization began not only to be seriously questioned but also challenged by newly emerging perspectives. These new perspectives—most notably, those labeled the life-span and human ecological perspectives—were marked by an emphasis on the physical and social context of human development (Bronfenbrenner 1977, 1979; Jenkins 1974; Lerner, Hultsch, and Dixon in press; Mischel 1977; Petrinovich 1979; Sarbin 1977). For instance, interest emerged in the fact that development is ongoing and that people live in a multileveled world consisting of their family, community, physical environment, and culture, all of which are mutually influential.

Several developmental thinkers maintained that as a consequence of these interrelations between people and their contexts, a potential for plasticity existed across the life span. Thus, developmental trajectories established at one phase of the life course are, at least in theory, susceptible to modification. Consequently, the constraints on development—for example as imposed by genes or early experience—were not as great as had been previously thought by advocates of noncontextual orientations (Brim and Kagan 1980; Lerner in press).

The basis of this book is this emerging intellectual perspective. We focus on what many scholars have identified as the key linkage between the developing person and his or her changing context: The child-family relationship (Belsky 1981; Lerner and Spanier 1978; Lewis and Lee-Painter 1974). Our goal is to describe key features of the reciprocal relations between infant, child, and adolescent development and changes in the family. Several key propositions, inherent in the life-span and ecological perspectives we adopt, will mark our presentation:

- Both children and the adult members of their families are developing organisms; as such, to understand child-family relations one must adopt a developmental perspective;

- Child development and family change are bidirectionally related. This means that children influence those who influence them; as such, children contribute to their own development;

- Children and their families are also reciprocally embedded in a broader ecology, composed, for instance, of the neighborhood or community, the work place, and of course the society and culture, which encompasses their general political and economic institutions and their symbols and values;

- Because of their being reciprocally linked to each other and to a changing ecology, there is a great potential for change—for plasticity—in human development. The presence of such plasticity offers considerable optimism about the potential fruitfulness of interventions aimed at enhancing the human condition.

PLAN OF THE BOOK

Our goal in this volume is to inform the reader about what is currently known of the child in the family. Toward this end we have divided the thirteen chapters of the book into five primary parts. Chapters 1 to 3 detail the conceptual foundations of the volume, starting first with an introduction to the life-span and ecological perspectives on human development.

In Chapter 2 we address the evolutionary basis of the child in the family; that is, we consider how changes in the ecology of prehistoric man and associated changes in the biology of early man converged to create a highly dependent human organism in need of high levels of parental care for which the family provided a structure. In Chapter 3 we change our focus from evolutionary to contemporary history, and look at the structure and functioning of the family and how it has changed over the past century, especially the past several decades. It is our contention that only when one realizes that the high levels of divorce, maternal employment, teenage parenthood, and reduced birth rates of today represent dramatic changes from the recent past can the development of the child in the family of today be understood.

Having provided the conceptual foundations of this inquiry into the child in the family in the first three chapters, we focus on the psychological and behavioral interior of the family in the five subsequent chapters that comprise Part II, Parent-Child Relations. Thus, in Chapters 4, 5, and 6 we consider, respectively, parental influence on child development during infancy, childhood, and adolescence. Then, in Chapter 7, we adopt a less chronological and more process-oriented approach to the general topic of parent-child relations as we consider ways in which children influence the care their parents provide. Our purpose here is to document the fact that the parent-child relationship is bidirectional in nature, with influence flowing from parent to child and from child to parent. We build upon this process of reciprocal influence in Chapter 8 when we consider research evidence indicating not only that parents and children affect each other, but that the nature and quality of the marital relationship shapes and is shaped by what transpires in the parent-child subsystem of the family. Our aim is to embed the study of the child in a family system perspective that emphasizes interdependent roles (parent, child, spouse) and relationships (marital, parent-child).

In Part III of this book, Families in Conflict, attention is turned away from what is known about the child's development in "typical" families to the study of children growing up in families in conflict. Thus, in Chapter 9 the nature and developmental impact of divorce becomes the central focus of inquiry, and in Chapter 10 we consider the prevalence, causes, and consequences of child abuse and neglect.

The final two substantive chapters of this volume, constituting Part IV, Contemporary Issues, address vital themes. In Chapter 10 the dual worker family is discussed, with special emphases on the effect of maternal employment on child development and the type, usage, and impact of supplementary, nonparental day care. In Chapter 12, teenage parenthood receives our attention, specifically its origins and frequency, and the impact it has on both the teenager who gives birth while still in the formative years of her own development and on the offspring raised by such an individual.

Finally, in Chapter 13, we make some concluding remarks about the material covered in the entire volume. We return to and underscore many of the major themes introduced in the first three chapters on conceptual foundations. We trust that this context will by then seem both logical and familiar to the student coming to the end of the book.

ACKNOWLEDGMENTS

Our work on this book was greatly facilitated by our previous collaborative scholarly endeavors—both among ourselves and with other colleagues—as well as by our respective solitary endeavors. We thank our many collaborators for all the stimulation they provided, and would like to mention Nancy A. Busch-Rossnagel, Frank Furstenberg, Jr., Paul C. Glick, David F. Hultsch, Jacqueline V. Lerner, and Judy Shea as meriting special thanks. Thanks also need to be extended to L. Alan Sroufe and Thomas Power for their thoughtful, and at times penetrating, critiques of the first draft of this volume. We should note that during the course of writing this book Jay Belsky was supported by grants from the National Science Foundation, The Division of Maternal and Child Health of the Department of Health and Human Services, the National Institute of Child Health and Human Development, and the March of Dimes Birth Defect Foundation; Richard M. Lerner was supported by a grant from the John D. and Catherine T. MacArthur Foundation. We are grateful for this support.

We also want to thank Lisa Caplan for assisting us with our editorial duties for the manuscript, and extend special gratitude to Joy Barger and Kathie Hooven for their excellent and professional secretarial and typing work. Finally—and most importantly—we are indebted to our children and our families for their constant love and support before, during, and after this project.

J.B.
R.M.L.
G.B.S.

Contents

PART I Conceptual Foundations

PART II Parent-Child Relations

PART III Families in Conflict

PART IV Contemporary Issues

Conceptual Foundations

<table>
<tr><td>CHAPTER

1</td><td># The Life-Span and Ecological Views of Human Development</td></tr>
</table>

As the title implies, the focus of this book is the child in the family. Why do the authors see it as crucial to consider child development in a family context? Although this entire book is, in a sense, an answer to this question, we should note that the perspectives we hold about human development require such a focus as a key to understanding human life. The two perspectives we hold—labeled the life-span view of human development and the ecological view of human development—combine to suggest that one cannot adequately understand the key features of child development unless the child is studied in the context in which he or she develops. This viewpoint, which has strong historical roots and thus has long been appreciated, has attracted renewed interest among students of child and family development. In particular, there are several key features of a contextual perspective that orient scholars in the field today. Four of these, briefly outlined here, will be further illustrated and elaborated on, as we proceed through the volume.

1. *There is a human ecology or context of human development.* This means that human existence is basically social (Tobach and Schneirla 1968), and that in their natural and typical condition humans exist along with other humans and with the products of human functioning. These products are the social institutions created by humans, such as the family, the economy, or the educational system (Bronfenbrenner 1979).

Unlike some animals, children are not born in isolation. Instead, human children are reared in the context of other developing people—

their parents, their siblings, their relatives, and their neighbors. Typically, the most significant of these child-other relationships exists in an institution that we commonly call the "family." Of course, the child and the family exist in a still broader ecology. And this wider social environment must always be kept in mind when considering the child in the family, since what goes on *beyond* the immediate boundaries of the family invariably affects and is affected by what transpires *within* the family. Consider, for example, how the safety of a neighborhood can influence the freedom parents grant their children in playing outside, away from the careful supervision of parents. Or, consider how child-rearing strategies might affect what goes on in the school. When parents are physically punitive and inclined to hit their children, the likelihood of children developing aggressive tendencies increases. Might it not be the case, then, that when schools are populated by children from families in which physical force is routinely used to exert control and settle parent-child and sibling disputes, such classrooms and playgrounds become more dangerous environments? Clearly the family affects the broader environment and is affected by it.

But it is not just the neighborhood and community contexts of child development that need to be considered in order to understand the child's development in the family. The broader sociocultural context, including the features of a particular historical period, plays an influential role in shaping a child's family experience and, thereby, his or her development. It is important to recognize also that the nuclear family typical of American society today has not always been the most common American family structure. Nor have cultural attitudes always encouraged the achievement of girls beyond the confines of the domestic family unit. Indeed, the extended family, in which children were exposed to people of a variety of ages on a more daily basis than they are today, was typical of the nineteenth century, and not until recently have girls on a large scale been stimulated to aspire beyond the traditional female role.

The point to be made, then, is that an appreciation of context is critical to gaining insight into child development. Since the family is the context in which children spend the most time and establish probably their most long-lasting and influential interpersonal relationships, it can be considered the most significant context of child development. While this alone would justify our interest in the study of the child in the family, there are other features of our life-span/ecological perspective that make this focus essential.

2. *Children and their families reciprocally influence each other.* Neither a child nor a family is a static entity. Children obviously develop, but so, too, do families. The structure of the family changes when additional children are added to it and when older children leave home. The functions of the family also change across the life-span of its members and across history. When a child is very young, the primary function of the family may be said to be *socialization*—the teaching of existing societal values to the new member of society—and provision of emotional support and nurturance. When the child is an adolescent or young adult, however, the family may serve as a source of social activities and of economic resources, such as helping to pay for the child's education or assisting him or her in launching his or her own family. In addition to changes in family functioning coordinated with the child's development, there are family changes that evolve in response to historical changes. The American family of the Revolutionary War era, for example, had as one of its major functions the production of economic resources—through farming or home-based "cottage" industries (like weaving); in contrast, the American family of today is primarily a resource-consuming unit.

The important message in our life-span/ecological perspective is *not* simply that changes occur at the level of the individual and of the family. Rather, the key feature of our perspective is that changes in each one influence the other: The child's development provides changes in the family and, similarly, changes in the family alter the child's development. Consider, for example, how a child's physical handicaps might limit the ability of parents to socialize outside of the home as much as they might like. The possibility certainly exists that such child-effects might place stress on the marriage and, thereby, the supportive care that parents can offer. Of course, changes in the marital relation or in the parents' behavior could arise from sources other than the child, such as the loss of a job by one spouse that altered the quality of the marriage. In any case, such familial changes are likely to influence the child—either *directly*, through the child's observation of them, or *indirectly*, through the effect they exert on processes of family functioning like marital and parent-child interaction.

In sum, developmental changes in the child affect changes in the familial context and changes in this context promote changes in the child.

3. *Children are producers of their own development.* Because children influence the world around them, and because this impact feeds back to influence them, children must be conceptualized as active agents in their own development. We do not mean to imply that children are themselves the only sources of influence on their development. Obviously, they are not. But, we should not overlook the fact that, in addition to parents, school, peer groups, the media, and other agents and agencies of influence, children play active roles in shaping the experiences they have and thereby contribute to their own growth and change.

This influence of the child is often intentional, as when a defiant child purposefully angers his or her parent and elicits more extreme punishment. But just as frequently, if not more often, the child's influence is unintended, as when his or her peer relationships create conflict between parents regarding how the child should be reared. Since children only gradually develop the capacity to intentionally manipulate others, it is quite likely that unintentional processes of influence outweigh intentional effects in their ultimate effect on the child's world and his or her own development.

4. *A multidisciplinary approach must be taken to studying children in their families.* Because children develop as a consequence of reciprocal interactions with their context, ·one must have knowledge of both children and their context. And since the context itself consists of many dimensions, a *multidisciplinary* approach to knowledge is crucial. In addition to psychology and sociology, then, we must appreciate economics, political science, history, anthropology, and even medicine and biology to fully understand child development in the family. After all, not only do the individual personalities and genetics of parents influence children (psychology, biology), but children and families are also affected by historical events like wars and depressions (history, economics), and more subtle social change, like the women's movement (sociology, anthropology). In fact, in our next chapter we discuss information from evolutionary biology and cultural and physical anthropology, information that allows us to understand the adaptive significance of the social nature of human functioning *and* the evolutionary bases of society, of the family, and of reciprocal child-family interactions.

CONCLUSION

We could say much more about the characteristics of our life-span and ecological perspectives about human development. It is enough to state at this point, however, that these perspectives suggest: (1) the need to conceptualize child development in a contextual manner; and (2) the centrality of the child-family relation. Indeed, the reciprocal interaction between child and family context not only underscores the potential for developmental change across life, since as the context changes so too can the individual, but this interaction also promotes the idea that human development is quite *plastic;* that is, is capable of considerable alteration over time. And this plasticity is of extreme significance to those hopeful of making positive changes in the world in which we live. Indeed, the implications of this plasticity are great. Since context shapes man and man shapes context, man can be regarded as a creative being possessing the ability, given the knowledge, to alter the course of individual lives. We should recognize that childhood does not represent the only time when such change and redirection are possible. Nevertheless, since the child is so rapidly developing during the opening years of life, childhood remains an ideal time to provide contexts capable of supporting optimal development, or to invest energies in manipulating contexts in order to encourage positive change.

2

The Evolutionary Basis of the Child in the Family

The notion of reciprocal relations between the individual and the context is a key feature not only of individual development, but also of the evolution of the human species, and of life more generally (Gould 1977; Johanson and Edey 1981; Lewontin and Levins 1978). Although much of the evolution of interdependent social relations has involved the family as *the* central institution of human development, the fact that the family as a social institution has itself evolved is not often recognized. In this chapter we discuss the social nature of human evolution; the role of the family in this evolution; and the evolutionary bases of human adaptation, bases which involve bidirectional relations between the developing child and the changing social world, especially the family. Subsequent chapters will build upon these ideas of reciprocal socialization, and of bidirectional relations between individual development and family change.

THE SOCIAL NATURE OF HUMAN EVOLUTION

Human development is both biological and social, since both biological and social adaptation are necessary if individuals are to meet the demands of their environment. Such adaptation is required because we must coexist with many others in our world who share everything from our natural resources to the space we live in to the food needed for sustenance.

Human evolution has involved an integration of biological and social functioning. To understand the nature of this synthesis it is necessary to discuss further the concept of "plasticity" introduced in

Chapter 1. *Plasticity* refers to the capability of an organism to show adaptive changes in its structure (e.g., the neural connections in its brain) or its function (e.g., the behaviors it has in its repertoire), or both, across the life span. Humans are the most plastic, or flexible, of all living organisms. That is, their development is least restricted by biogenetic programming and thus humans are capable of greater change than are all other forms of life. In fact, a key feature of the evolution of the human species is that individual development is characterized by morphological (i.e., structural) and behavioral (i.e., functional) changes allowing for considerable plasticity across life. The evolution of plasticity is relevant to a discussion of the social development of the human species, since the emergence of such flexibility was both a product and a producer of social behavior, which of course was required if humans were to function effectively in families.

Features of Human Evolution

To understand how the flexible nature of humans developed, and to appreciate its consequences for the family, we must consider changes that occurred in individual human development (ontogeny) over the course of man's evolutionary history. According to Stephen J. Gould (1977), a world-renowned scholar of evolution, evolution takes place when ontogeny is altered in one of two ways. First, evolution takes place when, at any stage of development, new characteristics are introduced into the organism that then have varying influences on later development. That is, if, as a consequence of a genetic mutation, a new characteristic for a species comes about, and if this new characteristic increases the organism's ability to survive, it will be this new characteristic that is passed on to future generations. For example, suppose only short-necked giraffes had existed, but, as a consequence of a mutation, long-necked giraffes had emerged; because giraffes are herbivorous (plant eaters) and have to compete with other herbivores for leaves, grass, and herbs that grow close to the ground, giraffes with long necks that could easily obtain leaves from trees would have had an advantage for survival. That mutation would have persevered.

The second way in which evolution occurs is when characteristics already present in the organism undergo changes in developmental timing, that is, the period during an organism's life when these characteristics emerge is altered. This second means by which species change is termed *heterochrony*. Specifically, heterochrony refers to changes in the relative time of appearance and rate of development for traits already present in evolutionary ancestors (Gould 1977, p. 2). To illustrate this concept, let us continue with our imaginary giraffes. Assume that long necks continued to be a characteristic of giraffes, but some giraffes reach the maximum neck length earlier in their development than others. If "earlier maturing" giraffes would deplete the available food supply before "later maturing" ones, obviously earlier maturing long-necked giraffes would have an advantage and would evolve. Thus, a characteristic already present—long necks—would appear earlier, and this change in *time of appearance* within the life-span would provide still another basis for the evolution of the species.

In human evolution, a specific type of heterochrony occurred that had important consequences for the development of human plasticity, and of the family. This type of heterochrony is labeled *neoteny* and involves a *slowing down* of the developmental process. It is currently thought that neoteny has been a major determinant of human evolution (Gould 1977). Specifically, by slowing down and thereby extending the period of rapid brain growth, which characteristically occurs before birth in higher vertebrates, from the prenatal period into the first postnatal years of life, neoteny served to increase brain size and the functional capacity of the human brain (Gould 1977, p. 9).

The implications of this delayed growth were profound for both the individual and the social group. First, and with respect to the individual, delayed growth caused the child to be exposed to the complex and intellectually stimulating social and physical environment outside of the womb at a time when the brain was still immature. These experiences dramatically enhance the learning capacity of the individual and provide the basis of the human species' remarkable plasticity.

But delayed growth did more than enhance human learning capacity. Most significantly, it created a less competent, more helpless organism. Whereas many animals are capable at birth of independent functioning, and others become independent over a relatively brief period of hours, days, or months, the human infant is strikingly limited in its skills for quite a long period of time. By making the child more dependent on others for its care and survival, neoteny in individual human development placed pressure on social groups to provide care for this evolving organism whose years of dependency were being extended. Without such special care, survival would have been virtually impossible. Quite possibly, it was just such pressure that played an important role in the establishment of family units, since families could guarantee a context in which the necessary increased and extended parental care could be provided.

Evolutionary pressures for the establishment of families may also have derived from the physical limits of humans to provide for their own self-defense. Since early man lacked fighting teeth, nails, and horns, but lived in open grasslands (called savannahs) that made him highly susceptible to attack from predators, group living and cooperation may have been essential for survival (Hogan, Johnson, and Emler 1978; Washburn,

1961). Indeed, from an evolutionary standpoint, it was probably more adaptive to act collectively by cooperating with others than to go it alone in isolation from the group. Accordingly, processes supporting social relations (e.g., attachment, empathy) probably were selected over the course of human evolution (Hogan, Johnson, and Emler 1978; Sahlins 1978). In this regard Lancaster and Whitten (1980, p. 15) have noted that humans

> can, then, accurately be described as cultural animals whose outstanding characteristics are sharing and reciprocity. The archaeological record, the study of modern primates, and the behavior of present-day hunter-gatherers all attest to the significance of those traits in human evolution. They led to that unique human invention—the family—the rock upon which all human experience is built.

Thus, in emphasizing the evolutionary and anthropological evidence supporting the notion that human functioning is social in nature, Lancaster and Whitten underscore a key idea of the present chapter: The family context is an important component of human functioning.

INDIVIDUAL AND FAMILY EVOLUTION: RECIPROCAL RELATIONS

Scientists who study fossil records (called paleoanthropologists) currently believe five characteristics separate man from other hominoids—a large brain; upright, two-legged locomotion; reduced front teeth with molar dominance; material culture; and unique sexual and reproductive behavior (e.g., of all primates only the human female's sexual behavior is not confined to the middle of her monthly menstrual cycle) (Fisher 1982). There is some dispute in modern anthropological theory, however, as to whether material culture or specific features of social relations, like intensified parenting or monogamous pair bonding, were primary in brain-behavior evolutionary relations. That is, some scientists believe that early human evolution was directly caused by brain expansion and material culture, whereas others believe that advanced brain development derived from an already established set of hominid characteristics that include intensified parenting and social relationships, monogamous pair bonding, specialized sexual-reproductive behavior, and bipedality (Johanson and Edey 1981; Lovejoy 1981). Despite this debate, consensus exists that the social functioning of hominids (be it interpreted as dyadic, familial, or cultural) was linked (i.e., reciprocally related) to the evolution of the human brain, irrespective of which came first. In other words, some connection is assumed by evolutionary biologists to exist between the unique social abilities humans developed and the expansion of their brains through the course of human evolutionary history.

To illustrate, Fisher (1982) notes that fourteen million years ago hominids were already exploring the expanding African woodlands and grasslands. During this period, the ancestors of humans (hominids) stopped living exclusively in trees and began to travel on four legs into the woodlands in order to search for food in low-limbed trees. On the basis of current observations indicating that chimpanzees use tools regularly, Fisher (1982) speculates that the most intelligent of these hominids may have employed sticks and stones as tools in order to pry up roots or smash nuts. Furthermore, she believes that hominids began to cooperate by coordinating efforts to hunt small animals, since this cooperation would increase the likelihood of gaining access to food. Fisher also notes that this form of cooperation, called "tolerated scrounging," is common among chimpanzees and baboons. Thus, the dependence of the individual on the group was supported, if not encouraged, by the enhanced likelihood that such social embeddedness (or interdependence) would lead to more food.

Two additional adaptive solutions other than tolerated scrounging had to be devised because the woodlands of that time were quite dangerous for relatively defenseless hominids (e.g., there was an abundance of tigers and leopards sharing the setting), and because the environment itself was changing significantly (fewer trees, with lower limbs, existed and stood further apart from each other). First, hominids began to travel in small, cohesive groups in order to protect themselves, and sticks and stones were picked up and thrown as "defensive tools" (providing a second basis for tool use). Fisher believes that despite the increase in group cohesion, which such adaptations stimulated and which was probably necessary for the emergence of families, male-female pair bonding did not exist (such relationship establishment is required to generate families as we know them). Instead, females had a monthly period of heat and males competed for the attention of estrous females. It was unlikely, she asserts, that at this time males aided females in caring for the young.

When, by about eight million years ago, the woodlands evolved into savannahs, the second major change was fostered among our hominid ancestors, one that led quite direcly to humans' neotenous brain of which we spoke earlier. Fisher (p. 20) describes this crucial change quite succinctly:

> Gradually, during the dry seasons, small groups of protohominids—the branch of hominids that leads to humans—must have been forced onto the plains, where life was even more dangerous; there were more open spaces, and even fewer trees to climb. By day, protohominids must have banded together, sleeping in trees or in protected, dried-up stream-beds at night. At this juncture, a major innovation occurred: Because of the dangers of savannah living, it seems that individuals soon discovered the practicality of gathering vegetables or small mammals and quickly carrying them back to a central location—perhaps to where they had slept the night before. They probably also discovered that sticks and stones were no longer available

every time they needed them, and that it was more practical to tote them as well. The innovation, of course, was carrying, and in order to carry efficiently they had to walk bipedally.

Because bipedalism was essential to survival in the savannah, it seems likely that this new upright stance evolved rapidly. Protohominids would never have evolved other human characteristics—such as bonding, kinship, language, culture, or a highly developed brain—if not for bipedalism. It is well known that bipedalism led, out of necessity, to major changes in the hominid skeleton. It seems a forgotten point, however, that a byproduct of that anatomical revolution was a reduction in the size of one, and perhaps two, major diameters of the pelvic inlet—the birth canal.

This structural change in the birth canal seemingly precipitated by upright walking, which itself was stimulated by the demands of the changing physical environment in which early hominids lived, significantly affected individual and family development. Specifically, reduction in the size of the birth canal created a major obstetrical difficulty because the head of the baby became too large to pass through it during the birth process. The evolutionary solution to this problem was a neotenous one—changing the timing of birth by having it occur earlier, at a time when the infant's head was less grown (in size) and thus could easily navigate the shrinking birth canal. This shorter gestational period increased the dependency of the now very immature human baby on others of its species, namely parents, and greatly extended the period of learning and, thereby, the plasticity of the organism. This increased dependency was a result of brain growth that extended into the postnatal period when the human organism would be exposed to an environment more complex and intellectually stimulating than that of the womb.

Implications for The Family

In certain respects, it was children, or at least highly dependent infants, whose prenatal development now extended into the postnatal period, that generated strong pressure for the emergence of pair bonding between man and woman, and with it the nuclear family. As Fisher (1982, p. 20) has argued, the presence of premature young left females with infants

requiring many extra weeks, even months, of care. Moreover, because mothers now walked bipedally, they had to carry their infants in their arms instead of on their backs. Females must have found it increasingly difficult to . . . chase after small animals, and join in hunting parties. Gone were the days when protohominid females could independently cope with their young.

In order to survive the female needed a mate, at least for the period of time following the birth of the infant when the mother was least able to fend for herself. Because of the press of this need, Fisher believes pair-bond relationships were developed, relationships that were advantageous not only to the mother and infant, but to the male as well:

Certainly an extended consortship provided tremendous benefits to females, but consorts may have been appealing to protohominid males as well—particularly in the dry season. By traveling with a mate, a male could share the nuts of one bush, the fruit of one tree, the eggs of one nest, and move on without waiting for a larger group. If he found no meat, he could depend on her to gather vegetables. During the consortship, he would not have had to compete with other males for sexual access to the female. Moreover, although he was unaware of it, if he attended to the offspring he sired by this female, they might live to pass on his genes. Thus males with even a slight predisposition to bond—to form an extended consortship—bred more, produced more offspring, and more of their young survived—spreading to each succeeding generation a disproportionate number of genes of both males and females with a tendency to bond.

In this fashion, bonding spread through the protohominid population (Fisher 1982, p. 21).

From the conjecture provided above, it is possible to envision a complex set of evolutionary relationships which coalesced to create a neotenous human born prematurely, with all the "handicaps" of such limited abilities, embedded in a social and familial context. Although Fisher's descriptions tend to cast these evolutionary relationships as if they progressed in a linear manner, with one development causing another and this other leading to a third, others view these developments from a more bidirectional, reciprocal perspective (Lovejoy 1981; Lewontin and Levins 1978). That is, it is not just that ecological changes led to social relationships, which in turn led to bipedalism and, in turn, to brain evolution. Instead, social relationships that led to brain evolution were then themselves altered when larger brained—and more plastic— organisms were involved in them. In turn, new social patterns may have extended the opportunities of humans into other arenas, thereby fostering further changes in the brain, in social relations, and so forth. Indeed, as Johanson and Edey (1981, pp. 325–326) describe it, Lovejoy's position is one that requires the examination of

> the mechanism of a complex feedback loop—in which several elements interact for mutual reinforcement. . . . If parental care is a good thing, it will be selected by the likelihood that the better mothers will be more apt to bring up children, and thus intensify any genetic tendency that exists in the population toward being better mothers. But increased parental care requires other things along with it. It requires a greater IQ on the part of the mother; she cannot increase parental care if she is not intellectually up to it. That means brain development—not only for the mother, but for the infant daughter too, for someday she will become a mother.
>
> In the case of primate evolution, the feedback does not just involve two elements whose influence moves from one to the other and vice versa. Rather, it involves many elements, all of them mutually reinforcing. For example, if an infant is to have a large brain, it must be given time to learn to use that brain before it has to face the world on its own. That means a long childhood. The best way to learn during childhood is to play. That means playmates which, in turn, means a group social system that provides them.

But if one is to function in such a group, one must learn acceptable social behavior. One can learn that properly only if one is intelligent. Therefore, social behavior ends up being linked with IQ (a loop back), with extended childhood (another loop), and finally with the energy investment and the parental care system which provides a brain capable of that IQ, and the entire feedback loop is complete.

It is important to emphasize that, on the basis of this conceptualization, all parts of the feedback system are considered to be cross connected. For example, if one is living in a group, the time spent finding food, being aware of predators and finding a mate can all be reduced by the very fact that one is in a group. As a consequence, more time can be spent on parental care (one loop), on play (another) and on social activity (another), all of which enhance intelligence (another) and result ultimately in fewer offspring (still another). The complete loop shows all poles connected to all others.

An illustration of this "complete loop," or system of reciprocal influence, is presented in Figure 2.1. This figure illustrates that the foundations of human plasticity and of the family evolved in a complex of bidirectional relationships among biological, individual, and social forces.

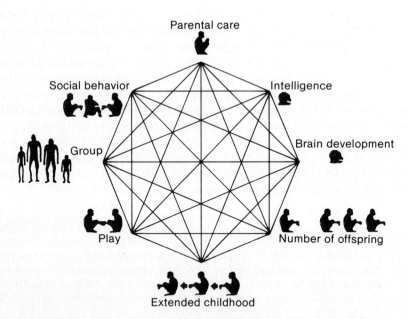

Figure 2.1 *Components of the system of reciprocal influences that Lovejoy believes was involved in the evolution human neoteny and social embeddedness.*

Source: Adapted from D.C. Johanson and M.A. Edey, *Lucy: The beginnings of humankind* (New York: Simon and Schuster, 1981), p. 327. Reprinted by permission.

CONCLUSION: FROM THE EVOLUTION OF THE FAMILY TO THE EVOLUTION OF SOCIETY

Social interaction has provided a combination of behaviors which allowed humanity to evolve, to be perpetuated and advanced, and therefore for social relations to be maintained. The structure of such social interactions may become institutionalized because they function to aid survival. In this way, society may evolve. A *society* is defined as any body of people living with a system of social rules governing the behavior of its people. But, as we have just seen that individuals need society for their survival, we will now see that society needs individuals as well.

As the settings within which humans lived changed and became more complex, more differentiated and complicated adaptational (survival) demands were placed on people. One social unit could not, for example, produce all the resources necessary for survival. Therefore, different units took on different roles, with some people becoming hunters, others cooks, others shepherds, and still others builders of homes or protectors of them. Role structure became more complex, more specialized, and more interpdependent as society evolved.

In order to assure that the roles maintaining society would be performed by people having the skills and commitments necessary for social survival, people began to engage in behavior to perpetuate the social order. One way to do this was to instruct children in the rules and tasks of that society in ways ensuring their eventual contribution to society's maintenance. As we noted earlier, the process by which members of one generation shape the behaviors and personalities of members of another generation is termed *socialization*; and one function of socialization is to ensure that there will be members of society capable of meeting the adaptational demands of people in that society. Although all societies teach their new members what to do, the precise attributes of what one has to do in order to survive will differ from one society to another.

In summary, society needs new individuals born into a social context that maximizes the likelihood of socially approved socialization. In order for society to survive, the new members must be committed to the society's maintenance and perpetuation. As such, society must assure that new members are efficiently and economically taught values that promote these goals. As a consequence, an institution is created in all societies that is the most efficient one for socializing new members. This core socialization unit is what we call the family, and it is given the function of bringing new members into the society within a context that ensures the stable continuation of the society.

As we have seen in this chapter, the emergence of the family in the course of human evolution was the result of a multiplicity of factors and processes. These included the physical environment in which man's evolutionary ancestors found themselves, biological changes in the birth process, as well as demands for gathering food and maintaining self-protection. In the same way that individuals and the families developed over macroevolutionary history, bidirectional processes of growth and change also characterize development within much shorter time spans, including individual and family histories. Several important changes which have taken place over the past several decades in the family are the focus of the next chapter.

The Changing American Family

Terms like "marriage" and "family," which we use every day, generate a great deal of discussion among scholars, and agreement over definitions is frequently difficult to achieve. Nevertheless, some family sociologists find it useful to consider the family as one *social system* located in the larger, more complex organization called society (Winch 1971). As a social system, the family can be studied in terms of its *structure*, the *functions* it performs, and the *interaction* found among its members.

> We can say that to qualify as a family. . .a social group must present differentiated positions, the relations among which bear designations of kinship. For example, a set of three actors bearing the designations of husband-father, wife-mother, and offspring would be recognized as a complete nuclear family. . . . This is a *structural* definition, and it leads to information answering such questions as to the make-up of the modal family of a society or of a sub-societal category.
>
> We can impose the requirement that to qualify as a familial system a social group must be engaged in one or more activities we recognize as familial, e.g., sexual gratification, reproduction, child-rearing. . . . This is a *functional* definition. A consequence of the functional definition is that we bring under scrutiny social systems not otherwise thought to be within the field of the family (Winch 1974, p. 23).

If we think of a family as a social group consisting of a husband, a wife, and children who carry out certain activities, what do we call a social group where there are no children? One parent? Or where there are all of the "required" persons but where certain traditional functions are not carried out? Winch (1971) argues that there may be different groups that some would consider families in which traditional familial functions are present but where structures are different (communes or group marriages, for example). Some groups that meet the structural definition of the family may be lacking function. This lack of function is characteristic, for example, of families on the verge of dissolution.

Alternative forms of marital or family relationships, then, are variations of or substitutes for traditional marriage or nuclear families. Winch (1971) uses the term *domestic family* to refer more generally to any family living in a single dwelling unit. A domestic family, therefore, could be a single adult or more than one adult who may or may not be legally married, with or without children, who perform many of the functions traditionally thought of as familial. With this attribute, we see that common residence is one other criterion that has traditionally been used to define the family. The term "household" can be used to designate this common residence. But this common residence is a limiting part of a definition of the family, since there may be some family structures that take up more than one household. Other cultures have been known to have families that live in more than one household (Eastern and tribal societies have a diversity of residential patterns), and very closely knit extended families in modern America fall within a definition of the family.

Family sociologists have debated whether the modern nuclear family is isolated from its network of kin. Although there appears to be a trend in this direction, proximity of kin still appears to be a major consideration in determining where a couple will live. Research also points to the great reliance on relatives for services, financial assistance, and other forms of material and emotional support. Despite modern-day mobility, it is surprising to find how many young couples resist the forces that might move them away from their families. In fact, most families still live within a short driving distance of relatives, some within walking distance.

THE ROLE OF THE FAMILY

The activity in a society is centered in its social institutions. A *social institution* is a part of society around which many of life's most important activities are organized. Examples of social institutions are the family, organized religions, the mass media, and the legal, educational, economic, and political systems. All social institutions change from time to time, and much of social change is based on the continuing evolution that can be seen in such institutions.

The social context of children is composed of other people (e.g., parents) and social institutions. Perhaps no social institution has as great an influence on development as the family. It is the basic social unit of society, encompassing reproduction, childbearing, and child rearing. Virtually all children in all cultures are socialized by families, although the form of the family unit may vary slightly. Thus, one way to define a family is as a unit of related individuals in which children are produced and reared.

In fulfilling its functions the present-day American family is confronted by new conditions and new demands. With increased urbanization there has been extensive proliferation of the number and types of groups, or aggregates, with which an individual may be affiliated (employees' union, PTA, Boy Scouts, church, and so forth). Some of these groups compete with the family for time, interest, support, and loyalty. Individuals are drawn away from the family in a great variety of directions, in contrast to earlier times when more demands were made on the individual by the family and less by "outside" groups. In today's society, for example, family commitments versus work demands may be a major source of marital conflict. These conflicting demands especially affect the modern woman, as more and more women enter the work force. However, both men and women often sacrifice family activities and commitments for the sake of career development, job security, and occupational status.

Nevertheless, from the standpoint of function, the family still has certain responsibilities that are usually thought of as services it provides for its members, especially children. These societal functions—the requirements necessary for a society to continue to exist—may be summarized as follows:

1. Replacement for dying members of the society.
2. Goods and services produced and distributed for the support of the members of the society.
3. Provision for accommodating conflicts and maintaining order, internally and externally.
4. Human replacements trained to become participating members of the society.
5. Procedures for dealing with emotional crises, for harmonizing the goals of individuals with the values of the society, and for maintaining a sense of purpose (Winch 1971, p. 13).

Some of these functions may be provided outside of the family. Children may be born to a woman who is not married; peer socialization takes place outside of the home, even though the family remains the central source of influence; and emotional support can come from a variety of sources, although that provided by parents to children, or children to parents, remains an important facet of family dynamics.

Historical Changes in the Family

Other societal functions include educational, economic, political, protective, and religious activities. Although the family plays a part in the performance of each of these functions, increasingly they are being taken over by institutions outside of the family. One example is found in the realm of education. Although parents play an important role in educating their children, more and more education is provided through formal schooling outside the home. Public school attendance, beginning at age five or six, is now virtually universal in the United States. Even at younger ages, large numbers of children attend preschools, nursery schools, Head Start programs, or some form of organized day-care program.

Similarly, the family's religious function has gradually shifted from the home to religious schools and churches. Contemporary American society has transferred the protective function, too, from the man of the house, who in colonial days was required to have firearms, to state and local police forces specially trained for this role. Even the recreational function has moved outside the home as we have come to rely increasingly on leisure opportunities created by a modern society: campers, spectator sports, golf courses, racquetball courts, tennis clubs, swimming pools, ten-speed bicycles, snowmobiles.

Probably the most striking change that has occurred to the American family over the past one hundred years involves its traditional economic function. As American society became industrialized, agriculture as a family enterprise diminished significantly. Today, the family farm that includes participating parents and children applies to only a tiny fraction of American society. Instead, most contemporary American children find that their economic role in the family is related primarily to consumption. Money is earned *outside* of the home, and the family's economic role is that of a spending unit.

One contemporary social scientist, Glen Elder (1974), has argued that the rise of industrialization, the passage of child labor laws, and legal requirements of compulsory school attendance have "conspired against" children by virtually denying them opportunities to contribute productively to the economic well-being of their families. Whereas children (especially males) were once perceived as economic assets (laborers in the family farm, business, and so forth), they are today more frequently perceived as financial liabilities. In fact, based on an analysis of child-rearing costs (food, clothing, housing, medical care, education, transportation, recreation, and other expenses) for a typical urban family in the United States, we can estimate that, in 1983 dollars, the eighteen-year costs of raising a child are approximately $80,000 to $100,000 (U.S. Department of Agriculture 1981). If we were to include the income not earned by mothers who leave their jobs to raise children, the costs of medical care during pregnancy and childbirth, and the expense of a college education, the figure would be substantially higher.

The family, then, is a structural unit that provides several important services to society. The most significant of these is related to children, who typically are reproduced, nurtured, and socialized as part of the family unit. In addition, the family confers social position on the child, gives the child his or her name, and often provides financial support through the college and young adulthood years. The family gives needed emotional support and plays a part in the education, religious training, and identity formation of the child.

Although social scientists emphasize the role of the parents and children in relation to each other, the family system is complex, and siblings and relatives in the extended family network may be quite influential in the overall socialization of the child. Many individuals upon reaching adolescence or adulthood are able to acknowledge the great impact in their development of a grandparent, aunt, uncle, brother, or sister.

The family, then, is the basic, nuclear unit in society. A society is composed of individuals. These individuals, however, are not entirely separate one from another. They occur and function as members of clusters of individuals. Some of these clusters are biologically produced and cohesive. The family is an outgrowth of both types of factors. The family is characterized by mutual aid and protection. It is an agency for the preservation and transmission of the cultural heritage of the group. In some cultures "family" suggests a structure different from that found in this country, but the central function is the same.

It is worth noting that the family also develops *parents*. As the family is a means of socializing children, so it is also a means of socializing adults. The opportunities for personal growth are as great in having children as they are in being children. Some parents contend, in fact, that not until the adoption of the parental role do they feel as if they truly are adults. In view of the financial and emotional responsibilities that parenting generates, we can easily understand how this social role exerts a maturing influence. Social theorists who speculate on the values of child rearing in the family versus child rearing by the state often base their arguments only on the welfare of the child. They do not think of parents and forget what might happen to them under some nontraditional scheme.

MARRIAGE AND THE FAMILY

The centrality of marriage and the family in the United States can hardly be disputed. Children are socialized for marriage from early childhood, and virtually all children, if asked, will say they intend to have children.

Such responses should not be unexpected, since television, school books, motion pictures, and the example presented by their parents suggest that marriage is expected. The mass media continue to confirm the centrality of marriage as the child matures. In America, where couples typically marry because they are in love, the great amount of attention devoted to love, romance, sex, and marriage has a powerful influence on individuals of all ages.

In some societies, marriages are arranged by parents, and the young persons who are involved in the union have little say in the matter. This practice seems highly unusual to most young Americans who believe that a marriage based on love cannot be created by individuals other than those in love. But marriage has different meanings. In some cases, an arranged marriage serves the important function of bringing two families together as much as it unites two individuals. Historically, marriages arranged amongst nobility often were strategically designed to prevent wars and create political alliances. In the society at large, economic considerations often were the primary determinants of marital relationships. Could the man be expected to support the bride? Would the union of two families bring financial benefits to each? The popular Broadway play, *Fiddler on the Roof*, which depicts life in peasant Russia in the last century, nicely portrays the role that love played—actually did not play—in marriages in traditional society. In one scene, Tevya, the husband, asks his wife of more than twenty years, Golda, "Do you love me?" After lengthy consideration, recalling the history of her marital bond, she concludes, "I suppose I do." What is apparent in watching this play is how small a role romantic feelings actually played in the establishment, and maintenance, of marital bonds. Life was demanding and survival was uncertain. A mate was conceptualized then as a partner who would hopefully make life easier and more certain. If that mate made life enjoyable, well, that was a fringe benefit.

The modern American system of dating, courtship, and marriage is different from that found in many traditional, less industrialized societies. The process leading to marriage has also changed considerably over the years. Many of these changes, which we discuss later, have come about because of the increasing importance of the marriage relationship. Although parent-child, sibling, peer group, and employee-employer relationships are considered important to most persons, it is the marriage relationship that captures our greatest interest. Only in rare cases do persons marry because they want to have children, or terminate a relationship because they are unable to. Although many couples eventually have children, the primary motivation to marry is likely to center on the rewards and satisfactions they expect to receive from a love-based, intimate relationship.

Why has marriage become increasingly important in America? For one, as our society has become more modern, technological, and urbanized, it also has become more impersonal. The rapidity of communication created by television and telephones, and the mobility of people traveling by automobile and airplane, has made America a fast-paced, forward-looking country. In a given day, most of us encounter dozens or even hundreds of persons. Contrast this with the society of colonial Americans, or the society of the post-Civil War farmer. In these earlier times, often only family members would be encountered in a given day. The impersonality fostered by our contact with hundreds of persons whom we never will really know has made marriage an even more important place for us to develop the close personal relationships most of us need.

Thus, marriage has taken on a greater role in the emotional gratification of its partners (Winch 1971). This important function was always a part of marriage in America, but it may become increasingly so. Contrast this situation with family functions that are declining in the family, such as educational and religious roles. Interestingly, the decline in these other functions has not influenced modern American marriage as much as the demands placed upon it by affectional and emotional needs. We expect a lot from marriage. The inability of many partners to meet this expectation undoubtedly contributes to our very high divorce rate.

Quality and Stability of Marriage

When trying to determine if the increase in divorce, which we will chronicle shortly, means that contemporary marriages are less happy than those of earlier generations, we must distinguish between marital stability (whether or not a marriage remains intact) and marital quality (how well an intact marriage is working). Marital stability indicates *outcome*, whereas marital quality relates to *process*, a couple's happiness *in* their relationship. This distinction helps us understand the argument that the quality of marital relationships has not changed, only stability. In his analysis of historical changes in the family, Goode (1963) argued that Americans have always looked back to the "classical family of Western nostalgia," but that this is a mirage. Even in 1960, a year when the divorce rate was only a fraction of what it is now, it excited alarm. One may wonder if there was ever or will ever be a time when the divorce rate will be viewed without alarm, and not defined as a threat to the institution of the family.

Numerous examples from nineteenth century literature, from Bronte's *Jane Eyre* to James's *The Ambassadors*, document the tragedy of marriages that remain intact structurally, yet have failed from the perspective of quality. Now, as then, marriage can be a source of both comedy and tragedy. The difference is that Americans are now more likely to seek divorce when a marriage is unhappy. This difference has oc-curred because much of the social stigma associated with divorce has dis-appeared (although it has not vanished entirely).

Although barriers to divorce have always existed, they have become much less formidable. Religious doctrine, for example, has diminished as a barrier to divorce. Furthermore, the need to maintain an appearance of marital stability for social reasons is less important today than a genera-tion ago. No-fault divorce laws have made it easier to obtain a divorce. There is also greater willingness on the part of women to leave a marriage that is intolerable to them because of physical or emotional abuse. This may be due to women's increasing financial independence and their sense of economic self-sufficiency. While all these changes have influenced marital stability, evidence that demonstrates marital quality has changed is difficult to find.

Trends in Marriage

The family seems likely to endure as long as marriage continues to re-main attractive. Young adults of today seem as committed to marriage as ever, but with one difference—the average age at first marriage has been delayed. The median age at first marriage is now about twenty-four years for males and about twenty-two years for females (U.S. Bureau of the Cen-sus 1980). This is an increase of nearly two full years since the 1950s. One reason that marriage may be postponed relates to the state of the economy (Davis 1972). Some young couples may not be financially secure enough to launch a marriage.

Perhaps the most persuasive argument centers around the increased freedoms experienced by young adults today. Many men and women become sexually experienced before the end of their adolescence, therefore the need for a sexual partner is less pressing. In addition, effec-tive methods of contraception virtually eliminate the chance of un-wanted pregnancies, which were fears and realities that in the past forced some early marriages. The phrase "shotgun wedding," which character-ized this situation, is rarely heard today.

Although the average age of marriage is increasing, we should note that this figure has always been greater for those at higher educational levels, and our population is becoming more highly educated. Thus, some marriages may be postponed because of specialized training, including undergraduate or graduate schooling. The increased movement of women into professional careers, and their associated economic independence and mobility, also works to delay some marriages.

Despite impressions in the media to the contrary, the proportion of teenage marriages has declined over the past decade (see Figure 3.1). Those who do marry in their teens, however, increase the prospect for divorce substantially. For example, women who marry at ages fourteen to seventeen are twice as likely to divorce as women who marry at ages eighteen or nineteen, who in turn are one and one-half times as likely to divorce as women who marry in their early twenties (Spanier and Glick 1981). Men who marry in their teens are about twice as likely to divorce as men who marry in their twenties. Premarital pregnancies, interrupted educations, parental opposition to the marriage, and lack of economic resources are undoubtedly related to the strong connection between age at marriage and marriage stability.

Nevertheless, marriage is still the norm in this society and is likely to continue so. In 1980 alone, nearly five million persons married, and the marriage rate continued a climb that began in 1976 (National Center for Health Statistics 1981a). The rate had declined through the first half of the decade, due in part to postponement of marriage for many individuals (see Figure 3.2).

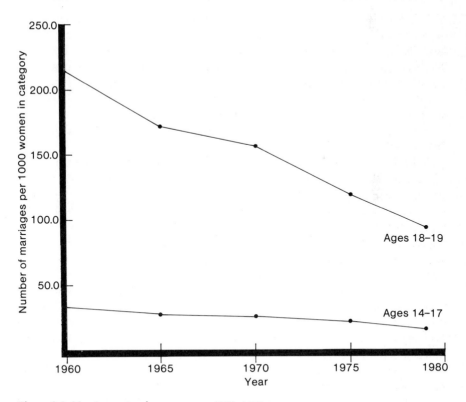

Figure 3.1 *Marriage rates for teenagers, 1960–1979.*

Source: National Center for Health Statistics, *Monthly Vital Statistics Reports,* "Advance Report: Final Marriage Statistics" (various nos.).

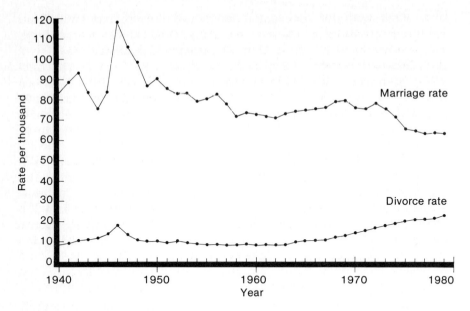

Figure 3.2 *Marriage and divorce rates of U.S. women 1940–1979.*

Source: National Center for Health Statistics, *Monthly Statistics Reports,* "Advance Report: Final Marriage Statistics" (various nos.).

Divorce Trends

Of all the trends relating to the family, none has had so profound an impact as the upturn in the divorce rates. Approximately 1.2 million divorces are now granted each year, involving more than 2.4 million adults and about 1.2 million children (Spanier and Glick 1981). (Some 50 million married couples reside in the United States.) Thus, divorce touches many lives every year. Although the increase in divorce seen during the past two decades (the rate has more than doubled) has finally slowed (see Figure 3.2), there is no evidence to suggest that the divorce rate will do anything other than level off. It is not likely to turn downward to any significant degree.

Projections based on Census Bureau and Vital Statistics Bureau data, and assumptions that future divorces will remain relatively constant, suggest that about one half of all first marriages formed in recent years are likely to end in divorce (National Center for Health Statistics 1980). Considering separation, divorce, remarriage, and redivorce, it is likely that a majority of all marriages among young adults today will not remain intact.

Numbers of this magnitude seemingly challenge the notion of family stability. One wonders how the future of the family can be assured when more than one half of all families are broken by separation or divorce. An optimist might note that approximately one half of those who divorce do so relatively early in their marriage, often before they have children. These divorced individuals may still look forward to a "traditional" family life following remarriage, with little obligation to a spouse from an earlier relationship. Moreover, many divorced persons with children develop acceptable, sometimes innovative, ways of coping with their disrupted status, and the concept of the family may still be maintained for them. The pessimist would point to the emotional, financial, and social damage that can be done by divorce, and there can be little argument with such an assessment.

Consider an important point for objectively evaluating the future of the family, obvious to some but missing from most discussions about the family: divorce is a response to an unsuccessful marriage relationship in which the spouses reject each other; *they are usually not rejecting the idea of marriage or the family per se*. Thus, divorce is not so much a statement about the viability of married life or about family stability, but rather a realization of poor mate selection, lack of personal commitment, disenchantment with one's partner, or some other personal or social problem surrounding a particular relationship. Persons approaching divorce usually report that they are no longer in love, that they have grown apart, or that they do not get along with each other anymore.

Who gets divorced? Divorce does not affect all social groups equally. Divorce rates are higher for blacks than for whites. Generally speaking, the higher the educational level, the lower the divorce rate. One interesting exception is women with graduate degrees; they have a disproportionately high divorce rate, due perhaps to increased economic security and social independence (Houseknecht and Spanier 1980). Although divorce occurs with couples of any age and circumstance, those who divorce tend to do so relatively earlier in their marriages. The peak period for divorce is two to five years after the marriage, a statistic that has not changed much (U.S. Bureau of the Census 1976). Given the time required to make the decision to divorce, separate, file, and wait for a final decree, this peak reflects evidence of serious marital problems very early in a relationship.

Examination of profiles of couples least likely to divorce shows the wife getting married in her late twenties, with only a bachelor's degree. The husband would be college educated as well and would have married no earlier than his late twenties. The couple would be white, upper-middle class, with two boys, or a boy and a girl, the oldest child born a few years after the wedding. Chances of divorce would be lessened further if they lived away from a large metropolitan area; if they were of the same religion; and if they went to church regularly (Spanier and Glick 1981). Recognize, though, that even this idealized couple is not immune from the possibility of divorce!

Remarriage Trends

The data on remarriage say more to some social scientists than do the data about marriage or divorce. Approximately 25 percent of divorced persons remarry within the first year following the termination of the marriage (U.S. Bureau of the Census 1976). Even though many recently divorced persons claim to be "soured" on marriage for a time after their divorce, one half have changed their minds and married again within three years (U.S. Bureau of the Census 1976).

CHILDREN AND PARENTHOOD

A generation ago, virtually all married women wanted children and had them, either through their own childbearing or adoption (Dejong and Sell 1975). Since that time, however, an increase in voluntary childlessness among women under thirty has developed (Dejong and Sell 1975). Nevertheless, the overwhelming majority of women still wish to have children, and there is no evidence to suggest that parenthood is going out of style. The decline in the birth rate seen in the United States in the early 1970s, for example, appears to have been due, in part, to the postponement of age at marriage, or a postponement in the age at birth of first child. Figure 3.3 indicates that despite an overall downward trend, the birth rate actually increased significantly between 1975 and 1980, after reaching an all-time low (National Center for Health Statistics 1981a).

Birth Rates

What about the overwhelming majority of couples who do become parents? A great deal of research indicates that young married couples desire fewer children than did couples in previous years, and that because of their more effective contraceptives, they succeed in reducing the size of their families. About three-fifths of all married women under the age of forty expect to have two or fewer children during their lifetime. This percentage is even higher for women who were in their late teens and twenties five to ten years ago, and are now completing their childbearing (U.S. Bureau of the Census 1978).

There are more than 3.5 million births in the United States each year. The birth rate in 1980 was 16.2 births per 1000 population. A look at birth rates during the twentieth century shows that the rate dropped to a low point in the 1930s, during the depression years, and then reached an all-time high following World War II. The "post-war baby boom" is an expression which refers to the relatively high period of fertility that followed the conclusion of the war, which began in 1945 and ended in the early 1960s, when the rate began to drop (National Center for Health Statistics 1981a).

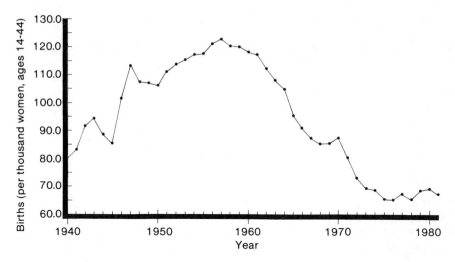

Figure 3.3 *Fertility rate of U.S. Women 1940–1981.*

Source: National Center for Health Statistics, *Monthly Vital Statistics Report* (various nos.).

As Figure 3.3 indicates, the birth rate declined through the 1960s and the first half of the decade of the 1970s, reaching a new low of 14.8 births per 1000 population in 1975. The rate then began a steady and pronounced increase between 1976 and 1980 (National Center for Health Statistics 1981a, 1981b). It is argued by demographers that the recent increase in the birth rate is actually due to postponement of births following marriage, and postponements of first marriages. On the other hand, the increase is also undoubtedly related to a growing interest in having children among recently married individuals. Perhaps parenthood was just not as attractive to those who entered adulthood in the 1960s and early 1970s.

Evidence that supports the idea that many women postponed their first pregnancies comes from the U.S. Bureau of Vital Statistics (National Center for Health Statistics 1982b). It is reported that more than 115,000 births in 1979 (the most recent year for which complete data are available on this topic) were to mothers in their thirties who were having their first child. This number represents a dramatic 73 percent increase from 1975, and more than twice as many as in 1970. The steady increase in first-birth rates for these women has occurred at a time when birth rates for women of other ages have either fallen or not changed significantly.

This trend can be highlighted by noting that the proportion of women aged twenty-five to twenty-nine who are unmarried nearly doubled during the 1970s. For example, for women born in 1950, 25 percent had had no children as of the end of 1979, compared with just 14 percent who were in this situation a decade earlier (National Center for Health Statistics 1982b).

In 1979, there were about 600,000 births to unmarried women, an increase of 10 percent over the previous year, and part of a trend of some years' duration. The increase has applied to both blacks and whites, although the increase is greater for whites. It should be noted that the increases in births to unmarried women reflect another factor, which is the growth in the number of unmarried women of childbearing age (National Center for Health Statistics 1981a).

Although part of the dramatic decrease witnessed in the 1970s can be attributed to a delay in marriage and childbearing among some women, the greatest part of the decrease is undoubtedly due to an actual desire among women to have fewer children than did women in previous generations. It is probably safe to say that the two-child family is becoming the norm in America and will likely remain so for some years to come. The tolerance for childless marriages and one-child families is increasing, too. Only a very small number of young couples expect to have more than three children. Part of the trend to smaller families may be due to the increased economic burden of child rearing. Since every decision to have an additional child means a decision to have a lower standard of living, many couples are weighing each childbearing decision very carefully.

Another trend that can be ascertained from research is the postponement of childbearing after the wedding. In earlier times, couples were expected to begin their families shortly after they were married. If several years passed without a pregnancy, the couple was often subjected to pressures from within the family, or a fertility problem was suspected. In modern America, most couples who are not confronted with a premarital pregnancy decide to wait a while before beginning their family. This is easily accomplished through the use of effective contraception. It is not uncommon for couples to wait several years.

Statistics show that traditionally blacks have higher fertility rates than whites, and that Roman Catholics have higher fertility rates than Protestants, who in turn have higher rates than Jews. These same comparisons also apply to the effectiveness of contraceptive use in these groups. About a decade ago, data from the National Fertility Studies began to suggest that while these differences still exist, they are diminishing. It is concluded that "American couples have changed their reproductive behavior radically . . . adjusting their fertility goals sharply downward, and increasing substantially their ability to stop childbearing at the wanted level. All parts of the population have shared in these developments, particularly those whose performance previously deviated most from the national averages (blacks and Catholics)" (Ryder and Westoff 1972). These trends have continued into the 1980s.

Family Size

Not only are women waiting longer before having children, but they are also having fewer children altogether. Figure 3.4 details graphically the percentage of families in the United States bearing zero, one, two, three, or four or more children from 1948–1981. Women now in their child-bearing years on the average desire two children (U.S. Bureau of the Census 1983). Given advances in contraceptive technology, effectiveness of contraceptive use, and reliance on voluntary sterilization (tubal ligation of vasectomy) among married couples who have completed their childbearing, today's women are much more likely than any time earlier in history to achieve their desired family size.

It is also likely that high divorce rates contribute to small family sizes, since many women interrupt their childbearing because of a divorce; often they do not have as many children during their lifetime as they would have had they not divorced. Other factors contributing to small family size are the movement of more women into the work force and an increased desire for a flexible lifestyle.

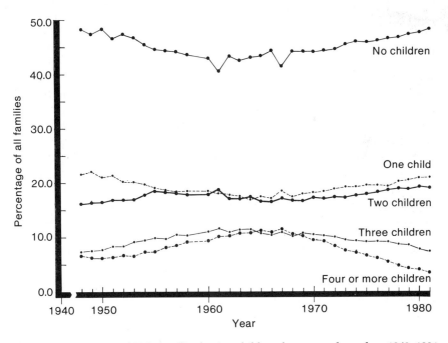

Figure 3.4 *Percentage of U.S. families having children, by year and number, 1948–1981.*

Source: U.S. Bureau of the Census, *Current Population Report* "Household and Family Characteristics" Series P-20 (various nos.).

Children and Divorce

Much of society's uneasiness with regard to family instability stems from its concern about children. About two of every five divorcing couples have no children under eighteen years of age when they divorce; three in five couples have at least one child (Spanier and Glick 1981). During the late 1970s, on the average, two children were involved in each divorce in which there were children under the ages of eighteen years. The impact of family disruption on children cannot be ignored. Psychologists such as Hetherington (1979) have summarized the problems children sometimes face following divorce—psychological stress, economic hardship, guilt, and discontinuity in parent-child relations, to name just a few (see Chapter 9).

On the other hand, Hetherington and other family experts suggest that it is far better for a child to grow up in a loving home with one parent than in a battleground with two. Some experts also point out that children are remarkably resilient, often showing an uncanny ability to survive oppressive family situations (Hetherington 1979). This has been demonstrated many times by children who appear well adjusted and seemingly unscarred by their family experience. There seems to be some truth in all of these assertions, but the data are not clear enough yet.

Single-Parent Families

The number of single-parent family households maintained by a man or woman increased substantially during the 1970s (see Figure 3.5). The dramatic increase during the decade in divorce and separation rates, as well as in the rate of births outside of marriage to females in their teens, has resulted in a rapid growth of one-parent households. Approximately three-fourths of white children and 94 percent of black children born out of wedlock are kept by their mothers (Zelnik and Kantner 1978). Households maintained by a man with children but no wife present increased by more than 60 percent, and households maintained by a woman with children but no husband present nearly doubled (U.S. Bureau of the Census 1980). This increase involves women of all races and classes. During the same time period, households maintained by married couples actually declined slightly, to 62 percent of all households.

There is a popular belief, spurred no doubt by recent movies such as *Kramer vs. Kramer* and affectionately written feature stories in newspapers and magazines, that a greater proportion of children are living with their fathers than ever before. Actually, the proportion of children living only with dad has remained small over the decade. Although the number of children living with only their father increased by about one-third between 1970 and 1979, from 747,000 to 997,000, the proportion of all children living with their father but not their mother still remains below two percent (Spanier and Glick 1981; U.S. Bureau of the Census 1980). By

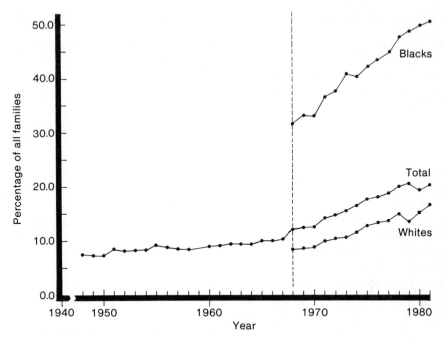

Figure 3.5 *Percentage of all families with own children under 18 maintained by only one parent: 1948–1981.*

Source: U.S. Bureau of the Census, *Current Population Reports* Series P-20 (various nos.).

contrast, 17 percent of children live only with their mothers. Only about one-tenth of the children living with a currently divorced parent live with their father; this percentage is about the same as it was in 1960. This is likely to change in the next decade, although slowly, and mostly among the middle and upper-middle classes.

There is some debate about the relative merits for the children of single-parent fatherhood versus single-parent motherhood, although Hetherington (1979) has found that there is little continuity between the quality of pre- and post-separation parent-child interaction, and particularly so for fathers. This finding challenges the assumptions behind the historical judicial guidepost known as the "tender years doctrine," a tradition of awarding young children to their mothers.

CONCLUSION: DIVERSITY OF LIFESTYLES

Apart from the documented rise in unmarried couples, it is interesting to examine the threats other lifestyles pose to the future of the family. It would be difficult to make a case that any form of interpersonal union, household arrangement, or family alternative is likely to replace the family as it is known for at least decades to come.

There is greater tolerance today of alternatives than ever before, as we have chronicled in this chapter. Indeed, most people have some acquaintances who are never married, separated, divorced and remarried, or living together outside marriage. Without too great a search, one can find examples of communal living, group marriage, homosexual couples, or single-parent adoptions. Yet those variations that are most common (remarried couples, for example) actually build upon the structure and function of marriages and families as they are typically defined. And those alternatives that depart most significantly from a reliance on traditional marriage and family structures (the commune, for example) are rare.

History tells us that alternatives to the family have always existed in the United States, but have never attracted large numbers. Communal living was the way of life for the Shakers, Hutterites, Moravians, and the Oneida community. Most contemporary communes are short-lived unless they have a strong ideological basis for their existence. Even then, they may face great challenges to their stability. Similar challenges are faced by other alternative living arrangements. We have no basis to expect the situation will change in the near future.

If the institution of the family changes in the future, the change is not likely to be found in its structural arrangements or in its functional tasks. Change will most likely occur in the dynamics of family interactions. In fact, family relationships will change as the times change. Family members will have to act toward each other differently, to meet each other's needs better than they have in the past, to communicate better about those needs, and to change their habits to perform more adequately the familial function—emotional support—that has become dominant in recent decades.

Having considered the broad historical and sociological context in which the family exists today, we next turn our attention, in Part II, to parent-child relations.

Parent-Child Relations

CHAPTER 4

Infancy: Parental Influences

To even the most casual observer it is strikingly apparent that families vary immensely in the manner in which they rear their children. For some parents comforting a distressed infant is considered essential to the provision of quality care. In other households, however, such a response would be regarded as spoiling the baby. With older children, some parents strictly punish a child's misbehavior, whereas others openly tolerate transgressions. Even when punishment is administered, it can take a variety of forms, ranging from the denial of privileges to scolding to severe physical beatings. Similarly, the tolerance parents display for misbehavior varies in form; in some households child behavior that violates parental standards is accepted as a result of the "stage" which the child is at, whereas in other homes virtually no standards exist, so it is difficult to determine if misbehavior has even been noticed.

The question that confronts every student of parenting involves the effect of various child-rearing regimens on child development. Concerns of this kind are not unique to this era or to professionals. They are most certainly as ancient as Western civilization, and quite probably predate even recorded history. Socrates, the main character of Plato's Greek dialogues, frequently expounded upon the proper way to raise the ideal citizen. A cursory reading of the Old Testament highlights frequent proclamations of how children ought to be cared for. And through the centuries child-rearing advice has continued unabated. In the eighteenth century, for example, the French philosopher Jean Jacques Rousseau published a small novel entitled *Emile* in which he offered a relatively formal theory of child rearing. And for anyone who might believe that theories of child rearing and advice to parents are things of the past, walk into any bookstore, pick up any magazine, or thumb through the pages of the weekend newspaper, and this myth will quickly be dispelled (Clarke-Stewart 1978b).

Careful scrutiny of ancient, as well as contemporary, child-rearing philosophies reveals that virtually all proclamations on this fascinating subject are founded upon varying basic assumptions about the nature of man and the human condition. As a case in point, contrast the antisocial characterization of the child that underlies the biblical injunction "spare the rod and spoil the child" with Rousseau's claim that proper child rearing requires letting children develop free from formal rules and regulations so that their natural prosocial inclinations can be realized. Given such different assumptions regarding human nature, it is not surprising that vastly different child care directives have been handed down through the ages—and continue to be transmitted even today.

Although we can trace interest in child rearing to ancient times, scientific investigation of the characteristics and consequences of various child-rearing practices is a modern phenomenon. Since the 1930s we have witnessed a movement away from speculation about parenting toward the systematic collection of empirical data. In fact, during the past half century incredible amounts of energy have been spent in attempts to validate various claims regarding the processes by which parents influence their children's development. Of special interest is the fact that the study of socialization has changed immensely during this time period. After years of studying *parental values and attitudes toward child rearing*, investigators abandoned this approach and switched their focus to *parental behavior*. Additionally, rather than retrospectively examining the experiences of children already grown up, researchers directed their attention to *children in the process of developing* and of being influenced by their parents.

Another major reorientation in the study of parent-child relations resulted from the cognitive revolution of the late 1950s and 1960s. This "revolution" was in part a result of Russia's successful launching of the spacecraft Sputnik, which warned of a technology gap between the United States and the U.S.S.R., and in part due to the rediscovery by Americans of Jean Piaget's seminal theory of intellectual development. As a result, students of socialization became increasingly concerned with how parents influence their children's cognitive-motivational, as well as socioemotional, development. These changes in the direction of research on parent-child relations, which began almost two decades ago, have resulted in the accumulation of studies which permit fairly reliable conclusions to be drawn about parental influence upon child development.

It is important to note that the knowledge accumulated to date speaks primarily to children growing up in the contemporary United

States. Further, within this time frame, most studies are of white middle-class children and, to a lesser extent, of children from black, economically disadvantaged families. Thus, it is by no means clear that current understanding of parent-child relations is informative with respect to family functioning in the past or, for that matter, far into the future. Also noteworthy is the fact that most research is correlational in nature. This means that the findings of most studies reflect empirical associations or relationships between parenting practices and measures of child functioning. The general tendency is to interpret such relationships in terms of parental influence on child development, even though correlational data cannot highlight actual patterns of cause and effect. As some have argued, it may be just as reasonable to interpret correlational findings in terms of child influence upon parenting (Bell 1968).

One of the major conceptual contributions of the 1970s, in fact, was the realization that socialization is a two-way street. That is, not only do parents influence children, but children influence parents. We can not say, however, that parent and child are of equal status when it comes to influencing what transpires in the parent-child relationship. Particularly in the infancy, preschool, and early childhood years, parents probably are the more powerful and controlling agents in most households. Consider as an example the fact that for the infant's behavior to have an effect on the parents, the parents must situate themselves within proximity of the child so that the child has an impact. One of the challenges associated with the conceptual breakthrough that emphasizes child as well as parent influence involves the sorting out of parent and child effects. How can such sorting out be accomplished scientifically, when the parent-child relationship is reciprocal and characterized by a complex feedback system whereby children influence parents who are in turn influenced by children and so on?

In light of the state of the art in the study of parent-child relationships, we have arranged this chapter and the two that follow to highlight what we regard as fairly consistent parent effects upon child development. Subsequently we consider processes by which children influence their parents, and then look more closely at marriage, parenting, and child development. Despite the currently limited state of our knowledge, the student, as well as the scientist, must learn to think dynamically about the interwoven parental and child influences in order to reflect the complexity of the ongoing interchange in this very special interpersonal system.

INFANCY: THE LIFE-SPAN PERSPECTIVE

The first two years of life have received special attention in the study of parent-child relations for a variety of reasons. Not only in psychoanalytic and attachment theory, but also among lay people the infant years and the child's first interpersonal relationship with mother are considered to be critical. Specifically, it has been assumed that early development determines, or at least places limits upon, development in later childhood, adolescence, and even adulthood. Since experiences that infants have in the first two years are assumed to exert the heaviest influence on later development, great attention has been paid to parent-infant relations during that period. If we can learn how parents affect infant development, and if infant development affects subsequent growth and change, then understanding the child's first relationships during infancy is the key to understanding the developmental process (Brim and Kagan 1980).

In recent years life-span theorists have challenged this set of assumptions most forcibly. They have argued, not unreasonably, that the human organism is open to change throughout the life course (Clarke and Clark 1976; Kagan, Kearsley and Zelazo 1978). While parenting practices may certainly influence infants, such influence and developmental effects need not determine future functioning. It is in the spirit of this awareness that we review parental influences upon child development during the first two years of life and argue against the assumption that because parenting during infancy influences infant functioning, the development of the child at this time necessarily determines future functioning. This is not to say, however, that child care and child development during this time are of no developmental consequence. Available evidence does suggest connections between early care and development and subsequent functioning. But when linkages are found between parenting during infancy, infant development, and future child behavior, they are likely to be accounted for by complex processes, not simple direct ones. For example, the infant whose parents foster intellectual competence and curiosity may develop into the toddler/preschooler who frequently asks questions of his parents and teachers, receives informative answers and, as a consequence, continues to display intellectual precocity in the preschool and school-age years. Thus, in this instance it would probably not appear to be the case that the intellectual brightness fostered by parents during infancy directly determines subsequent intelligence, but rather that a bidirectional and transactional process of parent-to-infant-to-parent-to-toddler-to-parent-to-preschooler effects characterize the connections that link together various developmental periods. We suspect that it will primarily be through such complex reciprocal pathways of influence that parental effects identified during infancy are connected to developmental outcomes and processes beyond the opening years of life.

INTELLECTUAL COMPETENCE

The task of measuring cognitive or intellectual development during infancy is by no means easy. Unlike the older child whose verbal skills (e.g., reading, speaking) can be used to tap underlying intellectual capacities, the infant offers no easy means of entry into the mind. After all, the Latin meaning of the word "infancy" is "without language." Thus, investigators have been forced to rely upon the manner in which children manipulate objects, either on their own in free exploration or in structured situations, in order to assess sensory-motor competencies, especially during the first twelve months of life. In the second year, simple comprehension and production of language plays an increasingly larger role in the conceptualization and measurement of infant cognitive-motivational development.

In order to examine parental influence upon infant cognitive development, researchers make systematic observations, either in the infant's home or in structured laboratory situations, of the frequency and style of mothers' interactions with their infants. Sometimes these assessments involve videotaping and subsequently coding recorded sequences of mother and infant behavior; sometimes they involve an analyses of handwritten narrative records describing the activities of mothers and their infants; and sometimes the assessments consist of global evaluations of maternal skill following extended periods of observation or the detailed coding of a set of specified maternal behaviors included on a behavioral checklist. Whichever strategy is employed to assess parenting, individual differences in the ways in which mothers behave toward their babies are then related to individual differences displayed by infants on one or more measures of infant cognitive functioning. These assessments of infant intelligence may take the form of standardized assessments, which rely heavily upon the infant's exploratory behavior, imitative capacities and rudimentary language; or they may involve measurement of the infant's free play activity and problem-solving skill.

In some investigations of parental influence on infant development, scholars employ correlational associations to link patterns of mothering with patterns of child functioning assessed at the same point in time; for example, at six months (Yarrow, Pedersen, and Rubenstein 1975). In other instances, researchers relate measures of parenting at one point in time (for example, nine months) to infant functioning at a somewhat later developmental period (for example, eighteen months — Clarke-Stewart 1973). And in other cases, the time span separating maternal and child assessments might be several years. Tulkin and Covitz (1975), for example, at six months (Yarrow, Pedersen, and Rubenstein 1975). In ing at six years, and Yarrow (Yarrow, Goodwin, Manheimer and Milowe 1973) linked mothering in the first half-year of life with child behavior at ten years.

Key Dimensions of Mothering

Across an extremely large number of observational studies, several key dimensions of maternal functioning emerge from the vast literature on parental influence during infancy as consistent predictors of individual differences in infant cognitive functioning. These predictors can be ordered along a continuum ranging from behaviors and activities denoting basic involvement (e.g., visually attending to baby) to those requiring more embellished interaction (e.g., responding to baby) (Goode 1980).

Attentiveness. At one end of this continuum, and defining the most limited extent of maternal involvement, are behaviors that require simple maternal *attentiveness* to the infant. In one of the first observational studies linking mothering during infancy with infant functioning, Rubenstein (1967) found that high levels of overall maternal attentiveness at five months (as indexed by the frequency with which mother looked at, touched, held, or spoke to the baby) predicted high levels of infant exploratory activity one month later. In what still remains the most comprehensive investigation to date, Clarke-Stewart (1973) found that the amount of time mother spent looking at her nine month old predicted performance on a standardized assessment of infant functioning nine months later. This study is important not simply because it involved a lower-class sample, in contrast to Rubenstein's middle-class families, but also because sophisticated data-analysis techniques indicated that the "flow of influence" between nine and eighteen months was more likely to be from mother to baby than from baby to mother.

To summarize, overall maternal attentiveness repeatedly has been found to be positively related to measures of infant functioning. Such measures include performance on standardized infant intelligence tests (Bell 1971; Clarke-Stewart 1973; Elardo, Bradley, and Caldwell 1975), assessments of language comprehension (Cohen, Beckwith, and Parmelee 1978), and measures of exploratory behavior (Rubenstein 1967). In interpreting these findings, it has been proposed that attentiveness itself may not be the important factor in the relationship between maternal behavior and infant competence. Rather, what also occurs when mothers are attending to their infants may be more crucial in influencing the infant's development. In other words, "attentiveness" may serve simply as a proxy for other maternal qualities and behaviors which more actively facilitate the infant's intellectual growth (Goode 1980).

Physical Contact. In certain respects, this same analysis may provide one reason why physical contact, an activity that requires more maternal involvement than merely attending to the baby, has also been linked to intellectual competence in infancy and beyond. In a study of infant information-processing, Lewis and Goldberg (1969) found that mothers who more frequently held their babies had twelve-week-old children who rapidly became bored watching a familiar visual display, but showed great interest in a novel one. More striking than these correlations, and those reported by Yarrow (1961) linking physical contact in the first six months with performance on standardized tests at six months, are studies that link parenting during infancy with cognitive functioning during childhood. In this regard, Tulkin and Covitz (1975) found that girls from middle-class families whose mothers held them frequently at ten months scored high on intelligence tests at six years. Furthermore, a follow-up analysis of Yarrow's (1961) babies revealed that those whose mothers frequently held them in their first six months of life scored higher on intelligence tests at ten years (Yarrow et al. 1973). The fact that all these babies had been adopted early in their first year indicates that the link between mothering and subsequent functioning in this instance was experientially rather than genetically transmitted. This does not mean, of course, that holding in infancy per se caused long-term intellectual achievement, as it is quite probable that the holding in early infancy which could have promoted optimal development was transformed into other age-appropriate parenting styles as children developed, and that it was these later patterns of child rearing, linked as they may be to earlier styles, that influenced intelligence during the school-age years.

A more recent investigation by Yarrow and his colleagues (1975) sheds some light upon the process by which physical contact might influence cognitive functioning during the later years. High frequency of maternal kinesthetic stimulation, that is, physical contact involving activity and movement, was found to predict high performance on activities requiring goal-directed behavior at six months, like reaching for an attractive object out of reach, pulling on a string in order to secure a ring attached to it, and working to obtain a toy wrapped up in a piece of paper. Moreover, follow-up assessments of these same infants when they were one year of age revealed that mastery motivation behaviors displayed in play situations (e.g., pushing a lever to produce a click and moving lights, reaching through a hole in a clear plexiglass box to obtain a toy from under the box) were more systematically related to such kinesthetic stimulation than to any other maternal behavior category assessed at six months. In an attempt to explain the psychological process at work in such a relationship, Yarrow and his colleagues postulated that rocking, jiggling, and other active movements of the infant's whole body maintains the infant in an optimal state of arousal (i.e., alertness), which then enables the child to attend to, respond to, and explore people, objects, and events in his or her environment. Such alertness and involvement is presumed to foster learning and thereby promote cognitive development.

Verbal Stimulation. While physical contact represents a higher degree of maternal involvement than mere visual attentiveness in most cases, a mother's speech to the child, and thus her verbal stimulation, represents even more embellished care. This is because such involvement, which signals more complex input on the mother's part, may demand more involvement on the child's part. For example, the mother who talks to her infant probably hopes to engage her infant's attention and may expect or try to elicit a response (e.g., smiling or vocalization) from the baby.

In examining the effects of maternal verbal or "vocal" stimulation upon infant functioning, a number of investigators have noted significant, positive relationships between such stimulation and infant competence, particularly in the second year of life (Beckwith 1971; Clarke-Stewart 1973; Cohen et al. 1978; Nelson 1973; Wachs 1976; Wachs, Uzgiris, and Hunt 1971; Cohen and Beckwith 1975; Engel and Keane 1975). Researchers have emphasized the significance of both the quantity and quality of maternal language input (Clarke-Stewart 1973; Nelson 1973; Yarrow 1961; Cohen and Beckwith 1975). Some investigators have focused on the relationships between maternal language and infant language competence (Cohen, Beckwith, and Parmelee 1978; Nelson 1973), whereas others have reported positive correlations between maternal verbal stimulation and more general measures of infant competence, such as standardized infant test scores (Beckwith 1971; Wachs, Uzgiris, and Hunt 1971; Engel and Keane 1975). For example, Clarke-Stewart (1973, 1978) found in her studies of maternal behavior at nine and fifteen months and infant performance on standardized tests at sixteen and eighteen months, that frequent speech by mother to infant predicted good performance on these assessments.

Material Stimulation. Stimulation with objects is another kind of maternal behavior that has been related to infant cognitive functioning. This kind of growth-promoting mothering involves deliberate attempts to involve the infant with the environment. Such efforts usually require more direct, active involvement than does simple attentiveness, physical contact, and even verbal stimulation.

Within this domain of maternal care, several degrees of involvement can be distinguished. The sheer number of toys which parents make available to their infants, for example, has been linked with cognitive functioning in infancy (Bell 1971). In an attempt to refine analyses of this dimension of early experience, Caldwell and her colleagues assessed the age-appropriateness of toys and learning experiences provided the child during the first two years and used such a measure to reliably predict intelligence test performance during the early elementary school years (Bradley and Caldwell 1976a, 1976b; Elardo, Bradley, and Caldwell 1975; see also Engel and Keane 1975). The mother's specific role in such material stimulation has also been emphasized. Clarke-Stewart (1973) found, for example, that the complexity of the child's play behavior in the laboratory at eighteen months was not influenced by the number of playthings provided at home. Rather, the best single predictor of the child's play behavior was the amount of stimulation with toys and objects that the infant received from mother at home at nine months. Thus, material stimulation can be seen to range from simple provision of toys, to provision of age-appropriate toys, to playing with these toys and other materials with the child.

Why should such stimulating caregiving facilitate the development of cognitive competence? One suggestion is that stimulating activity provides infants with information about the world and teaches them how to focus their attention on objects and events so as to be able to acquire information on their own. In an effort to empirically evaluate this hypothesis, Belsky, Goode, and Most (1980) experimentally manipulated the frequency with which mothers of one year olds directed their infants' attention to objects and events in their homes by giving them things, pointing out interesting events, and verbally highlighting unique properties of the world around them (e.g., "that's a big round ball"). As predicted, the babies of such mothers, in contrast to those assigned to a control group, displayed more focused and cognitively sophisticated exploratory behavior when observed several months later. Recently, Ruddy and Bornstein (1982) have reported evidence consistent with these findings. In fact, the frequency with which mothers directed their infants' attention to objects at four months strongly predicted vocabulary size at one year. A possible reason for this association is that in the course of providing material stimulation mothers are likely to rely heavily upon language to focus the child's attention and highlight particular properties of those things to which they draw their infant's attention.

Responsive Care. In addition to the sheer frequency with which infants experience cognitively stimulating care, the responsiveness of parental behavior also appears to be developmentally important to the infant. In a variety of correlational studies it has been found that infants whose parents contingently respond to their smiles, vocalizations, and other behaviors display greater intellectual competence both during infancy and at subsequent developmental periods than do their age mates whose parents are less responsive (e.g., Belsky 1979; Carew 1980; Yarrow et al. 1975; Clarke-Stewart 1973; Beckwith 1971; Hardy-Brown, Plomin, and DeFries 1981; Martin 1981; Martin, Maccoby and Jacklin 1981). Global evaluations of maternal emotional and verbal responsivity made when infants were six and twelve months of age, for example, have been linked to intelligence test performance at three years (Elardo, Bradley and Caldwell 1975). During early infancy, more detailed behavioral codings of mother's responsiveness to both infant vocalizations and cries have been found to predict the speed with which three month olds process familiar and novel visual information (Lewis and Goldberg 1969). And, as a final example illustrating this most consistent association between maternal responsiveness and infant competence, Carew (1980) reported that mothers whose preschoolers scored high on measures of intelligence at three years had been observed to be responsive and sensitive to their infants' behavior and needs at between twelve and twenty-four months of age.

In an attempt to explain why parental responsiveness and infant competence seem to go together, it has been proposed that parental behavior that is responsive to infant behavior enables the child to discover that she has control over the world and, thereby, encourages the child to engage in further activity. Lewis and Goldberg (1969) have spoken in terms of a generalized sense of efficacy that the infant develops, even in the first half of the first year, which, through the activity it encourages, generates experiences that are richly informative. It is likely then that it is the acquisition of such information, as well as the sense of control it affords the young child, that is responsible for the relationship between intellectual competence and responsive mothering.

Theoretical speculation about the relation of a sense of control to intellectual competence received empirical support from a series of experimental studies. In these investigations, Watson, Ramey and their colleagues systematically varied the degree to which three-to-six-month-old infants' behavior caused a mobile suspended over their cribs to move. Those infants provided with the opportunity to gain control over mobiles not only kicked more frequently to make the mobiles move, but also displayed enhanced learning capacities in other situations (Finkelstein and Ramey 1977; Ramey and Finkelstein 1978; Watson and Ramey 1972). If one makes a comparison between the mobile which responds to the baby's kicks and the caregiver who responds to the baby more generally, these experimental studies serve as a nice simulation or analogue, and provide a basis for concluding that responsiveness is not simply associated with infant competence, but influences it. Support for this conclusion can be found in a recent field rather than laboratory study which experimentally manipulated parents' actual responsiveness rather than the responsiveness of some object (like a mobile). Intervention administered over a three-month period to enhance the responsiveness of a group of working-class parents was found to facilitate both infants' exploratory behavior and information-processing ability (Riksen-Walraven 1978). Thus, there appear to be good empirical grounds for generalizing to parents (the animate environment) the work exploring the effect of a responsive inanimate environment on infant learning.

Restrictiveness. While the four dimensions of maternal behavior we have considered thus far have been phrased in positive terms and have been associated with positive infant outcomes, the next to be considered, restriction of exploration, has been found to relate negatively to infant functioning. Several investigators have focused specifically upon maternal physical and verbal restriction (Clarke-Stewart 1973; Tulkin and Kagan 1972; Engel and Keane 1975), whereas others have examined the amount of floor freedom infants and toddlers are provided (Ainsworth and Bell 1974; Beckwith et al. 1976; Stayton, Hogan, and Ainsworth 1971). For example, Clarke-Stewart found that frequent prohibitions at nine months predicted lower intellectual functioning at eighteen months. Similarly, Tulkin and Covitz (1975) found that lots of time spent physically restricted in a playpen and frequent verbal prohibitions at ten months forecast poor intelligence test performance when children were six years of age. In contrast, Wachs (1976) found that performance on cognitive assessments at twenty-one and twenty-four months positively covaried with high ratings of freedom to explore the environment between eighteen and twenty-three months (see also Beckwith et al. 1976). Similarly, Elardo, Bradley, and Caldwell (1975) observed that maternal avoidance of physical and verbal restrictions at six and twelve months forecast good performance on intelligence tests at three years.

Why should restriction undermine intellectual growth, as these several investigations indicate it does. The answer to this question probably resides in the effect of such restriction on infant activity and curiosity. By functioning to reduce the child's interest in the world, or at least limit the amount of time she has to pursue such interests, long periods of time spent in high chairs and in playpens, and frequent "no," "don't," and "stop that" undermine the child's information-gathering activity, upon which intellectual development is based. This, of course, is not to say that any and all restrictions are bad for the child. Clearly infants and especially toddlers require supervision involving appropriate restriction. From a developmental standpoint, freedom to explore an unprotected stairway or a household cabinet filled with dangerous medicines is unlikely to promote long-term intellectual competence. Too much of a good thing, in this case freedom from restrictions, is not necessarily in the child's best interest.

The same is true, most certainly, with respect to stimulating-response care. A caregiver, when insensitive to the arousal and attention limits of the infant, can overstimulate the baby. In this regard, it is of interest to note that Wachs and his colleagues (1971) found that extreme amounts of noise, activity, and disorganization in economically impoverished homes predicted poor intellectual performance. The suggestion was put forth, on the basis of this work, that in such situations sensory stimulation overloads the child's information-processing capacities, thereby resulting in intellectual deficits rather than benefits. The tendency of students learning about parental influences on child development to assume that more of a good thing, in this case sensory stimulation, is always better should be tempered by this telling finding.

On the basis of the preceding discussion it can be concluded that parents who promote optimal cognitive development during the infancy years function effectively as *sources of stimulation*, by speaking to and by playing with the infant, and as *mediators or filters of stimulation*, by directing infant attention to objects and events in the child's world and by restricting the toddler from engaging in dangerous activities. Although we have separately considered several major dimensions of parental care which have been consistently linked with child functioning—both during infancy and beyond—it would be mistaken to assume that these dimensions are unrelated. In fact, in the Clarke-Stewart (1973) investigation linking parenting at nine months with child functioning at eighteen months, mothers found to be attentive to their infants were materially and verbally stimulating, responsive, positively affectionate, and relatively nonrestrictive. Thus, Clarke-Stewart was led to conclude that although dimensions of caregiving can be teased apart for purposes of analysis, as we have done here, in the real world performance across them tends to be highly related.

SOCIOEMOTIONAL DEVELOPMENT

A primary social task for the infant is to establish a close emotional relationship with another human being (Sroufe 1979; Erikson 1959). The individual with whom the child develops this first *attachment relationship* is usually the mother, but always an individual who holds a special place in the baby's life. By the end of the first year, this is a person who the infant clings to when upset, orients toward following separation, and relies upon as a source of security so as to be able to move about the environment and freely explore.

Individual Differences in Attachment

Although all infants develop attachments to some individual, and usually to several persons eventually, individual differences in the quality of the infant-parent attachment relationship most certainly exist. Mary Ainsworth has developed a laboratory procedure for assessing such differences at the end of the first year (Ainsworth and Wittig 1969). This *Strange Situation Procedure*, as it is aptly called, involves placing the child in an unfamiliar room while alone with its parent, introducing a strange adult, twice separating the child from its parent by first having the mother leave the baby with the stranger and then completely alone in the room, and having the mother return after each of these brief infant-parent separations.

Close scrutiny of the child's approach and avoidance behavior directed toward mother, especially during reunion episodes following brief separations, is used to classify infants in terms of the security-insecurity of their attachment relationships. Children who by twelve to eighteen months can use their caregiver as a secure base from which to explore and may strongly and positively greet their mother following separation, and/or approach her to establish physical contact, are considered to have developed secure attachment relationships. Infants who, in contrast, mix greeting and proximity-seeking of caregiver with resistance to physical contact (anxious-resistant style), or who are inclined to avoid the caregiver by moving away from her, ignoring her, or refusing to look at her following separation (anxious-avoidant style), have been described as having established insecure attachment relationships. Such infants either find it difficult to use the mother as a secure base to facilitate exploration or seem to leave the side of the caregiver almost too readily and display lower quality exploratory behavior (Ainsworth 1979).

Importantly, individual differences observed in this highly stressful strange situation correspond to stable individual differences in behavior observed in the natural environment. Evidence substantiating this claim comes from a longitudinal study of the development of attachment relationships (Ainsworth et al. 1978). In this investigation it was found that infants judged to be securely attached on the basis of their behavior in the strange situation engaged in little crying at home, even when briefly separated from the parent, and positively greeted mother following such brief every-day separations. Moreover, securely attached babies frequently initiated close bodily contact with their mothers, responded positively once such contact was achieved, yet reacted positively too when such contact was terminated.

In contrast, insecurely attached infants, who have been found to represent about 25–35 percent of most samples, displayed generally more crying at home, and more anger and disturbances with respect to close bodily contact, such as avoidance or pushing away. Babies who in the strange situation are likely to resist physical contact and display anger toward mother following separation, are least likely to follow mother during brief in-home separations (as when mother walks into another room) or greet her positively upon reunion when mother reenters the room. Furthermore, these babies are least likely to initiate physical contact with mother. Babies who display insecurity by avoiding rather than resisting mother during reunion episodes in the strange situation are least likely to respond positively when picked up or held in the home, and respond negatively when such holding is terminated, as when mother puts the baby down (Ainsworth et al. 1978; Ainsworth, Bell, and Stayton 1972; Stayton, Ainsworth, and Main 1973; Stayton, Hogan, and Ainsworth 1971).

Consequences of Attachment

From a developmental perspective, it is of special interest that individual differences in attachment, as assessed in the strange situation, which we have seen relate systematically to behavior in the every-day home environment, appear to forecast future functioning beyond infancy in a quite predictable manner. Before considering work documenting this claim, it should be noted also that even by twelve months of age securely attached infants function differently than their insecurely attached counterparts in domains of development not directly related to relations with mother. In their original longitudinal study of the development of attachment behavior over the infant's first year, for example, Stayton, Hogan, and Ainsworth (1971) found securely attached infants to display more sophisticated modes of communication and to be more compliant than insecurely attached infants (see also Ainsworth et al. 1978). More specifically, these babies used more facial expressions, employed more gestures (e.g., waving bye-bye) and vocalizations, and engaged in less crying and other distress calls. Moreover, these infants were found to be especially skilled in limiting their own exploration of parts of the environment which curiosity compelled them toward but which past experience had taught them was off limits. Anyone who has watched a twelve month old point to an electrical outlet or some potentially breakable object and say "no-no," or shake his head from side to side while pointing at it, in order to inhibit his own behavior, has a good sense of just what such self-restriction looks like.

Beyond the first year, the results of a variety of investigations suggest that securely attached infants are more "competent" in a variety of ways. In one longitudinal study of black infants, Sylvia Bell (1978) found that securely attached infants and their mothers continued to display high levels of positive affect during play sessions across the second and third year of life, whereas anxiously attached infants and their mothers continued to display more negative affect. In a completely independent study it was found that by twenty-two months securely attached infants had developed into cooperative toddlers — cooperative with both mothers and a strange adult playmate in a laboratory play session, as well as with an infant tester when given an exam in a standard testing situation (Main 1973; Londerville and Main 1982; see also Thompson and Lamb 1981 for comparable findings). In still another investigation, this one following up at twenty-four months infants assessed in the strange situation at eighteen months, Matas, Arend and Sroufe (1978) found that when confronted with a problem too difficult for two year olds to solve on their own, securely attached infants were more likely to seek and accept their mothers' help, and displayed more pretend play and enthusiasm when engaged in free play. When these same toddlers were studied at the age of five, those who had been judged securely attached three and a half years earlier were found, in preschool, to adapt more resourcefully to changing personal and environmental circumstances than did other children (Arend, Gove, and Sroufe, 1979).

Researchers have also found behavior with age mates in preschool to be related to assessments of security of attachment during infancy. In one investigation linking attachment at fifteen months with behavior with peers at three and a half years, Waters, Wippman, and Sroufe (1979) found that those infants classified as securely attached displayed the most interpersonal and personal competence. Specifically, the securely attached infants were observed to be more self-directed in their activity, more curious, more sought out by other children, less withdrawn, more likely to be leaders, and more sympathetic to the distress of peers than age mates judged insecure as infants. Lieberman (1977), Pastor (1981), and Easterbrooks and Lamb (1979) have observed also that securely attached infants display more mature forms of interaction with peers during the toddler and preschool years. By more mature we mean here that securely attached infants develop into children who engage in more frequent sharing and show stronger inclination to initiate and maintain interaction with age mates.

Familial Origins of Attachment

On the basis of the work just reviewed, there appears to be consistent evidence documenting continuity between organization of attachment to mother at one year and organization of socioemotional behavior up to at least five years. The fact that quality of attachment predicts problem-solving and exploratory behavior, as well as orientation toward age mates, strange adults, and parents is most intriguing. Having considered individual differences in quality of attachment and their developmental consequences, the major question with which we concern ourselves in this book on the child in the family focuses upon the developmental and familial origins of such qualitative differences in infant-parent relationships. In general, two types of explanations of such developmental differences have been offered; one stresses variation in experience in mother-infant interaction (Ainsworth 1979), while the other emphasizes potentially stable characteristics of individuality in the child (Chess and Thomas 1982). While these two explanations are by no means mutually exclusive, the issue of origins has been approached, for the most part, as if they were. In what follows we first consider evidence supporting the notion that family experience determines individual differences and then that suggesting the presence of stable temperamental variation. We plan to show that these competing explanations can be integrated.

Mother's Role. Mary Ainsworth (1979) has proposed that the primary determinant of individual differences in quality of attachment is the experience the infant has over the course of the first year of life in interacting with its mother. The mother's degree of sensitivity in responding to infant signals is most significant in this regard. Note that the sheer quantity of time spent with the infant is not considered to be as important as the mother's ability to behave in an appropriately responsive and positively oriented manner toward the baby, supporting its developmental competencies and accepting its developmental limits. This is not to say, however, that quantity of involvement is unimportant. If nothing else, the amount of time a caregiver spends with a child facilitates the learning of the behavioral signals that the baby emits. Without awareness of the baby's signals, it is difficult to see how sensitivity is possible. As a result of their ability to read their infants' often subtle cues and respond in a manner that addresses the baby's needs in a timely manner, sensitive caregivers are hypothesized to promote in the infant a basic trust of the world that is founded upon the experience of being warmly loved and cared for in a manner that is predictable rather than inconsistent.

The results of several analyses carried out as part of Ainsworth's longitudinal study of the mother-infant relationship provide support for her thesis. This is the case whether one looks at sensitivity to signals relevant to feeding (Ainsworth and Bell 1969), responsiveness to crying (Bell and Ainsworth 1972), the pacing in close face-to-face interaction of behavior contingent upon infant behavioral cues (Blehar, Lieberman, and Ainsworth 1977), and similar contingent responsiveness to infant cues in the context of close bodily contact (Blehar, Ainsworth, and Main 1978). More specifically, in these studies mothers of securely attached infants were found, across the infants' first year, to be more responsive to infant crying (see also Crockenberg 1981), to hold their infants more tenderly and carefully, to display greater consideration of infant behavior when initiating and terminating breast feeding, and to be more responsive to infant emotional expressions during face-to-face encounters (Ainsworth et al. 1978).

Interestingly, a recent study conducted in Germany aimed at replicating many of these results emanating from Ainsworth's longitudinal investigation of twenty-six middle-class infants reared in Baltimore provides support for the contention that maternal behavior is critically important (Grossman and Grossman 1982). At two, six, and ten months of age, forty-nine mother-infant pairs were repeatedly observed at home and detailed narrative descriptions of interaction were recorded. At the end of each observation, mothers were rated on a sensitivity scale. High scores on this global rating (at three and six months) *predicted*, as expected, prompt response to infant crying, less frequent ignoring of crying, more frequent pick ups in response to crying, and more affectionate behavior during holding. The results that indicated that infants whose mothers were rated as most sensitive sought close bodily contact most often, responded most positively when picked up, and protested least when put down also replicated Ainsworth's findings. In light of these results, the findings that infants judged securely attached at twelve months on the basis of strange situation behavior had mothers rated more sensitive at two and six months should not be surprising. The fact that this investigation reproduced Ainsworth's findings with another sample, in another country, provides strong support for the claim that maternal sensitivity to infant cues and signals plays a critical role in determining the quality of infant-mother attachment.

Both the original Baltimore investigation carried out by Ainsworth and the German study just cited relied heavily upon global ratings of maternal sensitivity based upon extended home observations of mother-infant interaction. In an effort to pursue the issue of the determinants of individual difference in attachment using more refined behavioral analysis, Belsky, Rovine, and Taylor (1984) studied mothers and their babies at home when infants were one, three, and nine months of age. They hypothesized that those infants later to be appraised as securely attached would have experienced neither too much nor too little stimulating maternal involvement. An intermediate level of reciprocal interaction was presumed to index sensitivity, since it would neither overstimulate nor understimulate the child. Analyses revealed that, as predicted, babies appraised as securely attached at twelve months had received an intermediate level of stimulation at each of the three ages at which mother-infant interaction had been observed, whereas anxious-avoidant children averaged the highest levels and anxious-resistant the lowest level of reciprocal interaction.

The significance of sensitivity is also highlighted in several controlled and finely detailed behavioral studies of face-to-face interaction between mothers and infants in the first half-year of life. In one such investigation, Ricks (1982) found that mothers who at three and six months displayed more skill in maintaining infant attention and elaborating upon infant communicative signals had children, at twelve months, more likely to be classified as securely attached on the basis of their strange-situation behavior. Langhorst and Fogel (1982) have reported comparable data showing that avoidance of mother during strange-situation reunion episodes was infrequent at twelve months for infants whose mothers, at three months, scored high on several measures assessing mother's skill at coordinating their attention and activity with that of their babies during videotaped face-to-face interactions.

Infant's Role. Although all the evidence just reviewed suggests that quality of mothering determines quality of infant-parent attachment, we would be mistaken to assume that the infant plays merely a passive role in the developing relationship. In this regard, the results of three studies are important. In one investigation linking newborn behavior with security of attachment at one year, Waters, Vaughn, and Egeland (1980) found, in assessing one hundred infants from economically disadvantaged families, that babies later evaluated as insecurely attached displayed, as newborns, signs of unresponsiveness, motor immaturity, and problems with physiological regulation. Even though these differences between securely attached and insecurely attached infants were evident only seven days after, but not ten days after birth, they nevertheless suggest that it may be more difficult to provide sensitive responsive care to some babies than to others. Those infants whose signals are unclear, whose biological rhythms are highly irregular, and who experienced much distress caused by physiological processes, are likely to try the patience, skill, and, thereby, sensitivity of most any parent. Evidence in support of this contention comes from a follow-up analysis of these same babies. In an effort to examine the antecedents of maternal sensitivity, Vaughn, Crichton, and Egeland (1982) found that the same characteristics of the newborn that Waters, Vaughn and Egeland (1980) found predicted security of attachment at twelve months, also contributed significantly to the prediction of maternal behavior at three and six months, especially maternal sensitivity.

Joint Contribution. On the basis of such work we find evidence of both a maternal and child contribution to the child's developing relationship with his or her mother. Sensitive caregiving, it seems, is influenced, but not totally determined, by characteristics of the infant. In some cases caregivers will be able to overcome the limits of difficult-to-care-for infants, respond sensitively, and thereby provide the interactional experiences that seem to foster secure attachments. In other households, however, this may not be the case, and in these instances we can speak in terms of the infant affecting the care he receives and, thereby, producing his own development. Note, however, that in another household the very same infant behaviors may not have undermined maternal functioning. It is important to recognize, then, that the effect of the infant will depend upon those that he or she may affect. The same is no doubt true with respect to parenting. The care that one child finds to be overstimulating may not be experienced as such by another child.

A recent study by Crockenberg (1981) proves informative with respect to the notions just advanced. In her longitudinal study of the mother-infant relationship, this investigator found high levels of newborn irritability to be associated with insecure attachment, but only when mothers also reported having little support from friends and relatives. Under such conditions it would seem that the depletion of psychological resources caused by caring for a highly irritable baby, and required to maintain a sensitive, responsive orientation toward the infant, is not balanced by the provision of assistance from others. When such support is available, however, even an irritable baby does not seem to be sufficient to lead to insecure infant-parent attachments.

Consideration of the Crockenberg (1981) and Vaughn, Crichton, and Egeland (1982) investigations, and the work we summarized earlier on maternal sensitivity, suggests that quality of attachment is a result of early interactional experience, which is itself determined by characteristics of the mother, the infant, and the broader context in which the mother-infant relationship develops (i.e., family, community). While we have seen that quality of attachment is related to contemporaneous behavioral functioning, and forecasts subsequent development, it is inappropriate to conclude that early experience necessarily determines later development. Undoubtedly what we are observing are developmental paths characterized by a continually supportive and growth-promoting parent-child relationship as well as other positive experiences. These paths, of course, may well result from the social skills and trust that the securely attached infant has developed in his early parent-infant relationships. If this trust is undermined, especially by a change in the parent-child relationship or by some other experience, the links between early attachment and subsequent development that have been discerned should not be expected. Development, both within and beyond the family, is a dynamic process open to continual modification and refinement.

Since the quality of the socioemotional bond established between infant and mother seems to be strongly influenced by the interactional history that the infant has experienced with this person over the course of its first year of life, it stands to reason that the quality of attachment to the father may be distinct from that to the mother. After all, interactional experience with the father is quite likely to differ from that experienced with the mother. The empirical evidence gathered to date consistently indicates that this is indeed the case. Not only do infants establish attachment relationships with their fathers by the end of the first year which vary in terms of quality, but the quality of these relationships are independent of the quality of the infant-mother relationship (Belsky, Garduque, and Hrncir 1984; Grossman et al. 1981; Lamb et al. 1982; Main and Weston 1981). Thus, knowing the security or insecurity of the infant-mother tie does not permit one to predict the quality of the infant-father tie.

FATHER'S INFLUENCE

It must be pointed out that the role of the father during infancy has been neglected (Lamb 1976; Parke 1978). Consequently, much less is known about the influence fathers exert upon infant development than that exerted by mothers. Indeed, while many studies have documented the role of stimulating, responsive, nonrestrictive, positively toned, and sensitive mothering in promoting optimal infant development, only a handful of investigations have examined relationships between patterns of fathering and infant functioning. We remain, therefore, on much shakier ground in trying to draw conclusions regarding the kind of fathering that promotes cognitive as well as social development during the infant years.

From a theoretical standpoint there is reason to believe that the same patterns of care identified as being developmentally influential for the mother function in a similar way for the father. This similarity occurs because the processes by which stimulating, responsive, and nonrestrictive care are assumed to promote infant competence do not appear dependent upon the gender of the individual providing such care. It is conceivable, nevertheless, that for fathers processes of influence may be distinct. The truth is that at this time we simply do not know. The only conclusion research currently permits is that the quantity of the father's involvement is related to infant outcome. That is, infants whose fathers are highly involved with them appear to be more intellectually competent and socially oriented toward their fathers (Belsky 1981). This result has been reported in studies examining infants' manner of greeting fathers following brief separations (Chibucos and Kail 1981; Kotelchuck 1972; Pedersen and Robson 1969; Ross et al. 1973) and in investigations examining the correlates of individual differences in free exploration (Belsky 1980), on structured exploratory tasks (Pedersen, Rubenstein, and Yarrow 1979) and on Piagetian-based measures of infant cognitive functioning (Wachs, Uzgiris, and Hunt 1971). Beyond this general finding, it has been suggested that father's play behavior may be particularly influential (Clarke-Stewart 1978; Parke 1978), that he may exert greater influence on sons than on daughters (Easterbrooks and Goldberg 1983; Pedersen, Rubinstein, and Yarrow 1979), and that he may influence his children by drawing them into the world beyond their intimate relationship with their mother (Belsky 1980). Since little evidence exists on these points, they must be considered as tentative hypotheses in need of empirical confirmation (Belsky 1981).

Three additional points need to be made regarding fathers before proceeding to the next chapter to consider parental influence during the preschool and childhood years. First, processes of father influence may be distinct because of the secondary caregiver role that the large majority of fathers play in American society, especially during the infancy years. Second, and quite possibly a result of this secondary caregiver role, fathers' style of interaction appears distinct from that of mothers. Specifically, in several different studies play has been found to be the special province of fathers. Although most fathers interact less with their infants than do mothers (Belsky, Gilstrap, and Rovine 1983; Frodi et al. 1982), the average father spends a greater percentage of his time in playful, especially highly arousing, interaction (Parke 1978; Lamb 1981). Moreover, he is less likely to hold his infant for purposes of caregiving and comforting, though he appears equally capable of providing sensitive care when it is required — either because a mother has left the baby in the father's care or because research investigators structure situations in which there is little else for the father to do. Given such differences in the style and quantity of fathering, the possibility exists that fathers exert a unique, but still undetermined, influence upon infant functioning. The possibility must also be entertained, however, that fathers exert no special influence at all, at least not one that can be detected during the period of infancy. We will see when we consider older children that conclusions need not be hedged in such ambiguous terms since fathers have been well studied in the preschool period.

For a volume such as this with a focus on the child *in* the family, one further comment is in order regarding fathers. It may be more appropriate to conceptualize the father as a member of a family system rather than as an individual, and thus to think about the interrelation of patterns of mothering and fathering and how this influences infant development (Belsky 1980; Clarke-Stewart 1978). Indeed, it may be the case that it is the similarity or difference between what the infant gets from mother and from father that is most developmentally significant. Currently, we can only speculate on this issue, since the study of parent-infant relations has traditionally been carried out within the discipline of psychology, with its emphasis upon individuals and individual relationships. Concern for the family is only now emerging in the study of parent-infant relations, primarily as a result of the interdisciplinary orientation from which this book is derived (Belsky 1981; Lerner and Spanier 1978). Only when research is conducted from such a family perspective will it be possible to draw strong conclusions regarding the combined influence of mothering and fathering.

CONCLUSION

The evidence reviewed in this first of three chapters focused upon parental influences clearly indicates that the quality of care parents, especially mothers, provide during infancy exerts an impact upon child development. Without a caregiver, who is usually a parent, the infant could not survive. But parents seem to affect infant functioning beyond such an obvious influence. Care that is attentive, verbally and materially stimulating, responsive, positively affectionate, and not too restricting seems to promote both intellectual competence and security of attachment. Of course, such care must be given, but how it is provided is equally important. There seems to be an optimal level of involvement and, most significantly, care seems best that is sensitive to the individual limits and skills of the child. Not every baby is the same, so what is appropriate for one may be less appropriate for another.

What all this suggests is that there is no single way to care for a baby. In point of fact, beyond the experience of extremely poor care, it is likely that most babies will bounce back from the potentially limiting consequences of less-than-optimal care. In this regard, Scarr-Salapatek (1976) has pointed out that infant development is so highly "canalized" by evolutionary pressures that the quality of care offered in most caregiving environments will be sufficient to stimulate normal development. It is her contention, in fact, that the baby must be subjected to extreme stress before its own "self-righting" tendencies will not function to move it toward normal development. Support for this idea is found in cross-cultural work indicating that in contexts like Holland where infants do not get anywhere near the levels of intense interactional involvement from their mothers that many middle-class American babies receive (Rebelsky 1972) development still proceeds normally.

All this is not to say that especially high quality care cannot get the baby off to a very good start. In point of fact, the wealth of data considered in this chapter suggests that it very well can. Furthermore, the identification of the influential dimensions of high quality care is significant from the perspective of applied science. Our awareness of that which promotes optimal development carries with it the potential of informed efforts to positively influence development. Indeed, interventions directed toward infants at risk for some later problem are most likely to be effective when they are supported by knowledge generated through basic scientific research.

In view of the plasticity in human development mentioned in the opening chapters, we should not be surprised that intervention efforts during infancy have proven successful when lessons learned through basic scientific inquiry have been applied. Programs geared toward providing infants with more responsive and verbally and materially stimulating care have succeeded in enhancing early development. Often the expectation is that the provision of such early intervention will buffer the child against subsequent stress and assure optimal development. Unfortunately, this is unlikely to be the case. Since development is characterized by plasticity, stress as well as support will affect children. The principal lesson to be learned, then, by students, scientists, and policymakers alike, is that experience influences human development. Supportive experiences promote optimal functioning, while stress, especially in large quantities, risks undermining such valued growth. No period of development, including infancy, should be considered all important. Just because the early years are loving, caring, and stimulating, is no reason to presume that later years do not matter. Analogously, just because the opening years of life are stressful provides no basis for giving up hope. The plasticity of our character dictates the ever-lasting potential for change—both positive and negative (Lerner, in press).

CHAPTER 5

CHILDHOOD: PARENTAL INFLUENCES

The preschool period encompasses the time following infancy (two to three years of age) and prior to school entry (five to six years of age). Although the developmental changes that characterize the first two years of life are nothing short of dramatic, the next three to four also display great transformation. The blossoming of verbal-linguistic competencies is especially noteworthy as children become increasingly able to express their thoughts and feelings with words, describe the world around themselves, and query their parents and communicate effectively with age mates. It is a time, be it spent in preschool or day care, or in the neighborhood, when the child becomes increasingly able to effectively engage peers in play that is both cooperative and industrious. It is a time also of moving away from the close attachments of infancy, without breaking the relationships already established, and venturing forth to explore the social and object world beyond the confines of the nuclear family. As Erik Erikson (1950) so nicely said, the preschool years are a period of autonomy and initiative.

As in infancy, children differ markedly in the manner in which they cope with these developmental changes. For some, peers represent aversive sources of social stimulation and are to be avoided or aggressed against, whereas for others peers are great social attractions. Some children find the process of detachment from a caregiver exceedingly stressful and continue to crave contact in a dependent manner which, in certain contexts (e.g., day care), will be developmentally dysfunctional during the preschool years. Other children welcome the autonomy that the toddler and preschool years seem to be so much about; some of these children, however, will be forced to struggle with parents who feel uncomfortable with letting such a small child move out beyond their sphere of immediate control. And, as would be expected, some preschoolers master language and many other intellectual skills rather easily and are thus effective interpersonal agents and problem solvers, whereas others, failing to do so, experience stress and failure, especially in preacademic skills.

With formal entry into elementary school, the demands made upon the developing individual change. To get a better sense of the exact nature of these changes, reflect upon the experience of preschool and elementary school. Whereas in nursery school or kindergarten some efforts are made to orient the child toward academic activities like reading and writing, in the early grades such activity becomes central to the mission of schooling. Note that success in learning these and other skills (like arithmetic, spelling, and so forth) rests upon abilities other than mere intelligence. In addition to being smart, or at least intellectually capable of mastering school subjects, the child needs to be oriented or motivated toward acquiring the competencies that schools are designed to promote. Such motivation to perform well in school and function successfully at assigned tasks has been called achievement motivation.

School involves more than an emphasis on intelligence and achievement, however. Unless one is very rich, or handicapped in some way, and thus receives special one-to-one tutoring, the education system demands that the child be able to get along with age mates and cooperate with adults in positions of authority. Consequently, the ability to engage peers in a friendly manner and with a prosocial orientation (as opposed to an antisocial orientation) are important personal assets during the school-age years.

From the standpoint of the new student, it is important to recognize that schooling, at least as practiced in most American schools, is an extremely evaluative enterprise. As we all know, performance evaluations in the form of tests, grades, and report cards are used to measure academic success. Not only is it the case that such evaluative processes affect the school-age child's personal opinion of herself, but it is also true that the self-esteem and confidence the child brings from the family to school influence academic performance and relations with peers.

Our prime interest in this section is the familial origins of developmental differences in capacities such as intelligence, social competence, and sex-role orientation. Undoubtedly, earlier experiences and congenital differences are responsible for some of the differences that exist between children. But research also indicates that, to a sizable degree, such differences result from the different parental care that children experience in their families during the preschool and childhood years. It is just such variation, and its impact upon children's developmental competence during the childhood years, that is the focus of this chapter.

INTELLECTUAL COMPETENCE

Standardized tests of IQ serve as the primary means of assessing intellectual competence in efforts to identify the parental determinants of this dimension of child functioning. Other strategies of assessing intellectual competence during the preschool years focus upon basic cognitive skills, like concept sorting and classification, or upon preacademic skills such as reading readiness. Interestingly, results across investigations are fairly consistent despite the different measures of intellectual functioning that are used. The reason for this, no doubt, is that virtually all measures of intelligence during the preschool, childhood, and adulthood years are heavily weighted, whatever their differences, in terms of verbal-symbolic abilities, that is, the capacity to produce and understand language and manipulate symbols, be they letters of the alphabet or numbers (as in arithmetic and mathematics).

The sensitive, warm, loving orientation of mothers that was identified as promoting optimal development during the infant years still functions to promote cognitive competence during the preschool years (Hess and Shipman 1965; Sears, Maccoby, and Levin 1957; Whiteman and Deutsch 1968). During this developmental period sensitivity continues to denote an acceptance of the child's developmental limits and an understanding of the developmental challenges that are to be confronted. This guideline translates into providing the child with the freedom to explore the world and to express feelings. In a sense, then, intellectual competence is facilitated by supporting the developmental tendency toward autonomy.

The role that maternal warmth plays in fostering achievement and cognitive functioning during the preschool years is nicely illustrated in an early study by Radin (1971). Black and white lower-class mothers were observed interacting with their children in their homes. The children had previously taken standard intelligence tests upon entrance to preschool and were tested again at the conclusion of their participation in a preschool program. It was hypothesized that there would be a positive relationship between observed maternal warmth and intellectual development of the child upon entrance to school. It was also predicted that gain in IQ during the year would be positively associated with maternal warmth even after taking into consideration the effect of the teacher's behavior and the child's initial level of intellectual functioning. In this study, maternal warmth was operationally defined as the mother's use of (1) reinforcement, be it physical or verbal; (2) consultation with the child, or asking him to share in some decision; and (3) sensitivity to the child, or anticipating his requests or feelings.

Not only were the hypotheses confirmed, but it was also discovered that maternal warmth predicted academic or achievement motivation. That is, preschoolers whose mothers displayed more warmth toward their offspring at home scored higher on intelligence tests before starting school, gained more in intelligence during the school year, and were more motivated to achieve and identify with the teacher. These findings led Radin (1971, p. 1564) to conclude that "observable use of maternal reinforcement, consultation with the child, and sensitivity to his needs are related to cognitive growth."

The intellectually stimulating parent of the preschooler does more, however, than merely let the child follow his own inclination. She also challenges him and encourages mastery of the developmental tasks the child confronts. Thus, she encourages independence, by requiring that he try to solve problems on his own, yet is available to provide supportive assistance as needed. She also takes time to read to the child and to explain how the world works. A willingness to both answer and encourage questions is another part of the developmentally facilitative package of cognitively stimulating care.

The quality of of mother's language also seems to be related to intellectual functioning. Stimulating parents use words and sentences that the child understands or is close to understanding, thereby providing her with a sense of mastery and challenging her intellectual faculties. Parents such as these also take time to elaborate or expand upon what the child has said, clarifying ambiguities in the child's speech and highlighting distinctions in the way words and phrases are used. In a sense, then, intellectual competence, especially with respect to linguistic skill, is fostered when parents adopt and enjoy the role of teacher.

A study involving social class comparisons of maternal language behavior highlights the role of maternal language in children's language functioning and general intellectual functioning. On the basis of the observations that lower-class children perform less well than middle-class children on tests of intelligence and are less successful when it comes to academic achievement (e.g., Deutsch and Brown 1964; Kennedy, Van de Riet and White 1963), Hess and Shipman (1965) set out to compare the verbal interchange that transpires between black mothers from four different social classes and their preschoolers. It was expected that the language of middle-class mothers would be more elaborate whereas that of lower-class mothers would be more restricted and thus less cognitively stimulating (Bernstein 1961). Observations of maternal teaching behavior in a laboratory setting provided support for this contention, thereby offering evidence that variation in children's intellectual development may be, in part, a function of variation in maternal language behavior. Specifically, it was found that middle-class mothers were more likely than lower-class mothers to use abstract words and complex grammatical structures in their sentences and to generally rely more on verbal than nonverbal means of communication.

The intellectual abilities of the school-age child have been linked repeatedly to experiences of the child during the preschool period. Mother's earlier involvement in the child's play, and her tendency to respond to questions, read to him, and accompany him on frequent outings beyond the confines of the home have been linked to the older child's general verbal ability (Clarke-Stewart 1977). During the school-age period, we employ the phrase "verbal ability" to denote skill in reading, in speaking, and in understanding spoken language.

A recent report by Bradley and Caldwell (1976b) nicely documents the relationship between early care and cognitive functioning at the beginning of school. In this investigation of forty-nine children first studied at two years of age, it was found that children from families in which mothers had been more emotionally and verbally responsive, more generally involved in their children's activities, but less restrictive and punishing, scored higher on tests of intellectual functioning at four and a half. In a more recent study, Gottfreid and Gottfreid (1984) have reported similar data, but demonstrated that the link between early parental care and later child functioning could be accounted for principally by the quality of care children experienced at the end of the preschool years. In other words, it seems to be the continuing supportive and stimulating care that fosters intellectual development during the late preschool years, not the care received several years earlier.

During the school years themselves, the intellectual development of boys and girls appears to differentially relate to the quality of the mother-child relationship. Whereas in the case of boys a continued close relationship with mother seems to facilitate intellectually superior performance, in the case of daughters, a progressively more distant relationship seems most intellectually facilitative (Clarke-Stewart 1977). Before drawing the conclusion that close mother-daughter relationships are not in the child's best interest, the effect of historical time needs to be considered.

Most investigations into mothers' influence on intellectual development were conducted in a period when maternal employment was not as commonplace as it is today. What the effects just summarized may be indexing, then, are the influence of maternal employment on female intellectual development. As we will learn in a later chapter, mother's working may have a beneficial effect on daughter's intellectual development in part because it reduces the likelihood of a daughter's strong identification with a nonworking mother and thus with a role which, by tradition, discourages the manipulation of intellectual ideas (Clarke-Stewart 1977). It may not be the case then, as a first reading of the above paragraph suggests, that a distant mother-daughter relationship facilitates intellectual development; rather, it is more likely that a close nonworking mother-daughter relationship has discouraged intellectual stimulation in the past through the operation of traditional female roles. If such intellectual stimulation occurs in the mother-daughter relationships, regardless of whether the mother is working, it is likely that intellectual development will be facilitated.

It appears that for both sons and daughters intellectual competence, as measured by IQ tests, is promoted by both the quantity and quality of fathering, though the relationships seem far stronger for sons (Lamb 1981; Radin 1976). Indeed, not only is there some evidence that fathering influences boys' development and not girls' (Jordon, Radin, and Epstein 1975), but the reason for this may lie in the fact that mixed messages, which themselves undermine the intellectual development of girls (Radin and Epstein 1975), often characterize father-daughter interactions. Where fathering has been found to impact boys' and even girls' cognitive development, it is high levels of father involvement coupled with an accepting and nurturant orientation, plus time spent actively involved in teaching, that has been implicated as growth-promoting. Radin (1973) documented such an effect in the case of boys by demonstrating that individual differences in paternal nurturance measured at four years of age forecast performance on tests of intelligence taken when their sons were five years old. It was assumed that the process of identifying with a warm, nurturant father is what mediates the relationship between fathering and boys' intellectual functioning.

The father's influence on development is especially pronounced in the area of achievement motivation during the school-age years (Radin 1981; Clarke-Stewart 1977). Paternal encouragement of intellectual performance and achievement is related to achievement in the case of boys (Crandall, Dewey, Katkovsky, and Preston 1964; Hurley 1967; Soloman 1969; Katz 1967). The father's own success, achievement motivation, and nurturance (Radin 1981; Clarke-Stewart 1977) also promote male achievement. In the case of daughters, father's friendliness to daughter and wife seem to be associated with achievement (Clarke-Stewart 1977). However, when loving fathers demean the value of intellectual performance, their daughter's achievement orientation is undermined (Biller, 1974a; Lamb, Owen, and Chase-Lansdale 1979). Fathers who are nurturant toward, but have low expectations of their daughters also seem to retard achievement orientation (Honzik 1967; Nelson 1971).

Mothers also play an important role in children's orientation toward achievement; indeed it is their demand for achievement that seems particularly significant from a developmental standpoint. Achievement standards that are both high and explicit, like "I expect you to do well in science," are just what seem to energize a positive orientation toward performance. The parent who encourages achievement during the school-age years is the one who values education and deliberately rewards school success. Showing an interest in the child's daily school work, exam performance, and course grades, and encouraging good study habits while praising positive performance facilitate achievement. So too does fostering an intellectual atmosphere in the home, modeling structured work habits, and serving as the child's own teacher where appropriate (Crandall, Preston, and Radson, 1960; Kagan and Moss 1962; Rosen and D'Andrade 1959).

One of the challenges preschoolers face as they venture out beyond the confines of the nuclear family and confront the responsibilities of autonomy and initiative is learning to regulate their own impulses and behavior. That is, they need to learn when certain ways of functioning are expected (e.g., being considerate and polite) and when they are inappropriate (e.g., being loud and active). Not surprisingly, given the significance of this developmental challenge, the strategy parents employ to control their preschooler's behavior also influences intellectual competence. Parents who exercise control in an absolute manner, by relying primarily upon their power or upon appeal to formal rules, tend not to promote optimal cognitive development. Instead, reliance upon reasoning and appeals to the child's feelings serve as the primary strategy of parental control in families in which preschoolers flourish intellectually.

If one thinks carefully about how appeals to reason and feelings are experienced by the child, in contrast to power assertion or rules, it becomes clear why this strategy should facilitate cognitive functioning. When a parent reasons with a child or makes an appeal to how the child feels, encouragement is provided to think about what is going on. This process of thinking is not only cognitively stimulating in the immediate situation, but if adopted and exercised on the child's own, continues to stimulate intellectual functioning (e.g., Clarke-Stewart 1977; Baumrind 1971; Hess and Shipman 1967; Radin 1972).

As an example, consider the child who is prohibited from running at full speed through the house. An appeal to power informs the child to stop simply because the parent said so; an appeal to a rule requires the child to stop running simply because such behavior is not permitted in the house. Neither appeal stimulates thought; each merely requires the child to change her behavior. An appeal to reason, in contrast, which points out that the child may fall and get hurt, or may accidentally break something, requires that the child consider the consequences of her actions.

The use of reason, of course, can be carried too far. As noted in the discussion of parenting during infancy, more is not always better. Achieving the proper balance between power and reason is developmentally very important. And as we will see when we consider socioemotional development, even reasoning parents must be prepared to assert their legitimate authority when required. Reasoning is not always immediately effective in establishing control and in situations where control is immediately essential (i.e., ones involving physical safety), alternative control strategies are required. This does not mean, of course, that reasoning is wasted in such situations, especially if targeted at or near the child's level of understanding. Most likely the effects of reasoning accumulate over time and teach the child that reasoning is the preferred medium for exercising control.

In summary, the most effective pattern of parenting for facilitating children's success in school as well as their general intellectual development, seems to involve being nurturant without being too restrictive, responsive yet not overly controlling, and stimulating but not too directive. An orientation toward independence, and a family structure that expects and rewards such behavior, fit the developmental needs of the child—at least as so far as intellectual competence is concerned (e.g., Bayley and Schaefer 1964; Clarke-Stewart 1977; Hess, 1969; Honzik 1967). McCall's (1974) comparison of children displaying increases and declines in intellectual functioning between two and eleven years of age underscores this conclusion quite nicely. Parents whose children's IQs increased were found to be substantially rewarding of their children's behavior, clear in their disciplinary policies, medium to severe in their efforts to control the child, and highly encouraging of intellectual acceleration. Parents whose children's IQs declined, in contrast, were found to be either the most severe or the most lenient with respect to punishment following their children's misbehavior, and rarely encouraged accelerated or mature behavior. In the next section, we will see that these very differences in child rearing correspond not only to the development of intelligence but to social functioning a well.

SOCIOEMOTIONAL COMPETENCE

A prominent series of reports by Baumrind (1967, 1968, 1971, 1972) usefully summarizes much of what is known about parental influence upon social competence during the preschool years. In this research, Baumrind identified three broad types of parents and characteristics of their children that seemed to result from the child-rearing and disciplinary practices experienced at home. It is significant that the clusters of parenting behaviors that Baumrind identified as generally going together, and the patterns of child functioning that seemed to result from these styles of care, are relatively consistent with the findings of other studies.

One type of parent Baumrind identified and labeled as being *authoritarian* tries to shape, control, and evaluate the behavior and attitudes of the child in accordance with a preestablished absolute standard of behavior. Such authoritarian parents stress the value of obedience to their authority and, as a result, are likely to favor punitive, forceful disciplinary measures to curb "self-will" whenever the child's behaviors or beliefs conflict with what the parent thinks is correct. Such parents believe in respect for authority and adhere to an orientation that places heavy emphasis upon the preservation of order and traditional social structure. Thus, the authoritarian parent does not encourage verbal give and take, but instead requires that the child accept the word of the parent as defining correct conduct (Baumrind 1968, p. 261).

Interestingly, parents such as this, who tend to display high levels of control but only modest levels of warmth in parenting, have children who can be described as conflicted-irritable. Such children tend to be less cheerful and more moody than others, as well as apprehensive, unhappy, easily annoyed, passively hostile, and vulnerable to stress. Certainly one would be hard-pressed to describe such children as competent in any sense of the word.

A second type of parent Baumrind identifies is labeled the *permissive parent.* This type of caregiver attempts to behave toward the child's behaviors, desires, and impulses in a nonpunishing, accepting, and affirming manner. The parent consults with the child about decisions regarding family "policy," and explains to the child the basis of family rules. But the permissive parent does *not* present himself or herself to the child as an active "agent" with the responsibility for shaping or modifying the child's present or future behavior. Rather, this type of parent presents himself or herself as a family "resource" for the child, someone to use as the child wishes. Thus, this parent largely allows the child to govern his or her own behavior. As such, the permissive parent avoids exercising control over the child and, in fact, often does not encourage the child to obey external (social) standards. Thus, reason, but little overt power, is used by this parent in his or her attempts to rear the child (Baumrind 1968, p. 256).

While the experience of permissive rearing, characterized by much warmth but little overt control, sounds attractive, for preschoolers trying to master the process of self-regulation in a world that they do not fully understand, this "freedom-to-be" appears developmentally inappropriate. Evidence to support this claim comes from Baumrind's (1967) observation that permissively reared children tend to be impulsive-aggressive. More specifically, these children display very low levels of self-reliance, are frequently out of control, and tend to have a difficult time inhibiting their impulses. In terms of mood, however, permissively reared children are more cheerful than the conflicted-irritable children of authoritarian parents, probably as a result of the warmth they experience at the hands of their noncontrolling parents.

The third type of parent Baumrind identified is labeled the

authoritative parent. Parents who received this label were the most nurturant in Baumrind's studies, as demonstrated by their high use of positive reinforcement and infrequent use of punishment; they were also the most responsive to their children's demands for attention. By no means was it the case, however, that these loving parents indulged their children. Quite the contrary; in fact, authoritative parents were very ready to direct and control the child—but in a manner that displayed awareness of their children's thoughts, feelings, and point of view, as well as of their developmental capabilities. While such parents were strongly unwilling to yield to unpleasant demands, especially when communicated by crying, whining, and nagging, they did alter their positions upon considering arguments put forth by their young children. It is important to note that, in addition to being loving and controlling, authoritative parents were demanding of mature, independent behavior from their children and frequently explained to them the rationale behind their disciplinary and other controlling actions.

It might be said that this third type of parent understands the responsibilities and obligations of child rearing and is willing to exercise legitimate authority. Contrast the authoritative style of parenting with the permissive parent who seems to fail to recognize the responsibilities of child rearing, specifically with regard to setting limits and having expectations. Contrast the authoritative parent also with the authoritarian parent who seems to take advantage of the power inherent in the parenting role without considering the child's developmental limits or need for maintaining a sense of self-integrity.

Not surprisingly, it was the children of authoritative parents who looked the most socially competent, so much so in fact that Baumrind characterized them as energetic-friendly and instrumentally competent. These preschoolers tended to approach novel or even stressful situations with great curiosity and interest, and also tended to display high levels of self-reliance, self-control, cheerfulness, and friendly relations with age mates.

Findings from other studies suggest the presence of the three parenting types identified by Baumrind and support the notion that the different parenting styles have contrasting roles in children's development. In one such investigation, Becker et al. (1962) interviewed parents of young children and found that parental use of reasoning was related to parental warmth and that, in turn, restrictiveness on the part of parents was related to their use of power, punishment, and physical means to assert their authority. Coopersmith (1967) found that mothers who were accepting, supportive, caring, concerned, and loving, *and* who enforced established rules consistently, but sought the views of the child in a context of free and open discussion, had sons who were higher in self-esteem than did mothers who treated their sons harshly, gave little guidance, and enforced rules inconsistently. Similarly, Mussen et al. (1970) reported that girls who showed high levels of self-esteem, honesty, and altruism had warm, intimate interactions with their mothers. Although corresponding relations were not found with the boys Mussen et al. (1970) studied, Sears (1970) found that when at least one parent was warm and accepting, both male and female children were likely to have high self-esteem. In this regard, a recent report by Rutter (1979) indicates that a good relationship with one parent may "buffer" the child from the potentially detrimental effects of a poor relationship with the other parent. Clearly this suggests that children with two parents may be at an advantage relative to those with just one, since they have an alternative relationship to fall back upon in the event that one parent-child relationship sours.

Endsley et al. (1979) assessed the relations between various maternal interaction patterns and children's curiosity. The frequency with which mothers (1) oriented their children to explore novel materials presented in a laboratory play situation; (2) responded positively to their children's exploration; (3) answered their children's questions; and (4) explored the novel materials themselves, was highly related to high levels of child curiosity. However, authoritarian mothers were less likely to display these behaviors than were nonauthoritarian mothers; thus, their children displayed less curiosity. Similarly, Jones, Richel, and Smith (1980) found that maternal restrictiveness was associated with evasive problem-solving strategies in their preschool children; in turn, the more restrictive mothers were, the less their children used personal appeal and negotiation problem-solving strategies. In turn, maternal nurturance was related to children's reliance on authority. Thus, the Endsley et al. (1979) and the Jones et al. (1980) studies (as well as others [e.g., Schaffer & Crook, 1980]), add to the evidence cited above which indicates that the different child-rearing patterns identified by Baumrind are associated with differences in child development.

Discipline

Hoffman (1970) identified several parental disciplinary strategies that are, in part, compatible with aspects of the parenting types described by Baumrind (1967, 1968, 1971, 1972). Parents who use *power-assertive discipline* employ physical punishment, threats of punishment, and physical attempts to control their child's behavior. Parents who use psychological discipline may employ one or both of the following techniques: (1) *love withdrawal*, which involves the parent's temporarily taking away love from the child because the child's actions have made the parent feel disappointed or ashamed; and (2) *induction*, which involves parental use of rationality and explanation in attempts to influence the child's behavior. Thus, at least insofar as power assertiveness and induction are concerned, there seems to be some consistency between Hoffman's descriptions and those pertaining to the authoritarian and the authoritative parent, respectively. When one examines work on the general consequences of these various disciplinary practices one discovers, quite interestingly, that it is just the inductive patterns of controlling children's behavior which Baumrind's work on the authoritative parent would suggest would be most effective in positively influencing children's prosocial functioning that indeed is successful in achieving this goal.

Hoffman (1970) has found, for example, that the frequent use of power assertion by a parent is associated with weak moral development in the school-age child. Indeed, children of parents who use power-assertion techniques frequently tend to show high levels of aggressive behavior themselves (Anthony 1970; Chwast 1972; Feshbach and Feshbach 1972). In general, aggression seems to be fostered by parenting that is hostile, coercive, and physically punitive. Several psychological processes are responsible for this relationship. First, physically punitive disciplinary practices function as a model of aggression that the child is likely to imitate. Second, the frequent use of such hostile discipline teaches the child that physical action in the form of aggression is one viable way to solve interpersonal disputes. And finally, the experience of such hostile care serves to demean the child and thereby places him at a psychosocial disadvantage when it comes to engaging age mates in a prosocial manner. Aggression may simply be a response that comes all too easily to a child who thinks poorly of himself and frequently fails to attract the good wishes of others, as he would like to (Clarke-Stewart 1977; Hoffman 1970; Lefkowitz, Walder and Eron 1963; Radin 1973).

The effectiveness of disciplinary actions in controlling behavior is increased when parents are consistent in its use and vary punishment in terms of the severity of the child's misbehavior. It has been found, for example, that inconsistent parental discipline or parental conflict over discipline is associated with aggressive and delinquent behavior in children (Hetherington, Cox and Cox 1978; Patterson 1977, 1978). However, when efforts to regulate the child's behavior are systematically implemented, as when the practice of two parents are in harmony with each other, and when punishment varies in terms of the degree of the child's transgression, rather than as a function of parental mood, its effectiveness is greatly enhanced. Thus, discipline that relies upon processes of reasoning or induction, is consistently enforced, and varies systematically, is most likely to be effective in controlling children's misbehavior.

To achieve understanding of why the use of reasoning and inductive approaches to discipline are so effective, consider being told in an angry, hostile manner that you should not have hit another child or taken your brother's bike, and contrast this style of discipline with a more controlled manner that explores exactly what the child did, finds out why he did it, and makes him consider the interpersonal consequences of his actions. A child experiencing the first kind of discipline walks away feeling demeaned and possibly even angry, whereas a child experiencing the second approach gains insight into why he did what he did, why it was unacceptable, and how he might have handled the situation differently — and all in an atmosphere communicating concern and care yet not hostility. Most important for future functioning, this inductive approach to discipline leaves the child with information and insight that serves to guide subsequent activity. It is just such learning, which takes place through discipline, that accounts for why inductive discipline during the school-age years tends to promote the development of conscience and self-control.

Disciplinary practices that rely upon induction are especially effective when parents are loving and nurturant. Hoffman (1970, 1975) found, for example, that although love withdrawal was not consistently related to moral functioning, disciplinary practices that relied upon reasoning were associated with moral development when parents were warm and caring in their general orientation toward the child. Why should this be the case? When parents are regarded as nurturant, there seems to be intrinsic incentive to the child to value their desires and developmental goals, and thus to behave in a way that meets their expectancies and, thereby, pleases them.

It is important at this time to recall McCall's (1974) longitudinal study of the parental correlates of varying patterns of intellectual development across the preschool and childhood years. His findings that children displaying intellectual increase over the school-age years had warm, controlling, and reasoning parents are remarkably similar to those of Hoffman and Baumrind — yet with respect to intellectual functioning. It would appear, then, that the same kind of parenting Baumrind labeled authoritative, namely that which is loving *and* controlling, and which she found to be associated with instrumental competence during the preschool years, also tends to promote moral and intellectual development once the child enters school.

SEX-ROLE DEVELOPMENT

Instrumental competence, moral development, and intellectual achievement are not the only developmental consequences of parenting that have been investigated during the preschool and school-age years. Investigators have made great efforts also to understand the role parents play in the development of their children's sex-role identification, that is, their tendency to act in a way that is traditionally masculine or feminine. More specifically, sex-role typing is the process whereby children acquire the motives, values, and behaviors regarded by their culture as character-istically masculine or feminine. While sex-role attitudes and standards are changing, most adults and children still maintain rather traditional and stereotyped conceptions of sex roles. Males in our society are re-garded as more assertive, independent, dominant, and competent in deal-ing with problems in the environment. Females, on the other hand, are considered to be more submissive, warm, emotional, and sensitive to in-terpersonal situations (Hetherington, Cox and Cox 1978).

To fully understand the nature of parental influence on sex-role de-velopment, it is important to point out differences in the characteristic manner in which mothers and fathers behave toward their preschoolers. At least in middle-class households, fathers are more inclined to be emo-tionally distant, instrumental, physical in their punishment, and de-manding. This is especially true of father-son relationships. Mothers, in contrast, tend to be more emotionally expressive, nurturant, rewarding, responsive, playful, accepting, and verbal (Clarke-Stewart 1977). We must recognize that these differences are based upon the average father and average mother, and that such behavior is open to alteration, such as displayed in some nontraditional households. Even within dual-worker families, however, behavior patterns of mothers and fathers are more traditional than nontraditional (Frodi et al. 1982).

The evidence indicates that parents treat sons and daughters in ways that promote sex-role-stereotyped functioning. A recent study by Block (1982), in fact, of more than 1,000 parents found that sons were en-couraged more than daughters to be competitive and achievement-striving (see also Frey and Slaby 1979), independent, and to control their feelings (i.e., boys don't cry), whereas girls were encouraged to be warm and physically and emotionally expressive. While these findings are derived from parental reports, which are known to not always map di-rectly on to parental behavior, observational data tend to substantiate these differences. In one investigation of two year olds, for example, bids by daughters for help and assistance were encouraged whereas similar dependency bids made by sons did not receive the same attentive, positive response (Fagot 1978). Other observational studies provide sup-port for the contention that behavior by parents encourages traditional sex roles. Baumrind (1979) found that boys were encouraged to be domi-nant, while Block (1973; Block, Block, and Harrington 1974) found that girls were encouraged to engage in interpersonal activities, and to talk about their concerns and feelings. Further, daughters were provided more comfort by parents when distressed.

In addition to patterns of parenting that directly encourage tradi-tionally masculine and feminine behavior on the part of their offspring, researchers have linked other characteristics of mothers and fathers to children's sex-role development during the preschool years. Most importantly, the general nurturance and warmth that children experience at the hands of their parents seem to affect the degree to which they will model and imitate behavior displayed by their parent of the same sex (Mussen and Rutherford 1963; Payne and Mussen 1956). In the case of daughters this was shown in an early study in which preschool girls were more likely to imitate the behavior of their mothers during a drawing task if mother was regarded as nurturant in contrast to nonnurturant (Mussen and Parker 1965). In the case of sons, a doll play study revealed that those boys who displayed the most characteristically masculine behavior outside the play situation made the father doll appear more nurturant and rewarding (Mussen and Distler 1959). The assumption in this investigation, of course, was that children were modeling the father doll's behavior after their own father's behavior.

Fathers' power and dominance in the family, especially when coupled with a warm and nurturant style, has also been linked to sons' masculinity, though it is unrelated to daughters' femininity (Mussen and Distler 1959; Biller 1969; Hetherington 1966). In the case of sons and daughters alike, fathers' own masculinity seems to promote traditional sex roles in children of both genders (Hetherington, Cox and Cox, 1978). This complementary influence of fathers on daughters reveals some interesting differences in processes of male and female development, as does research on the development of father-absent children.

The fact that fathers' masculinity, but not mothers' femininity, is associated with daughters' sex-role development suggests that girls acquire their sex-roles through a process of *reciprocal role learning*. That is, daughters learn how to be female by complementing fathers' maleness. A "lock 'n' key" analogy nicely captures the essence of this process of reciprocal roles. If a similar process were at work in boys' development, mothers' femininity would be systematically associated with sons' masculinity. As already noted, this is not the case. Indeed, all evidence suggests that identification with father, and imitation and modeling of his behavior, are the psychological processes of primary importance to males. Thus we find that boys with nurturant and powerful fathers are likely to be strongly masculine. Exactly why boys and girls should learn their sex-roles through different processes remains one of the unsolved mysteries of human development.

Boys and girls may differ in the process of acquiring their sex-role behavior in other ways. While there is some evidence that a sensitive period in male sex-role development may exist, no such evidence has been presented in the case of female sex-role development. Evidence that supports this notion, and the theory that boys become masculine by identifying with and modeling their fathers, comes from the study of children without fathers. Boys whose fathers leave home (because of death, desertion, or divorce) before they reach the age of five (but not after) grow up to be less traditionally masculine than do boys whose fathers are present and involved with them, or whose fathers leave home after this critical age (Hetherington and Deur 1971; Hetherington 1966; LeCorgne and Laosa 1976; Drake and McDougall 1977). That is, father-absent boys tend to be less aggressive, more dependent, and display a more feminine style of dealing with conflict (i.e., greater use of verbal than physical aggression). Interestingly, and importantly, the apparently detrimental effect of father absence on male development is lessened if an alternate male role model (uncle, older brother, neighbor) is available to the male child. In other words, if father leaves home before his son is five, but another male is involved in his life during this time, his masculinity is not nearly as severely compromised. This observation is extremely significant as it highlights the fact that while the period prior to five years of age is important to male sex-role development, it is not the father's presence per se that is critical, but the presence of a male role model. Mere presence alone, however, is not sufficient, as children whose fathers are physically present but psychologically and behaviorally unavailable seem to develop in the same way as children whose fathers are completely absent.

For years, boys reared in father-absent homes have been described in negative terms because of their failure to develop in the traditional masculine manner. The role that context plays in human development is most apparent as sex-role ideology changes and greater variability in the ways that boys and girls behave is tolerated, if not encouraged. Indeed, it is conceivable that the time may come when traditionally masculine behavior styles are no longer culturally valued and the male from the father-absent home who displays more traditionally female styles of behaving is seen to have certain advantages, as he more closely approximates a new ideal of androgynous, rather than gender-determined, personality.

CONCLUSION

Throughout this and the preceding chapter dealing with infancy, we have considered the state of current knowledge regarding parental influences upon child development. Although the available evidence certainly indicates that the manner in which parents rear their offspring affects their children's functioning, it would be inappropriate to ascribe too much influence to parents. Undoubtedly there are limits to the impact that parents have on children, if for no other reason than that there exist a variety of other agents and agencies of influence—like the peer group, the school, siblings, and the media, that affect the child. As we will see in the next chapter, which focuses upon adolescence, as children age they come into increasing contact with these other sources of influence. While the toddler, for example, may spend a little bit of time in a play group, the adolescent, in contrast, will spend more time in contact with age mates than with her parents. This is not to say that absolute quantity of time is the most important determinant of parents' or peers' influence. The warmth of the relationship that the child has with these social agents seems to be especially important. But time in contact with others is significant, too.

Consider, for instance, how a peer group can affect a child's intellectual and social development. Friends who value achievement will undoubtedly establish a climate in which studying and doing well in school is valued. Similarly, when friends value athletic competition and engage in sports frequently, it is likely that cooperative skills will be fostered as a function of the time spent being part of a team.

Even though children are influenced by persons other than parents, this does not mean that parents are not influential. We should recognize that what the child does outside of the family can be quite strongly influenced by the family. While it may be true, for example, that a child's aggressiveness is greatly affected by the peer group in which he or she participates, it is also true that selection of a peer group can be affected by parents. Parental influence here can be direct, as when parents restrict children's contact with certain age mates, or it may be indirect, as when the quality of care the child received fosters an aggressive orientation, which itself directs the child toward a group of peers that takes pride in behaving in an antisocial manner. This illustration of an indirect influence highlights, of course, the complex ways in which parents can influence their offspring's developmental trajectories and how children, through the selection of a peer group, function to produce their own development.

CHAPTER 6

Adolescence: Family Relationships and Other Contextual Relations

A s children reach adolescence a host of individual and contextual changes occur. For instance, changes associated with puberty alter the adolescent's body, and, socially, new school settings (junior and senior high schools) and arenas of activity, like part-time employment (Steinberg et al. 1982), are entered. Such changes do not require adolescents to leave their families, but during this developmental period the child's social horizons are broadened and less time is spent in the family setting. In addition, it is often the individual changes of adolescence, such as emerging sexual maturity, that promote this alteration in orientation from family to, for example, peers (Freud 1969). In other words, the family may not so much lose its influence on the adolescent as it must share its influence with other socializing agents. In fact, some theorists contend that it is the key developmental task of adolescence to establish the separation of self from parents (Erikson 1959, 1963, 1968; Freud 1969). Thus, they claim that unless the child defines him- or herself as different from his or her parents, the child can never be in a position to make an independent contribution to society's maintenance and perpetuation (Lerner and Spanier 1980). Because of adolescents' need to establish themselves as independent from their parents—the "older generation"—many theorists say that the adolescent period should be marked by several key phenomena:

First, intensely experienced differences of opinion, and strongly evident differences in behavior, between the younger, adolescent generation and the older, parental one should exist. For this reason theorists have argued that a "generation gap" should exist (see Adelson 1970; Gallatin 1975; Lerner and Spanier 1980, for reviews);

Second, adolescents should be more oriented to, and influenced by, peers than parents. That is, because of the need to establish a separate sense of self, one distinct from one's family, adolescents should be prone to move to a social setting where there is less of a constraint on their attempts at self-definition; one available social setting will be composed of other people facing a similar developmental task and, of course, this social setting is the peer group. Thus, the idea here is that adolescents should have as their primary social "objects" peers, not parents (Freud 1969);

Finally, theorists who claim that these first two phenomena characterize adolescence also point out that breaking long-held family ties is not easy, either emotionally or behaviorally. The adolescent is still attached to his/her parents, but has at the same time a compelling need to break with them. This situation represents an approach-avoidance conflict which can create considerable stress for the adolescent and his family. As such, theorists describing this process conclude that the adolescent period is inevitably filled with conflict and stress. In fact, adolescence is often described as a period of "storm and stress" (Freud 1969; Hall 1904); and indeed this view of the adolescent period is the one stereotypically held in society (Anthony 1969) and depicted in the mass media (Gallatin 1975).

In order to understand the child in the family during adolescence, then, it is necessary to view the person and family in a broader contextual perspective. One must understand the concomitant role of the peer group and the societal pressures upon the adolescent for finding a separate definition of self or, to use Erikson's (1959, 1963, 1968) terms, *an identity*. Moreover, in attempting to attain this broader understanding we need to evaluate ideas that speak directly to the nature of *inter*generational, adolescent-parent relations, to *intra*generational, adolescent-peer relations, and to individual adolescent emotional developments. In this chapter we consider all these topics. To facilitate discussion it is useful to overview the nature of the child's transition from childhood to adolescence and depict some components of the adolescent experience that occur as a consequence of the combination of individual and contextual changes characterizing this developmental period. Indeed, we will try to explain precisely why and how the person making the transition from childhood to adolescence is faced with a challenge of re-creating his or her self-definition—a developmental task we have noted is regarded as the core problem of adolescence—precisely because of the combination of changes involved in adolescence. In succeeding sections we indicate some of the issues and facts pertinent to many of these change processes. Following this discussion we will return to the issue of self-definition, or identity.

THE ADOLESCENT'S TRANSITIONAL EXPERIENCES

The most obvious changes that adolescents go through are those associated with their anatomy and physiology. New hormones are produced by the endocrine glands, and these generate alterations in the primary sexual characteristics with the emergence of secondary sexual characteristics. The "child" thus begins to look and feel different. There is also a change in emotional functioning as a consequence of these physical and hormonal changes. New hormones that induce sexual changes produce new drives and new feelings. In combination with changing social influences such as peer pressure and the mass media, and a renewed or accelerated interest in members of the other sex, the individual becomes more sexually oriented.

All these physical, psychological, and emotional changes are complicated by the fact that the person is also undergoing congnitive changes. New thought capabilities come to characterize the adolescent (Elkind 1967; Piaget 1969, 1972). Rather than being tied to the concrete physical reality of what is, the adolescent becomes capable of dealing with hypothetical and abstract aspects of reality. He or she no longer sees the way the world is organized as the only way it could be arranged. He or she no longer takes as concrete, immutable things the system of government, the orders of parents, his or her status in the peer group, and the rules imposed on him or her by others. Rather, as the new thought capabilities that allow the person to think abstractly, hypothetically, and counter-factually come into existence, they allow the person to imagine how things *could be*. These imaginings could relate to government, self, parents' rules, or what he or she will do in life. In short, anything and everything becomes the focus of an adolescent's hypothetical, counter-factual, and imaginary thinking.

For both psychological and sociological reasons, the major focus of the adolescent's concerns becomes the adolescent himself or herself. First, psychologically, the adolescent's inner processes are all going through changes, and the physical, physiological, emotional, and cognitive components of the person are undergoing major alterations. Now, with any object being able to be thought of in a new, different, hypothetical way, and with the individual changing so radically, he or she appropriately focuses inward to try to understand what is going on.

The person will ask: What is the nature of this change? What will it do to me? What will I become? Am I the same person that I think I am? As all of these uncertainties are being introduced, another set of problems arises. At the very time he or she may be least prepared to deal with further complications and uncertainties, the adolescent in our society typically is asked to make a choice, a decision about what he or she is going to do when grown. Society, perhaps in the form of parents or teachers, want adolescents to choose a role. Thus, in today's society, as soon as they go into junior high or early in high school, the adult world asks them to choose between a college preparatory program or a non-college preparatory program. By approximately age thirteen, adolescents must begin to put themselves on a path that will affect what will happen years and years later.

The important point being made here is that at precisely the time in life when adolescents seem least ready to make a long-term choice, they often are asked to do so. In order to reconcile the changes being experienced, and to cope with the demands made on them, American adolescents have to make choices. To say what they will do, to commit themselves to a role, they have to know what their capabilities are. They have to know what they can do well and what they want to do. In short, they have to know themselves.

Many adolescents are, understandably, in a dilemma. They cannot answer the social-role questions without settling other questions about themselves. The answers to one set of questions are interdependent with the answers to the others. A feeling of crisis may emerge, one that requires finding out precisely who one is now. This really is a question of self-definition, of self-identification. Erikson (1959) labels this dilemma the *identity crisis*.

To summarize, the adolescent—because of the impact of all these changes converging on him or her—may be described as in a state of crisis, a state of search for self-definition. Accordingly, the adolescent moves through his or her days attempting to find a place, or role, in society. Such definition will provide a set of rules for beliefs, attitudes, and values (an "ideology") and a prescription for behaviors (a role) that will enable the persons to know what they will "do with themselves" in the world. They will try to find out if they can begin to think like someone who engages in particular behaviors (e.g., being a doctor, a lawyer, a nurse, or a telephone operator).

Thus, the search for identity arises as a consequence of the combined influence of the changes the adolescent undergoes and, in turn, resolution of one's identity is a means of reconciling problems created by the combination of these changes. As noted, we will consider some of the major facts and issues involved in several of these change processes. Our discussion will necessarily lead to a reconsideration of the issue of identity. However, our journey will lead us first through the most salient of the new social settings for the adolescent—the peer group—wherein many of the attempts at identity are tested and evaluated. In turn, because the adolescent does not typically leave the family, we will next consider the nature of the adolescent's family context and the actual influence of peers and parents on the adolescent's behavior. These discussions will allow us to evaluate issues pertinent to the generation gap and whether the adolescent period is necessarily stormy and stressful. Finally, this discussion will close with an evaluation of the role of family relations in facilitating or hindering the adolescent's key emotional development task—the establishment of an identity.

PEER RELATIONS IN ADOLESCENCE

The study of peer relations is sometimes referred to as the study of *intragenerational* relationships because peers are members of the same generation. The study of adolescent-parent relationships, which crosses generations, is the study of *intergenerational* relationships. A *generation* is a group of people born during one period of history. Thus, peer relations are sometimes called intragenerational relations because peers are born within the same generation. The length of a generation is the span of time between one's birth and the birth of one's children. In the United States this period averages about 25 years.

Perhaps the most notable social phenomenon of adolescence is the emergence of the marked salience of peer groups. Peers have the ability to make an adolescent feel on top of the world or at the bottom of the social ladder. Peers hold the key to adolescent popularity or rejection. Peers informally instruct the adolescent on how to talk, how to dress, and how to eat. And it is often the intensity of the way one conforms to peer group norms that serves as a basis of parent-adolescent conflict.

Peer groups certainly exist in childhood, but they become more central to the individual during adolescence. The adolescent comes to rely heavily on the peer group for support, security, and guidance. Marked peer-group importance probably emerges because there is a great need for such support, security, and guidance during these years of transition, and it is easiest to find such things among others who are undergoing the same transition and with whom much time is spent. From the standpoint of the adolescent, the peer group has much to offer: it is a sounding board that gives constant feedback that all is well (or not so well) as adolescence progresses; it answers some of the important questions of adolescence (for example, about sexual relations and drug and alcohol use); and, by virtue of its size, it helps legitimize any behaviors or activities in which its members engage.

All peer groups change over time. During adolescence, persons begin new types of interaction with members of the opposite sex, including dating. They move into a new school environment (junior high or high school), and they engage in a multitude of activities that may be new to them (for example, organized sports, dances, after-school clubs). All of these new experiences can be mildly threatening if approached alone. The peer group often provides group support to its individual members so that these transitions become less formidable. Thus, it can be argued that influential peer groups emerge during adolescence to help the individual through some new transitions, and provide support, security, and guidance to the persons involved.

In addition to the peer group's influence there is another part of the social context that is quite influential for adolescents. This, of course, is the family. During adolescence, family relations have been examined primarily in terms of their influence relative to peers.

THE RELATIVE INFLUENCE OF PARENTS AND PEERS

Adolescents exist simultaneously within both family and peer groups, and one may ask how such dual commitments influence the adolescent's behavior and socialization. Do the family and peer relationships that adolescents have contribute in similar ways to development, or is one set of relationships more influential? There are data to suggest that both parents and peers are important. However, depending on the context and meaning of the social relationship, either parents or peers may be shown to be *more* influential.

Despite the alleged presence of a generation gap between adolescents and their parents (Adelson 1970; Gallatin 1975), and the belief that stormy and stressful adolescent periods inevitably arise as a consequence of these gaps, scientific research indicates that *among fourteen- to eighteen-year-old male and female adolescents, there are few, if any, serious disagreements with parents* (Douvan and Adelson 1966). This perhaps surprising finding stands in contrast to reports derived from anecdotal accounts, from clinical case studies, and from literary depictions of the adolescent years (Gallatin 1975). The majority of the pertinent scientific findings derive essentially from relatively large-scale questionnaire and interview studies. While other methodological approaches to studying adolescent-parent and adolescent-peer relations (intensive home-based behavioral observations, for instance) might present us with a different set of findings—perhaps one more consistent with the popular lore about adolescents—it is the case that we must currently rely on the extant empirical literature.

As noted, this literature speaks with a surprisingly consistent voice. Douvan and Adelson (1966) report that in choosing their peers adolescents are oriented toward those who have attitudes and values consistent with those maintained by the parents and adopted by the adolescents themselves. Similarly, Smith (1976), in a more recent study of over 1,000 sixth- through twelfth-grade urban and suburban black and white adolescents, found that the family, more so than the peer group, influences the adolescent to seek the advice and consider the opinions of parents. Kandel and Lesser (1972) report similar findings. Together, these data also suggest that the alleged movement away from parents and toward peers (Freud, 1969) is not generally characteristic of the adolescent period.

Indeed, although there are data indicating that during adolescence the person spends more time with peers than with parents (Bandura 1964; Douvan and Adelson 1966), this shift in time commitments does not necessarily indicate a corresponding alteration from parental to peer influence. For instance, Costanzo and Shaw (1966) found that conformity to peer group norms increased between seven and twelve years of age for males and for females, but it declined thereafter. Floyd and South (1972) studied sixth, eighth, tenth, and twelfth grade male and female orientation to parents and peers. Although they found less orientation to parents and more orientation to peers in the older age groups, there was still a trend toward mixed orientation—to both parents and peers—in these older age groups. Thus, not only are the influences of parents and peers compatible with respect to the values and behavioral orientations of the adolescents with whom these parents and peers interact (Douvan and Adelson 1966), but at older ages adolescents show an orientation to be influenced simultaneously by both these generational groups (Floyd and South 1972).

In fact, not only does it appear that this dual influence exists, but also it seems that the generational group that is more influential at any particular time depends upon the issue adolescents are confronting. Floyd and South (1972) found that when parents were seen as the better source of information about a particular issue, adolescents were more parent- than peer-oriented. Larson (1972) also found that the demands of the particular choice situation determined adolescents' choice, regardless of the direction of parent or peer pressures. This was true despite the fact that the fourth, ninth, and twelfth graders Larson (1972) studied more often complied with parental than with peer desires. Similarly, Brittain (1963) found that both parents and peers influence adolescents, depending on the issue at hand, with adolescent females being more likely to accept the advice of parents concerning the future and the advice of peers concerning school-related issues. Another study reported data consistent with these findings. Kandel and Lesser (1969) found that 85 percent of middle-class adolescents and 82 percent of lower-class adolescents were influenced directly by parents in formulating future goals (in this case concerning educational plans). Because of the prominence and importance of education and educational attainments in modern society, it is of particular interest to focus on the body of work designed specifically to assess the relative influence of family and peers on education.

Family and Peer Influences on Education

The family and peers influence both aspirations about and actual outcomes of the adolescent's accomplishments in school. According to information from the U.S. Bureau of the Census (1978), the college aspirations of high school seniors tend to be correlated with the educational attainment of the head of the household in which they live. About 70 percent of students living in households in which the head had completed at least one year of college had definite college plans themselves. When the head of the household had completed high school, but not any college, only 45 percent of students had definite college plans. Of those living in families having a household head who had not completed high school, only 35 percent had definite college plans.

Over and above parents' own education, there are particular types of parent-child relationships during adolescence that appear to facilitate successful school functioning. Morrow and Wilson (1961) found that high-achieving adolescents, as compared to a group of low achievers, tended to come from families where they were involved in family decisions, where ideas and activities were shared by family members, and where parents were likely to give approval and praise of the adolescent's performance and show trust in the adolescent's competence. In turn, low-achieving adolescents came from families marked by parental dominance and restrictiveness (Morrow and Wilson 1961). Moreover, both Morrow and Wilson (1961) and Shaw and White (1965) found that high-achieving adolescents tend to identify with their parents while low-achieving adolescents do not.

Other researchers have also reported that the type of parenting studied found by Morrow and Wilson (1961) is systematically related to adolescent high-school achievement. Both Swift (1967) and Rehberg and Westby (1967) report, for example, that parental encouragement and rewards are associated with better adolescent school performance. Similarly, Wolf (1964) discovered that parent-child interactions that involve encouragement to achieve and the development of language skills are highly correlated with intelligence. Recall that these are many of the same characteristics of parenting found to be related to school achievement and intelligence at younger ages.

Peers also influence adolescents' aspirations and educational performance. And, in most cases, there is convergence between family and peer influences. Rigsby and McDill (1972), in a study of over 20,000 adolescents, found that there was a positive relation between the proportion of peers perceived to have college plans, the actual proportion of college plans, and adolescents' own likelihood of planning for college. Similarly, Kandel and Lesser (1969) observed that when adolescent peer relationships are characterized by closeness and intimacy, there is a great deal of correspondence between the educational aspirations of the peers and of the adolescent. Importantly, most adolescents' educational plans (57 percent) agreed with peers and parents. In turn, among those adolescents who disagreed with their parents, there was also a great likelihood (50 percent) that they would disagree with peers as well. Moreover, in those cases where there was a discrepancy between parent and peer orientations, it was most likely that the parental orientation prevailed (Kandel and Lesser, 1969).

The "Contemporary" Social Context and the Relative Influence of Parents and Peers

The social context changes and as a consequence so too do the issues of immediate, current concern to different age groups. For example, in the 1960s youth found issues of war and peace to be of prime saliency, whereas in the 1970s domestic economic issues were seen by youth as more prominent. When an issue is of immediate contemporary relevance, do parents or peers exert greater influence on the adolescent?

As with the previously reviewed research, studies in this area show an orientation to parents and peers, depending on the issue of contemporary concern. Chand, Crider, and Willets (1975), for example, found agreement between adolescents and parents on issues related to religion and marriage, but not on issues related to sex and drugs. Similarly, Kelley (1972) found high parent-adolescent similarity on moral issues, but not on issues pertinent to style of dress, hair length, and hours of sleep.

It is important to note that although several studies indicate that groups of adolescents and parents have somewhat different attitudes about issues of contemporary social concern (e.g., war, drug use, and sexuality), most of these differences reflect contrasts in attitude intensity rather than attitude direction (Lerner et al. 1975; Lerner and Knapp 1975; Lerner et al. 1972; Weinstock and Lerner 1972). That is, rather than one generational group agreeing with an issue while the other group disagrees (a directional difference), most generational group differences involved just different levels of agreement (a matter of intensity). For example, in regard to a statement such as "Birth control devices and information should be made available to all who desire them," one study found that adolescents showed strong agreement with the item, while their mothers showed moderate agreement with the item (Lerner and Knapp 1975).

Finally, consistent with the above data indicating influences by both peers and parents, there is evidence suggesting that adolescents perceive their own attitudes as lying between these two generational groups. In one study adolescents were asked to rate their own attitudes towards a list of thirty-six statements pertaining to the issues of contemporary social concern noted above; in addition, they rated these same statements in terms of how they thought their peers would respond to them; lastly, they responded in terms of how they thought their parents would answer. The adolescents tended to see their own attitudes as lying *between* those of others of their own generation and those of their parent's generation (with twenty-seven—or 75 percent—of the thirty-six items). Adolescents tended to place their own positions between the "conservative" end of the continuum, where they tended to put parents, and the "liberal" end, where they tended to place peers. Interestingly, adolescents think their peers are more liberal than they actually are. In essence, this means that adolescents think their friends are, for example, using more drugs and having more sex than is actually the case.

In sum, the available evidence indicates that adolescents and their parents do not have many major differences in attitudes and values. Apparently, the impact of the intra- and intergenerational social contexts often is compatible. Indeed, adolescents tend to perceive that their values lie between those of their parents and peers. With this knowledge about intra- and intergenerational relations in adolescence we can now directly focus on the issue of the generation gap. This evaluation of adolescent-parent relations will facilitate our discussion, in the succeeding section, of the role of family relations in identity development.

THE GENERATION GAP

Despite the character of the influence of parents and peers that actually exists for the adolescent, there are recurring reports in the media and elsewhere that suggest that significant disparities exist between adolescents and their parents. When social scientists discuss such differences between the generations, the term *generation gap* is often used. The presence of such a gap would suggest a basis for conflict between adolescents and their parents.

The research we have considered already suggests that when the *actual* attitudes of adolescents and their parents are compared, few major differences in attitude can be found, although intensity differences often do exist. However, most studies find even this type of intergenerational disparity to occur in only a minority of attitude comparisons between generations (Lerner et al. 1975; Lerner and Knapp 1975; Lerner et al. 1972). These data suggest that the purported generation gap may be more apparent than real (Adelson 1970).

Nevertheless, there are both empirical and theoretical reasons to expect a generation gap to exist to some degree. There are data showing that adolescents and parents do not perceive the influence of social relationships accurately. Adolescents perceive their parents to be less influential than they actually are while parents perceive that they are more influential than they actually are (Bengtson and Troll 1978; Lerner 1975; Lerner and Knapp 1975). For example, two studies compared the actual and the perceived attitudes of adolescents and parents (Lerner et al. 1975; Lerner and Knapp 1975). Actual intergenerational differences in attitudes about issues of contemporary societal concern occurred with fewer than 30 percent of the comparisons made in either study by Lerner and his colleagues. However, in both investigations, adolescents *over-*

estimated the magnitude of the differences that existed between themselves and their parents; they saw their parents as having attitudes less congruent with their own than was actually the case. In both studies, parents *underestimated* the extent of differences between themselves and their children; they saw their children as having attitudes very consistent with their own. Thus, although only a small and selective generation gap can be said to actually exist, parents underestimate this division while adolescents overestimate it.

Both psychological and sociological theorists have suggested reasons for the existence of these different perceptions regarding the generation gap. Erikson (1959, 1963) believes adolescence is a period in life which involves the establishment of a sense of personal identity, or self-definition. Other theorists (e.g., Elkind 1967; Piaget 1950, 1970) stress that adolescence is, as well, a period involving the development of new thought capabilities; these capabilities lead adolescents to believe their ideas are not only new in their own lives, but in general as well. Together, then, adolescents need to establish their own identities, and tend to believe in the uniqueness of their thoughts. These orientations may lead them to believe they are quite different from those around them—especially their parents. This might result in their overemphasizing and magnifying whatever differences actually exist (Lerner 1975).

A sociological approach suggests why parents might minimize differences between themselves and their children. Bengtson and Kuypers (1971) suggest that members of the parental generational group have a stake in maximizing consistency between themselves and members of their children's generation. The parents have "invested" in society—for example, by pursuing their careers and accumulating society's resources. Because they want to protect this investment, they rear their children—the new members of society—in ways that maintain the society in which they have invested. It may be that as a consequence of such a "generational stake" (Bengtson and Kuypers 1971; Bengtson and Troll 1978), parents are oriented to believing they have produced children who—because they agree with parental attitudes—will protect their investment. This orientation is consistent with one Erikson (1959, 1963) describes; he believes that adults have a psychosocial need to feel they have generated children who will perpetuate society. This idea, as well as the generational stake idea, suggests that parents may be oriented to minimizing whatever differences exist between themselves and the adolescent children.

In summary, both theory and research combine to suggest that the adolescent's social context is composed of not one, but several, generation gaps. First, there exists a relatively minor and selective set of differences between adolescents and their parents. However, in addition to this actual gap, there exist two perceived gaps: the overestimated one of the adolescents and the underestimated one of the parents. The potential presence and function of these gaps makes the social context of the adolescent a complex, diverse setting; we continue to see this complexity as we now examine the role of the social context in a central feature of adolescent development — identity.

THE ROLE OF THE SOCIAL CONTEXT IN ADOLESCENT IDENTITY DEVELOPMENT

We have already noted that a key feature of adolescents' personality development — their identity development — involves their cognitive and perceptual orientation to their parents. In other words, the parents provide a stimulus source around which the adolescents organize cognitive and perceptual components of their ego identity. Parents are more than passive stimulus sources, however. Considerable evidence shows that the nature of adolescents' interactions with their parents, as well as with other people in their social context, influences identity development. Of course, there are good theoretical reasons to expect that individual adolescent development is reciprocally linked to social interaction.

Since achieving an identity denotes finding a role meeting society's demands, identity-development processes are basically interpersonal ones. They link the person to society in a way that facilitates both individual and social maintenance and survival. One might expect, then, that people who have achieved identity should engage in interpersonal relationships useful in advancing this individual and social functioning, i.e., intimate relations. Orlofsky, Marcia, and Lesser (1973) found evidence of just such a relation. In a study of fifty-three college males, they reported that those subjects who were ranked as achieving an identity were among those who had the greatest capacity for intimate interpersonal relationships. The interpersonal relationships of adolescents who had not achieved an identity tended to be stereotyped, superficial, and hence not very intimate. Similarly, Kacerguis and Adams (1981) studied forty-four male and forty-four female college students, and found that those people of either sex who were in this Identity Achievement category were more likely to be engaged in intimate relationships than were males or females in non-identity achievement categories. People in these other groups were much more variable in their level of intimacy.

Because identity links the adolescent to his or her social world, a basis of the different interpersonal styles of adolescents that indicate the presence or absence of identity achievement may lie in their social interaction history; perhaps this involves the family, since the family is the major social institution structuring those societal demands to which the person must adapt.

Several studies suggest that parental personal and interpersonal characteristics may be transmitted to their offspring, in the context of the family milieu the parents help create, to foster identity development. LaVoie (1976) reports that male high school students high in identity reported less regulation and control by their mothers and fathers, and more frequent praise by their fathers, than did males low in identity. Similarly, LaVoie found that high-identity high school females reported less maternal restrictiveness and greater freedom to discuss problems with their mothers and fathers than did low-identity females. Thus, *high-identity adolescents appear to be characterized by a family milieu involving less parental restrictiveness and better child-parent communication than do low-identity adolescents*. Waterman and Waterman (1971) and Matteson (1974) provide further data to support this conclusion. Note how consistent these facilitative styles of parenting are with those discussed in the preceding two chapters focused on infancy and childhood.

In their longitudinal study of college freshman, Waterman and Waterman (1971) found that those students who showed stable identity-achievement status for the entire year, which many did not, scored significantly higher on a measure of family independence than did those students who changed out of the Achievement status. In the study by Matteson (1974), involving ninth-grade students, a measure of adolescent self-esteem and of communication with parents was taken. In addition, the parents of the adolescents completed questionnaires about parent-adolescent communication and their own marital communication. Matteson reported that adolescents with low self-esteem viewed communication with their parents as less facilitative than did adolescents with high self-esteem. Moreover, parents of low self-esteem adolescents perceived their communication with their spouses as less facilitative, and rated their marriages as less satisfying, than did parents of adolescents with high self-esteem. Thus, characteristics of family milieu relating to communication quality among *all* family members and to patterns of parental control appear to relate to identity development.

Of course, milieus having such characteristics need not be just conventional American familial ones. Although there have been few studies, other types of family structures, on the one hand, or other types of social milieus, on the other, can promote such development. In this regard, Long, Henderson, and Platt (1973) studied fifty-one Israeli male and female adolescents, aged eleven to thirteen years, reared in a *kibbutzim,* and compared them to two groups of youths of the same age reared in more traditional family settings. In the kibbutzim family system children are reared collectively by adults who are not necessarily their parents. In fact, in this system children may often spend at most a few hours a day with either biological parent. And in the kibbutzim system the individual's contribution to the group is emphasized, as is equality of all group members despite their age or role. The adolescents reared in this setting showed more social interest and higher self-esteem than those adolescents reared in other settings.

The college environment is another nonfamilial social milieu that supports open communication of ideas and minimal restrictiveness of search for roles. Sanford (1962) has speculated that because of these properties the college experience promotes movement toward identity achievement. The longitudinal data of Waterman and Waterman (1971), Waterman, Geary, and Waterman (1974), and Waterman and Goldman (1976) support this view. Most college students experience an identity crisis during their college years and, of these, 75 percent reach the achievement status.

Although further research is needed to evaluate the appropriateness of these interpretations, it does appear that if an adolescent is placed in a social setting, including the family, involving openness of social communication and minimal restrictiveness on role search, an adaptive coordination between self and society will be attained. An identity will be achieved.

CONCLUSION

In this final chapter on parental influence, we have learned that the experience of the child in the family influences both cognitive and personality development. In adolescence the family influence functions in concert with the influence of the peer group. Not surprisingly, then, most adolescents are not mere replicas of their parents. This is not to say, of course, that peers and parents pull the individual adolescent in opposite directions. As we have shown, peer influence and family influence are often complementary and usually not conflictual. Thus, whatever the nature of popular stereotypes, the generation gap is more myth than reality, and the storm and stress characterization of adolescence in the family is more the exception than the rule. Of course, variation exists in the experience of adolescents and their families. And, as we will see in the next chapter, such variation in family experience is often of the individual child's own making.

Having reviewed patterns of parental influence from infancy through adolescence in this and the previous two chapters, it is reasonable to ask before considering a child's effects on parenting whether there is any evidence of continuity in parenting over time. For example, is it the case that the mother who is sensitively responsive and appropriately stimulating to her infant will then adopt an authoritative approach to her preschool and school-age child, and will be comfortable in trusting her adolescent with a high degree of autonomy apart from a great deal of external control? In view of the documented benefits of each of these seemingly developmentally appropriate approaches to parenting, there is surprisingly little evidence on this issue. In point of fact, we know almost nothing about how parental functioning at one age relates to that at another age.

There is reason to expect that there would be some continuity over time. Presumably, the responsive, stimulating caregiver of an infant, the authoritative parent of a preschooler, and the nonrestrictive parent of an adolescent share a common skill—the ability to recognize and respond to the developmental capacities of their offspring and the challenges their children face. One might expect that the parent who can diagnose and provide what is appropriate at one age would be able to do so at another.

But this may not be the case. Some parents enjoy caring for dependent babies but find it difficult to care for autonomous adolescents. Alternatively, it may be the ever-growing independence of the school-age and adolescent child that some parents like, while the clingy dependence of the infant or toddler is something they find to be difficult to handle. In such cases there would seem to be more reason to expect discontinuity to characterize parenting across developmental periods than continuity.

| CHAPTER | **Child Effects** |
| 7 | **on Parenting** |

The preceding chapters were devoted to detailing what is currently known about how parents influence the development of their offspring throughout infancy, childhood, and adolescence. We have noted in several places already that the parent-child relationship is bidirectional in nature, with parents influencing children and children influencing parents. This reciprocal process of influence occurs at both micro and molar levels of analysis. From a microanalytic standpoint, we can see that when a parent tickles a three month old, the baby is likely to smile in response to this stimulation, and that this response is likely to evoke a smile or further tickling from the parent. Thus, at the level of discrete interactive behavior, a chain of interaction characterizes the developing parent-child relationship. At a more molar level of analysis, we can think about bidirectionality by considering how an aggressive or disobedient child might elicit punitive and hostile care and about how such care then feeds back over time, to promote still further aggression.

The identification of the actual starting point of such complex chains of reciprocal influence is quite difficult. Indeed, consideration of this problem frequently leads one to conclude that the behavior of the parent and of the child are so inextricably intertwined that we are dealing with a "chicken-egg" dilemma. Which comes first? For purposes of this chapter we are not as concerned with which influence actually comes first as we are with the ways in which children can influence parenting. In contrast to the preceding chapter, in which we adopted a developmental framework to consider parental influences during the infancy and preschool years before considering the school-age and adolescent years, in this chapter we employ a more topical approach. That is, we consider first ways in which the age or developmental status of the child and the child's gender influence parenting, and then examine the way in which other domains of individual difference, including temperament and risk for developmental delay, affect parenting.

Before embarking upon an examination of such child effects two points need to be made. First, the impact of the child upon the parent is very likely to be mediated by the parents' own characteristics of individuality, including his or her own level of psychological development (Sameroff 1975). Thus, when certain characteristics of the child harmoniously intermesh with the parent's behavioral tendencies, smooth, synchronous, and developmentally facilitative interactions are likely to take place. Consider, for example, how an adolescent fascinated with mathematics is likely to get along with a father who happens to be an engineer. In contrast to such good-fitting characteristics of parent and child, it is likely that difficult and possibly developmentally problematic relationships will emerge when parent and child characteristics do not complement each other. As an example, consider the experience of a dyad in which the mother is looking forward to the opportunity to hold her baby physically close and express love in this manner yet has an infant who tends to find close bodily contact, though not more distal interpersonal stimulation, disturbing. Clearly the prospects of conflict, or at least disappointment, are great in such a mother-infant relationship. The point to be made here is that the goodness-of-fit that exists between child and parent is likely to be an important determinant of just how children will affect the care they receive.

A second point that needs to be underscored regarding child effects involves the developmental implications of children's impact upon their parents. Since children, as we shall argue, do influence their parents' behavior, and since, as we have already seen, parents influence their children's development, the possibility must be entertained that children serve as "producers" of, or at least contributors to, their own development (Lerner and Busch-Rossnagel 1981). That is, by initiating processes whereby parents are affected by the child and then serve to influence the child, children can strongly impact their own developmental trajectories. As an example, consider the unassertive preschooler who places few demands for attention on his parents. If, in response to the child, the parents require little of him, then the potentially positive effect of stimulating parental involvement on intellectual competence may not be experienced. Thus, the child in this instance has served, inadvertently, to undermine his own functioning—by failing to elicit a certain quality of care.

But the possibility must be entertained that even aspects of the child that serve to encourage or discourage growth-facilitating parental involvement are, in actuality, dependent on the parent, that is, they only exert their influence as a function of the parent. Indeed, we noted in an earlier chapter that the same characteristic of the child may lead to differing developmental outcomes *if* expressed in significantly different parental/familial contexts; that is, the feedback the child gets depends critically on who his/her characteristics are stimulating (and therefore on the demands, attitudes, behaviors, and so forth of these significant others). Child effects *cannot* be understood independent of the context within which they are expressed. It must be noted, too, that aspects of the child's behavior that are regarded as attractive or unattractive and influence parental care may actually be a product of the experience the child has had in the family. Furthermore, many of the "child effects" we will chronicle can only occur if the parents respond in a certain manner. Parents, then, as much create what we will be calling child effects as do the children. Neither parent nor child can be completely understood apart from the reciprocal parent-child relationship. Thus, while a child effect could often be labeled a parental effect, for heuristic purposes we nevertheless speak in terms of parent and child effects, as we think such analysis underscores the complex nature of the parent-child relationship.

Our capacity to conceptualize the dynamic processes through which children influence the care they receive exceeds our current scientific ability to empirically measure and capture such reciprocal processes of influence (Lerner, Skinner, and Sorell 1980). As a result, we rely in this chapter mostly upon research findings that document unidirectional child-to-adult effects. At times we consider such effects in terms of the goodness-of-fit between parent and child and in terms of extended processes whereby children contribute to their own development. When we do not explore such implications of the material reviewed, the reader will be well served to reflect upon such processes. Our goal here is to assist in, and provide the opportunity for, thinking dynamically about parent-child relations.

GENDER

Probably the first information that parents receive regarding their child concerns its gender. Either they ask "Is it a boy or a girl," or the obstetrician or nurse/midwife pronounces "It's a boy" or "It's a girl" very shortly following delivery of the newborn. As most of us know all too well, what gender we are strongly influences the ways in which people treat us. The hope of many is that such effects of child gender on parents' and others' behavior will decrease as contemporary American society continues to change so that boys and girls and men and women are treated more equally. Some doubt exists as to whether completely equal treatment, and complete absence of consideration of an individual's gender, will ever be fully realized or should be realized. Only history will determine whether such a state of affairs comes to characterize interpersonal relationships. We know now, however, that children's gender remains a strong determinant of parental treatment. Indeed, this is one of the most powerful child effects that there is.

The effect of child gender in shaping parental behavior is evident as early as the opening days of life. In a study conducted by Rubin, Provenzano, and Luria (1974), it was discovered that parents were more likely to describe their newborns as softer, smaller, cuter, less attentive, and more delicate if they were girls than if they were boys. Fathers were more sex-typed than mothers in their perceptions, reading more strength, size, coordination, and alertness into their sons' characters, even without necessarily ever handling their newborns. It should come as little surprise, then, that parents treat their offspring differently—throughout childhood and adolescence—since they confront their offspring with preconceived notions of what boys and girls are like even before they have had much opportunity to get to know them.

The differential treatment that boys and girls experience is evident in both parents' behavior during the infancy years but, as will be the case throughout childhood, tends to be more marked for father-son relationships. Several observational investigations of father-infant interaction reveal that fathers prefer to interact with, and behave in a different manner toward, boys than girls (Parke 1978). Fathers have been found, for example, as early as the first days, weeks, and months of life to look more at sons than at daughters and to provide sons with more visual and tactile stimulation. Some evidence also indicates that fathers are more likely to engage in routine caregiving (e.g., diapering, feeding) if their offspring are male. In the second year of life, fathers verbalize more to boys and engage them in play more regularly. This differential interest in, and involvement with, sons in infancy should also not be surprising, as even before the child is born fathers show a general preference for having a son (Hoffman 1977).

The quality of mother's behavior during infancy is also susceptible to gender effects, though not as strongly as father's. The one dimension of behavior for which consistent effects of gender have been observed is maternal verbal activity. During the infancy years mothers, on the average, are more likely to talk to girls and are more verbally responsive to their daughters' vocalizations (Lewis and Ban 1971). The fact that girls tend to be more verbally skilled throughout childhood suggests two possible interpretations of the finding that mothers talk more to daughters. Girls may be more oriented to verbal stimulation and thereby elicit more such behavior from mother, or the extra verbal input that daughters receive may facilitate their language development. Of course, both processes may be at work simultaneously. To the extent that they are, we observe a process whereby children, in this case infants, produce their own development.

Gender effects become especially pronounced during the preschool years. In one study of two year olds, boys received parental encouragement to play with toys that could be regarded as traditionally masculine (such as pull toys, blocks, trucks) whereas girls were encouraged to play with dolls, to dance, and to dress up in mother's clothes (traditionally feminine activities). Importantly, while parents discouraged boys from playing with dolls, less rigorous efforts were made to inhibit girls' running, jumping, and climbing (Fagot 1978).

Exactly what is going on in these efforts should be self-evident. As children get older, more explicit efforts are made to have them behave in a manner consistent with traditional sex roles. But these data also highlight a general pattern of socialization that is true throughout childhood, namely, greater pressure and effort are placed upon boys to conform to masculine ideals than upon girls to conform to feminine ones. In fact, the available evidence indicates that parents, particularly fathers, tend to react more negatively to feminine behaviors in boys than to masculine behaviors in girls. As Emmerich (1959) suggested quite some time ago, the basic developmental task for boys seems to be learning not to be a girl, whereas for girls it is learning not to be a baby. Consider, in this regard, the labels we use to characterize male and female children who engage in opposite-sex play. Boys are negatively labeled "sissies," whereas girls receive the more neutral label "tomboy."

As children grow older, the effect of child gender upon parental behavior remains pronounced. Girls are encouraged to maintain close family ties and to be more dependent. Boys, in contrast, are encouraged to explore more, to achieve more, and to be more independent and competitive. Traditionally, fathers have displayed a special concern for the achievement of their sons, and are likely to stress the importance of a career and occupational success (Block 1976). Daughters, in contrast, are more likely to be encouraged to focus upon interpersonal relationships rather than performance in achievement settings (Block, Block, and Harrington 1974).

Possibly as a result of the strong investment in certain kinds of developmental outcomes for males, boys are also more likely to experience more power assertion and less induction (i.e., reasoning) in disciplinary encounters with parents than are girls (Zussman 1978; Block 1982). Complementing this pattern of parent-son, parent-daughter relations is the finding that higher levels of overall interaction, especially affectionate interchange, seems to take place between parents and daughters (Noller 1978).

Before these "effects" of child gender on parenting attitudes and behavior are etched in stone, it is important to consider a point made earlier in this volume. What is true today may not be true tomorrow. Context is an extremely important determinant of how social systems, in this case parent-child relations, function. Thus, there is a need to recognize that the gender effects summarized here are by no means inevitable. Human development and parent-child relations are remarkably labile, that is, subject to change. Most of the studies summarized in this section were conducted on rather traditional middle-class families in the 1960s and 1970s. If it were 1990 or the year 2000, it is quite possible that the effects just reported would be different. Indeed, certain elements of society would be quite pleased if no gender effects at all were discernible.

If such social change is to occur, it will not come easily and will take a fair amount of time. One thing the past decade has taught us rather convincingly is that our ideology or belief systems often change more rapidly than our behavior. A case in point is a recent study of nontraditional families in Sweden where fathers are offered paid paternity leave for three months during their infants' first year of life. Analyses of patterns of mothering and fathering, which compared parents in nontraditional families where fathers took such leave and became primary caregivers for at least part of the first year with traditional families where mothers were full-time primary caregivers, revealed few differences between supposedly liberated and nonliberated families when infants were three, eight and sixteen months of age (Lamb et al. 1982). This is not to say that social change is not possible in the parenting role; quite the contrary, just witness the greater involvement that fathers currently display with infants than has been the case in the past. The point to be made is simply that behavioral change often takes longer than attitudinal change. With respect to the effects of child gender upon parenting, this "rule" is also likely to apply.

A second comment regarding gender effects involve their general impact upon the child's sex role development. Although parenting practices vary, on the average, depending upon whether the child is male or female, the sex-typed treatment of children does not appear to be as influential in sex-role development as one might suspect. Indeed, other factors, such as father's power, nurturance, and masculinity, appear to be of prime importance — in the development of both traditional masculinity in sons and femininity in daughters.

DEVELOPMENTAL STATUS

Next to gender, the characteristics of the child that probably exerts the most pronounced impact upon the parenting he receives is his age or developmental status. After all, it is babies who are cuddled and smothered with physical affection when they fall down and hurt themselves, not adolescents. While the child's age influences parenting in a variety of ways, it is important to note that it is rarely age per se that is the true source of the influence. Age, we might say, is simply a "marker" variable, that is, a summarizing index that subsumes a variety of characteristics that truly influence parental behavior. Age, after all, systematically covaries with physical size, cognitive ability, and motor coordination. Thus, it is likely that effects which appear to be determined by age are most likely a result of these more subtle developmental processes.

It is of special interest to note that the newborn infant enters the world apparently "designed" by processes of evolution to elicit care from its parents despite, or quite possibly because of, its limited developmental status. There was a time when young infants, especially newborns, were regarded as helpless, unable to support their own well-being. After two decades of research during which tremendous strides were made in detailing the abilities and limitations of the young infant, we speak now of the "competent" newborn (Stone, Smith, and Murphy 1973). The competencies of the young infant are especially evident in the subtle ways in which its developmental limits serve to elicit care. In fact, the skills that the newborn does possess tend to effectively capture adult attention and facilitate effective adult-infant interactions (Goldberg 1977). Consider, for example, the cry of the newborn. While clearly limited in its communicative sophistication, the cry is remarkably effective in drawing adult attention because of its inherently aversive qualities. Analogously, the very configuration of the infant's face is judged to be especially cute by adults, apparently as a result of the relative size of the forehead and eyes, the flattened nose, broad cheeks, and the magnitude of the head in comparison with the rest of the body (Hildebrandt and Fitzgerald 1979). In sum, there seems to be an essential "dovetailing" of infant abilities and caregiver proclivities, such that the stimulus characteristics of the young infant fit nicely with the behavioral tendencies of the caregiver. It is in this process of observing the dovetailing of infant and caregiver characteristics that we return to the earlier introduced concept of goodness-of-fit.

The effect of the infant's behavior upon the caregiver becomes most pronounced when various developmental landmarks are attained. Consider, for example, the emergence of the infant social smile around three months of age. Prior to this time infants offer little of what might be regarded as clearly positive social feedback. Thus, the experience of early caregiving is most certainly one of "giving" more than "getting" for most parents. With the emergence of the reliable social smile, however, the nature of parent-infant relations changes remarkably. Now the infant provides true social rewards and the effect of such reward is most pronounced. Time spent smiling and in face-to-face interaction increases, and parents will often report that they finally feel that the baby is truly human.

With further development during infancy, locomotion in the form of crawling and walking takes place and, when driven by or at least coupled with the infant's curiosity, creates a new challenge to parents. To some mothers and fathers, the child's inquisitive forays into closets and cupboards pose a serious problem and restrictions become frequent and forceful. In the previous chapter we noted the potentially negative effect of frequent restriction on intellectual development. Since such restriction may derive directly from the infant's increased locomotor capacity, and undermine the infant's motivation to explore, we get a sense of how the infant can produce its own development. Note, however, that whether or not locomotion and curiosity serve to elicit frequent restriction, with all its cognitive costs, will be determined by the characteristics of the caregiver. A parent interested in teaching her child about the world may take advantage of the child's movements into cupboards and closets by turning them into learning and teaching encounters, thereby facilitating cognitive development. The very fact that such a parent reacts so differently than the restrictive parent we first considered highlights the consequence of the relationship between characteristics of child and parent. More specifically, a mismatch between parent desires and child behaviors can easily result in increased restriction and a poor developmental prognosis, whereas a harmonious match can lead to increased teaching and learning and, thereby, a more positive forecast for the child's eventual intellectual competence.

The very nature of cognitively stimulating parenting styles undergoes modification as the infant and young child develop. Belsky, Goode, and Most (1980) found, for example, that from nine to eighteen months efforts by mothers to direct their infant's attention to objects and events in the world become increasingly verbal in style. More specifically, caregivers are much more likely to label things and verbally describe them, and spend less time pointing, showing, and actually demonstrating how things work, as their infants are transformed developmentally into toddlers. There can be little doubt that these changes in maternal behavior reflect a responsiveness to the ever-increasing linguistic competencies of the child.

Not only does the quantity of language input change as the child's developmental status changes, but so too does the quality of this input. Parents of young infants, in response to their children's limited communicative skills, exaggerate pronunciations and facial expressions in speaking to babies, and are likely to repeat often what they say. During the preschool years mothers employ more complex explanations with three than with two year olds (Reichle, Longhurst, and Stepanich 1978). These changes, interestingly enough, are much like the modifications an author makes depending on whether his or her readers are unfamiliar with or quite sophisticated in terms of the subject matter under discussion.

As children develop from the preschool years through adolescence, expectations of parents change in part as a function of children's developing competencies and of the contextual demands that are placed upon them. Several reviews of research suggest, for example, that with development comes increasing emphasis upon independent behavior, responsibility, and achievement (Becker 1964; Martin 1977). Thus, as children grow older, parents employ more reasoning, explanations, and giving and withholding of privileges, while at the same time displaying less physical affection, becoming less protective, and spending less time with their children (Maccoby 1980).

A recent longitudinal study examining changes in parenting between the time children are three and twelve years of age nicely illustrates these general trends (Roberts, Block, and Block 1981). Relative to the responses offered when children were three, mothers and fathers of twelve year olds were more likely to say that they encouraged the child to do better than others; that it was good for the child to play competitive games; and that they expected a great deal from the child. In addition to this increased emphasis on achievement, encouragement of independence increased, as revealed by responses to items focused upon teaching the child that she or he is responsible for what happens, and upon letting the child make his or her own decisions. A decrease in responses over time underscored the expression of positive affect—for example, being easygoing and relaxed with the child, joking and playing with the child, and expressing affection by hugging and kissing.

Changes in family dynamics are likely to accompany many of the cognitive and behavioral changes that these alterations in parenting practices are both a product and producer of. Clear evidence of this comes from several studies examining how the transition into adolescence, and especially the onset of puberty, influences parent-son relations. In an early study, Jacob (1974) found that, during mother-father-adolescent family interchanges, older boys (sixteen year olds) were more assertive toward their parents than younger children (eleven year olds). While this investigation revealed the likelihood that some transformation in family processes occurred during the transition to adolescence, and thus that developmental status affects parent-child relations, the exact causes of such change beyond the marker-variable chronological age could not be discerned.

In order to address this issue, Steinberg (Steinberg and Hill 1978; Steinberg 1981) studied family interaction on a sample of some thirty triads of parents and their first-born adolescent sons. Families were visited three times at six-month intervals in a longitudinal design in order to determine whether age, physical maturation, or cognitive skill was the source of the developmental changes Jacob's (1974) work highlighted. Like this earlier research, Steinberg found that as boys matured they asserted themselves against their mothers and, additionally, that mother-son conflict was most frequent at the time of most dramatic physical change during adolescence. As sons passed this puberty apex, conflict subsided somewhat, yet by the end of the pubertal cycle which transformed the sons' bodies from that of boys to that of men, adolescents were more influential in family decision-making and mothers were less influential relative to the power they possessed before adolescence. The fact that this research revealed that it was physical changes in the boys and not cognitive changes or merely changes in age, makes this piece of work extremely important in detailing how developmental status affects parent-child relations and family functioning. Indeed, the evidence suggests that with the social changes that accompany biological transformation during puberty comes a new sense of personal status for the male child in the family.

Probably the most dramatic effect of the child's developmental status on the care received is realized by considering the changing nature of what we have described as optimal parenting practices between infancy and the preschool/school-age years (Belsky, Robins, and Gamble 1984). To document this effect, we must first consider the similarity in growth-promoting parenting practices across ontogenic epochs. Across childhood, parenting that is sensitively attuned to the child's capabilities and to the developmental tasks the child faces seems to promote the kinds of outcomes for the child that Americans hold dear—security, independence, social competence, and intellectual achievement. In infancy this sensitivity translates into being able to read the child's often subtle cues and appropriately respond to his or her needs in reasonably brief periods of time. In childhood, sensitivity means continuing the warmth and affection provided in the early years, but increasing the demands for age-appropriate behavior. The parent during this period must be willing, and able, to direct the child's behavior and activities without squelching his or her developing independence and industry. Thus, the authoritative parent listens to the child and considers his or her point of view legitimate even when the parent disagrees.

The change in parenting that we have summarized is no doubt influenced by the changing nature of the child; it is not merely an automatic response to the child's age. For example, as the child's cognitive skills develop, reasoning and demands for delayed gratification become effective disciplinary strategies. Similar efforts, we are not surprised to learn, would be useless with an eight month old. Correspondingly, as the child becomes increasingly able to regulate his or her own behavior, parental control provides a useful scaffold to support such emerging competence. Ultimately, the sensitive and thus competent parent must be willing to let go of this control and permit the child to test his or her own limits and discover his or her own boundaries. Indeed, by the time the child reaches adolescence, the competent parent has set the stage so that the child has the building blocks to encounter successfully the transition from childhood to adolescence. In sum, such a developmental approach to parenting not only increases the likelihood of highly valued child outcomes, but also, from a scientific standpoint, illustrates the child's effect on his or her caregivers, and thus the bidirectional nature of the parent-child relationship: Children's capacities influence their parents' behavior, which in turn influences subsequent child development.

CHILDREN AT RISK

Children labeled "at risk" are those who are known, for some biological or psychosocial reason, to run an increased chance of experiencing developmental difficulties as they grow up. These biological or psychosocial risk factors seem to exert their influence upon the child directly or indirectly. When we speak of direct effects, we are referring to limitations that risk factors place upon the child's immediate behavior or functioning. For example, deaf children run an increased risk of language problems because of their inability to hear spoken language. Deaf children, or other children at risk for other reasons, may also have a higher probability of intellectual deficits as a result of the effect they have upon their parents and other individuals which feeds back to influence them. We call such effects indirect, since they flow from child to parent to child. An example of such an indirect effect, whereby the child contributes to its own development, or retardation thereof, would be the deaf child whose parents neglect him due to his hearing deficit, and who, as a result, is denied the social stimulation and interest that fosters a positive sense of self. In the following discussion, we consider the effect of two types of risk on parenting: prematurity and cerebral palsy.

Prematurity and Low Birth Weight

A premature or preterm baby is one who is born at or before thirty-seven and a half weeks gestational age (i.e., at least two and a half weeks before it is biologically due), and a low-birth-weight infant is one born weighing less than five and a half pounds (average birthweight being seven and a half pounds). During the past decade great efforts have been made to understand the unique developmental experiences of premature and low-birth-weight infants because they are known to be at risk, when reared under economically deprived circumstances, of experiencing a host of developmental difficulties (Birch and Gussow 1970). The assumption behind much research has been that if the experience of high-risk infants can be better understood, intervention efforts could be undertaken to prevent or remediate such developmental disturbances.

In many respects, the premature infant can be regarded as a "difficult" baby to care for. Biologically, such babies have more problems controlling their temperature during the neonatal period; they are more susceptible to early infection with all its devastating consequences for the newborn; and they are likely to have respiratory difficulties. Since prematurity defines a continuum of risk, from very preterm and lightweight infants to relatively older and heavy preterm babies, it should be of little surprise that the biological complications associated with prematurity and low birth weight are more likely the more premature and the smaller the baby is.

From a behavioral standpoint, preterm babies are frequently less alert, tend to be less responsive to stimulation, have weak motor movements and reflexes, poorer head control, and more irregular sleep patterns (Goldberg 1978). These characteristics early in life probably explain why, initially, caregivers are less actively involved with such infants. Specifically, parents of prematures have been found in the newborn period, in contrast to parents of full-term infants, to engage in less bodily contact with the baby, spend less time in close and focused face-to-face interaction, and to smile at and touch their infants less often (Goldberg 1978). These results, too, should come as little surprise, as parents are undoubtedly being affected by their infants' delicate physical status and often precarious medical condition.

As infants get older, the effect of the premature infant on patterns of parenting change rather dramatically. In fact, rather than doing less than mothers of term babies, as was the case during the newborn period, they tend to do more. Since the preterm baby is so much less responsive and alert, their parents are compelled to carry more of the interactional burden. That is, they have to work harder at maintaining social interaction than mothers of term infants since their infants seem so much less able to return social bids by being responsive (Goldberg 1978).

Some evidence suggests that this heightening of the caregiver's response may be counterproductive, since it tends to overload the preterm infant in terms of its capacity to deal with arousing stimuli. One of the great problems that parents of high-risk infants confront in trying to engage the child in interaction is the child's generally "narrower band of arousal." While levels of stimulation sufficient to capture the attention and interest of the term infant go unnoticed by the preterm infant, levels of stimulation regarded as moderate by the full-term baby frequently overwhelm the preterm baby, resulting in gaze aversion (turning away), if not outright distress (Field 1982). For the father who traditionally likes to engage his infant in highly arousing play, by tossing the baby in the air, tickling him or her vigorously, or bouncing him or her on the bed, problems may be encountered when such routinely pleasing activity is responded to by the child with distress. The challenge of fine tuning one's interactive style so as not to undershoot or overshoot the high-risk infant's attentional limits is great. Indeed, the failure of some parents to master this challenge may explain why, as we discuss in more detail later, premature infants run an increased risk of child abuse (Belsky 1978a, 1980).

Cerebral Palsy

It is often contended that the prototypical developmental disability is the child with CP (Capute and Palmer 1980); empirically, it is known that CP may interfere significantly with social interaction and emotional development, as well as with cognitive, language, and motor functioning (Denhoff 1981; Field 1980). In addition, the parents of CP children have reactions toward them, and interaction patterns with them, that differ from those shown by the parents of nonhandicapped children (Howard 1978; Kogan 1980; Kogan, Tyler, and Turner 1974). Furthermore, in at least some school settings, the nonhandicapped peers of mainstreamed CP children interact with them more negatively than is the case when nonhandicapped peers interact with other nonhandicapped children.

The significant motor handicap of the child with CP has been the distinguishing and highlighted feature of this disability (Capute and Palmer 1980). However, motor impairment may not be the most incapacitating handicapping condition for a CP child. The child may have associated developmental disabilities like mental retardation, learning disabilities, learning loss, visual impairment, seizures, cortical sensory deficits, emotional problems, and social interactional difficulties (Capute and Palmer, 1980; Denhoff 1981; Howard, 1978). For instance, 60 percent to 70 percent of CP children are mentally retarded, and the other 30 percent to 40 percent should be recognized as having received brain damage and thus being at risk for central perceptual abnormalities and a subsequent specific learning disability (Capute and Palmer 1980). Today, then, the motor impairment of CP is "seen as a neurodevelopmental marker for underlying associated dysfunctions" which, if overlooked or ignored, preclude optimal development (Capute and Palmer 1980, p. 66).

The initial response of the family to the handicapped child, in this case the child with CP, frequently includes shock, depression, guilt, denial, anger, sadness, and anxiety (Howard 1978). In addition, there seem to be particular child-rearing issues that parents of CP children face which highlight the manner in which children influence their caregivers. Call (1958) found three major problems among CP parents. First, they have difficulty in perceiving the child's actual handicap and actual abilities. Second, there is considerable difficulty in psychological separation between child and parent. Third, there is extended mutual behavioral interdependence of parent and child. Similarly, Shere (1955) found that when compared to how they treated their own nonhandicapped child, mothers tended to overextend help to their CP child and, in addition, babied him or her, discouraged curiosity, and overprotected the CP child from real and imagined danger. In turn, Kogan, Tyler, and Turner (1974) report a progressive reduction, over the course of their two-year longitudinal study, of friendly, warm, and positive interactions during play sessions between mothers and their CP children. Kogan (1980) attributes this change to the fact that mothers of CP children participate in interactions that are less rewarding and provide less positive feedback than received by mothers of normal children. However, Howard (1978) notes that the specific nature of parental reactions is dependent on several factors associated with both the parents' and the CP child's individuality.

In addition, Kogan (1980) reports that while it is difficult to change many of the CP child's behaviors that lead to negative or long-term maladaptive (at least for the child) parent-child interactions, it is possible to intervene with the parents, for example, to alter the attitudes, demands, and expectations they place on their child. Since there are few available guidelines to help parents set appropriate behavioral goals for their CP child (Kogan 1980), they may be prone to use the behavioral expectations and standards for normal children (Denhoff 1981). To the extent that this is the case, there will almost inevitably be a poor fit between the child and his or her parental context. However, since Howard (1978) has indicated that parental reactions toward the CP child vary in relation to both the child's individuality and the parent's attitudes and demands, and since Kogan's (1980) work suggests that such parental attributes may be successfully modified, one can potentially improve the fit between the characteristics of the CP child and those of parents by altering parent's expectations and demands.

It is important to note that rearing a handicapped child can influence parents in ways other than by affecting their parenting behavior. As we will see in Chapter 8, marital functioning may be enhanced or undermined by the stress resultant from caring for a biologically impaired child; and it seems that marital quality prior to the child's arrival is a major determinant of which of these two courses the child's effect will take (Gath 1978). The rearing of a disabled child may also influence the social relations parents have with both extended family and neighbors (Howard 1978). In this regard, McAllister and his colleagues (1973) found that the presence of a behaviorally retarded child was associated with less frequent visits with neighbors and, to a lesser extent, with relatives. Quite possibly, the inability to find a qualified babysitter to care for a handicapped child served to limit parental excursions beyond the home or, alternatively, members of families' social networks may simply have been less willing to socialize with the family because of the handicapped child. Whatever the exact cause of this association between the presence of a child with a handicapping condition and extrafamilial relations, it is clear that rearing an at-risk child can affect family functioning in diverse ways.

TEMPERAMENT: A SAMPLE CASE OF THE CHILD IN CONTEXT

Throughout this chapter, and indeed the entire book, we have emphasized that characteristics of the child must be viewed in the context of the family. Children with contrasting characteristics of individuality elicit different reactions from their parents and siblings, reactions which will likely feed back to the child, thereby affecting his or her further development. Note, however, that the exact same characteristics of individuality may have different consequences in different families. Consider, for example, the fact that a high activity level might mesh well with the child-rearing attitudes and practices of one set of parents, yet be in direct conflict with the parental orientation of another set of parents. To fully understand the effect of the child on his or her parents, then, the characteristics of individuality of parents must also be considered. It is our contention that virtually any feature of a child's psychological and behavioral development must be conceptualized as being influenced by and an influence on this context.

Yet, if one surveys the accumulated scientific literature pertinent to major features of a child's functioning, it would be clear that most often these characteristics have been studied apart from either their familial or their broader social context. Instead, features of psychological and behavioral functioning have been viewed as arising within the person and as influencing individual behavioral and psychological development. For example, self-esteem is conceptualized in Erikson's (1959, 1963) theory as a within-person characteristic, that is, as the feeling state about the self that arises as a consequence of other within-the-person changes—in Erikson's (1959, 1963) theory, the appropriate resolution of ego crises. Similarly, the changes in cognitive structure described by Piaget (1970) are thought to be brought about by the resolution of cognitive conflicts that occur within the person (cf., Riegel 1975, 1976a, 1976b).

There are several problems with this within-the-person or personological focus, especially as it pertains to the effect of the child on its caregivers. First, contextual variation cannot *only* speed up or slow down changes in the individual—a point acknowledged by personological theorists (cf., Emmerich 1968)—but it can also alter the very quality of these changes. For example, considerable evidence exists that the ego changes described by Erikson (1959, 1963) do not follow the stagelike sequence he specifies for both males and females, or for children from all family types, or from all cultures (see Lerner and Spanier 1980, for a review). A second, more technical problem is that personological developmentalists' attempts to explain all the differences—i.e., all the variation—in some individual characteristic by reference to other individual characteristics have not met with much success; that is, relatively small amounts of variation have been accounted for in this manner. A third problem has been that personological developmentalists have not attended to the *reciprocal* relations between individual characteristics and the contexts of development, relations that are becoming increasingly better documented each year. This is a crucial omission since, even if one ignores the possibility that within-the-person, or individual, attributes develop through reciprocal person-context interactions, one cannot deny that peoples' behaviors always occur in a context.

In sum, we believe several scientific benefits would accrue if features of individual behavioral and psychological functioning were studied as interactive with their social context. Much of the initial empirical evidence promoting this viewpoint derived from the study of one key feature of a child's individuality—temperament. Today, the study of this aspect of behavioral individuality still serves to highlight the necessity of studying child development in context. Indeed, the theoretical and empirical advances in the contextual study of temperament enable us to illustrate both the uses for a child-context focus and the limitations of an approach to the child that ignores this focus.

Definition of Temperament

As a result of an interest in the interrelation of person and context characteristics, two physicians, Alexander Thomas and Stella Chess, initiated the New York Longitudinal Study (NYLS) in 1956 in order to investigate the implications of individual differences in temperament. For these two investigators, temperament was conceptualized as the *stylistic* components of behavior, not *what* the person does, but *how* he or she does whatever is done. To clarify this distinction, consider the fact that a large portion of the young infant's behavioral repertoire could be described as involving eating, sleeping, and toileting. Since all infants display such behaviors, individual infants can not be easily discriminated on these dimensions. But if one infant nursed at regular intervals (e.g., every four hours), while another ate at irregular times, such discrimination could be achieved. In that the terms "regularity" or "irregularity" qualify eating, and specify the distinction between otherwise identical eating behaviors, the terms are used as designators of the stylistic aspect of behavior.

Thomas and Chess (1977) themselves focused upon nine specific attributes of behavioral style: activity level, rhythmicity (of biological functions), approach-withdrawal, adaptability (to new situations or people), intensity of reaction, threshold of responsiveness, quality of mood, distractibility, and attention span/persistence. In our view, it is just such stylistic characteristics of behavior that give a child's behavioral repertoire its key individual distinctiveness, especially at early ages (cf. Dunn 1980). It is this distinctiveness which, in turn, serves to mark the organism as a unique individual—to parents (especially experienced ones), and to teachers and others in the social network who must discriminate a particular child from among many in order to interact most appropriately. We are indicating then that the key significance of a definition of temperament as behavioral style is its impact on the social context of the person. But, how may such temperament-context relations be conceptualized, much less empirically investigated?

The Goodness-of-Fit Model

The approach we favor can be summarized in terms of the goodness-of-fit between person and context; it emphasizes the significance of a particular characteristic of individuality, like a high activity level, in a particular context, such as a small apartment. Conceptions of development which stress behavioral (Bandura 1978; Bijou 1976), organismic (Erikson 1968), or contextual (Schneirla 1957; Thomas and Chess 1981) mechanisms converge in suggesting that people may affect their own development. As a consequence of characteristics of physical (e.g., sex, body type, or facial attractiveness; Berscheid and Walster 1974) and/or psychological individuality (e.g., in regard to conceptual tempo, or temperament; Kagan 1966; Thomas and Chess 1977), people promote differential reactions in their socializing others; these reactions may feed back to people, increase the individuality of their developmental milieu, and provide a basis for their further development.

Through the establishment of such "circular functions" in development (Schneirla 1957), people may be conceived of as producers of their own development (Lerner and Busch-Rossnagel 1981). However, this circular functions idea needs to be extended; that is, in and of itself the notion is mute regarding the specific characteristics of the feedback (that is, its positive or negative valence) an organism will receive as a consequence of its individuality. Just as a person brings his or her characteristics of individuality to a particular social setting, there are demands placed on the person by virtue of the social and physical components of the setting. These demands may take the form of:

1. Attitudes, values, or stereotypes held by others in the context regarding the person's attributes (either his/her physical or behavioral characteristics);
2. The attributes (usually behavioral) of others in the context with whom the child must coordinate, or fit, his or her attributes (also, in this case, usually behavioral) for adaptive interactions to exist;
3. The physical characteristics of a setting (e.g., the presence or absence of access ramps for the motor handicapped) which require the person to possess certain attributes (again, usually behavioral abilities) for the most efficient interaction within the setting to occur.

The person's individuality, in differentially meeting these demands, provides a basis for the feedback he or she gets from the socializing environment. For example, considering the demand "domain" of attitudes, values, or stereotypes, teachers and parents may have relatively individual and distinct expectations about behaviors desired of their students and children, respectively. Teachers may want students who show little distractibility, since they would not want attention diverted from the lesson by other activity in the classroom. Parents, however, might desire their children to be moderately distractible, for example, when they require them to move from television-watching to dinner or to bed. Children whose behavioral individuality was either generally distractible or generally not distractible would thus differentially meet the demands of these two contexts. Problems of adaptation to school or to home might thus develop as a consequence of a child's lack of match (or "goodness of fit") in either or both settings.

Similarly, considering the second type of contextual demands that exist — those that arise as a consequence of the behavioral characteristics of others in the setting — problems of fit might occur when a child who is highly irregular in his biological functions (eating, sleep-wake cycles, toileting behaviors) interacts in a family setting composed of highly regular and behaviorally scheduled parents and siblings. In turn, considering the third type of contextual demands that exist — those that arise as a consequence of the physical characteristics of a setting — a child who has a low threshold for response and who also is highly distractible might find it problematic to perform efficiently in a setting with high noise levels (e.g., a crowded home, a school room situated near the street in a busy urban area) when tasks necessitating concentration and/or attention, such as studying, or taking an examination, are required.

Thomas and Chess (1977, 1980, 1981) and J. Lerner (in press) believe that adaptive psychological and social functioning do not derive directly from either the nature of the person's characteristics of individuality per se or the nature of the demands of the contexts within which the person functions. Rather, if a person's characteristics of individuality match (or "fit") the demands of a particular setting, then adaptive outcomes in that setting will accrue. Those people whose characteristics match most of the settings within which they exist should receive supportive or positive feedback from the contexts and should show evidence of the most adaptive behavioral development. In turn, of course, mismatched people, whose characteristics are incongruent with one or most settings, should show alternative developmental outcomes.

Empirical Evidence

Much of the research literature supporting the validity of the goodness-of-fit model is either derived directly from the Thomas and Chess NYLS or

is associated with independent research that has adopted their conceptualization of temperament. In the NYLS study, several groups of subjects provide data relevant to the issue of goodness of fit. One sample consisted of 133 white, middle-class, largely Jewish children of professional
parents, another of 95 Puerto Rican children living in New York City.
Each sample was studied from at least the first month of life onward.

As a first example illustrating the importance of the match between
child and context let us consider the impact of low regularity in
biological functioning or rhythmicity of behavior, particularly in regard
to sleep-wake cycles. The Puerto Rican parents studied by Thomas and
Chess (1977; Thomas et al. 1974; Korn, Note 4) placed virtually no
demands on their children as to when they should be awake or asleep. In
fact, these parents allowed their children to set their own individual
schedules, permitting them to go to sleep and wake up any time they
desired. In contrast, white, middle-class parents placed strong demands
on their young children, expecting them to sleep and wake up at specific
points during the day and to maintain these schedules day in and day out.
Consistent with predictions derived from the goodness-of-fit model, irregular sleep-wake cycles amongst children predicted problem behaviors
within the infancy period and throughout the first five years of life in
middle-class households (since such biologically irregular styles were
in conflict with contextual demands), but not in Puerto Rican households in which few demands were made and thus any sleep-wake cycle fit
the context (Thomas et al. 1974; Korn Note 4).

Thus, in the white-middle class sample early infant arrhythmicity
tended to be a problem, whereas in the Puerto Rican sample infant arrhythmicity was not a problem during this time of life; did not contribute
to a poor fit; and was not associated with adjustment problems in the first
five years of life. However, to underscore the importance of considering fit
with the demands of the context of development, we should note that arrhythmicity did begin to predict adjustment problems for the Puerto Rican
children when they entered the school system. Their lack of a regular sleep
pattern interfered with their getting sufficient rest to perform well in
school and, in addition, often caused them to be late for school (Thomas et
al. 1974; Korn, Note 4). Thus, before the age of five years, only one Puerto
Rican child who developed clinically identifiable problems between ages
five and nine years was diagnosed as having sleep problems. However,
almost 50 percent of the Puerto Rican children who developed clinically
identifiable problems between ages five and nine years were diagnosed as
having sleep problems. Obviously, characteristics of individuality that fit
one context, in this case the Puerto Rican home, may not fit another, that
is, the public school.

Another example of how the differential demands existing between
the two family contexts provide different pressures for adaptation
highlights the importance of differences in the demands of the physical

contexts of families. As noted by Thomas et al. (1974) and Korn (Note 4), overall there was a very low incidence of behavior problems in the Puerto Rican sample children in their first five years of life, especially when compared to the corresponding incidence in the white, middle-class children. However, if a problem was presented at this time among the Puerto Rican sample, it was most likely to be a problem of motor activity. In fact, across the first nine years of their lives, of those Puerto Rican children who developed clinical problems, 53 percent presented symptoms diagnosed as involving problematic motor activity (i.e., hyperactivity). Parents complained of excessive and uncontrollable motor activity in such cases. However, in the white, middle-class sample's clinical group only one child (a child with brain damage) was characterized in this way. To fully understand these differential problem rates, the physical features of the home must be considered.

In the Puerto Rican sample the families usually had several children and lived in small apartments. As a result, even average motor activity tended to impinge on others in the setting. Moreover, even in the case of the children with high activity levels, the Puerto Rican parents were reluctant to let their children out of the apartment because of the actual dangers of playing on the streets of East Harlem in New York City. In the white, middle-class sample, in contrast, parents had the financial resources to provide large apartments or houses for their families. These homes typically provided suitable play areas for the children both inside and outside the home. As a consequence, the presence of high activity levels in the homes of these families did not cause the problems for interaction that they did in the Puerto Rican group. Thus, as Thomas et al. (1974) emphasize, the mismatch between temperament attribute and physical environment accounted for the group difference in the import of high activity level for the development of behavioral problems.

Support both for the generalizability of the temperament attributes studied by Thomas and Chess (1977, 1980, 1981), as well as for the goodness-of-fit model, is provided in work carried out in other cultures. Super and Harkness studied infants in a rural farming community in Kenya, named Kokwet, and in suburban families living in the metropolitan Boston area. These investigators report that the nine dimensions of temperament studied in the NYLS "are not, by and large" artifacts of the American setting. In both the Kokwet and the Boston samples, the dimensions of mood, adaptability, intensity of reaction, and rhythmicity were identified in both interview and naturalistic observational data. However, because of the cultural differences between these two settings, the importance of these temperament attributes were quite different; and, as Super and Harkness (1981) report, children with the same temperament attribute scores had different fits, and different developmental outcomes, as a consequence of the different contextual demands they encountered in their different rearing cultures.

In many of the American households, physical space was altered in anticipation of the arrival of the baby (e.g., a room was decorated for the baby). Typically, the mother made arrangements to change her schedule once the baby arrived. However, in none of the American families was there more than one person generally at home during most of the day (i.e., typically, either the mother or a babysitter was present). This one-to-one ratio of caregiver-to-infant presents a limitation on the moment-to-moment flexibility of the caregiver; he or she cannot engage in non-caregiving activities when the infant makes anticipated (e.g., scheduled) or unanticipated demands.

The people of Kokwet (Kipsigis) create a much different environment for an infant. In the first few months of life, the baby is in the exclusive care of the mother and, in fact, is rarely separated from physical contact with her. Such constant and close physical contact is not at all characteristic of the mother-infant relationship in the Boston sample. Moreover, in Kokwet the mother is rarely alone with the infant. During the day an average of five additional people are in the house with her and the infant.

Some of the impact of these cultural differences may be seen by considering the dimensions of rhythmicity and adaptability. In the Boston sample the infant's activities are often highly temporally scheduled in order to meet the needs of both the mother and infant. In Kokwet, however, the baby spends much of his or her waking day being held or sitting on the lap of the mother, while she is pursuing her duties. As noted, if the mother needs a break or has to do a task where the infant cannot be carried, the infant is attended to by another nearby caregiver. Within this situation the infant is free to both sleep at will and nurse at the mother's breast virtually at will, as well, (since at most the mother is only a short walk away).

Thus, an infant who does not show rhythmicity of biological functions like sleeping and eating, would not have a problem of fitting the cultural demands imposed by the Kokwet setting. An infant in the Boston setting who had the same low level of rhythmicity, however, would not fit well with the demands imposed on him or her. Moreover, if this American infant was low in adaptability, the problems for fit to the schedule the mother tried to impose might be enhanced, and the potential problems for adequate development would be increased. In turn, an infant in Kokwet who had a low adaptability score would not have a poor fit because there is no schedule imposed on him or her to which adaptation is required.

Super and Harkness (1981) point out that there are several developmental consequences of these cultural differences in the meaning of temperament. For example, although it starts out similarly, by four months of age the sleep-wake cycle of Boston and Kokwet infants is quite different, with the average Boston infant sleeping for eight hours at night, and the average Kokwet infant continuing to wake briefly and nurse. In addition, maternal impressions of the infant are different in each setting. The Kokwet mothers are not concerned with characteristics like negative mood, low rhythmicity, and low adaptability, and do not view them as indicative of long-term problems. The American mothers in the Super and Harkness (1981) sample, however, have precisely the opposite evaluation of these temperament attributes. Thus, as in the NYLS data set, we see that the same temperament characteristics have a different impact on others as a consequence of being embedded in a different cultural context.

CONCLUSION

As noted earlier, children, especially as they get older, spend time in a variety of contexts other than the family. Importantly, there is evidence to document the fact that in the same way that children's characteristics of individuality match or mismatch family demand and thereby determine the nature of children's experience, the fit between individual child characteristics and the demands of other contexts also determine experience and influence developmental outcomes. In one set of studies, for example, it has been found that the degree to which children's temperaments fit or fail to fit teacher and peer expectations and demands predicts achievement and adjustment in school (J. Lerner, in press). In sum, then, there are both empirical and conceptual grounds for concluding that not only do children influence the care they receive, which feeds back to shape their own development, but that to fully understand the process by which children contribute to their own development characteristics of both the child and the family must be considered.

In certain respects the very concept of "child effects" may be misleading. The child's characteristics of individuality (e.g., gender, age, temperament) have meaning, and thus have consequences in particular contexts, and are defined by the people who inhabit the context (e.g., parents/family, peers/playground, teachers/school). An appropriate conclusion, therefore, would be that the influence of child characteristics on others is mediated, if not determined, by those others who engage the child, but only by writing in terms of "child effect" could the complexity of this contextual intertwining be appreciated.

<table>
<tr>
<td>

CHAPTER

8

</td>
<td>

Marriage, Parenting, and Child Development

</td>
</tr>
</table>

The study of the child in the family has been spread across several disciplines, most notably family sociology and developmental psychology. By tradition, family sociologists have been concerned with the nature and development of the marital relationship, and the impact that children have upon the marital dyad. Developmental psychologists, in contrast, have concerned themselves primarily with the characteristics of the parent-child relationship and its consequences for children. As a consequence of the two distinct foci of sociology and psychology, it has not been until very recently that we have moved toward an integrated view of the child in the family. Even today, such a multidisciplinary perspective is only just emerging (Belsky 1981; Lerner and Spanier 1978). One of the primary purposes of this volume is to "wed" disciplines that have displayed interest in the child in the family. In this chapter we plan to further such a multidisciplinary perspective by considering the impact that children have upon the marital relationship and the manner in which marriages both influence and are influenced by parenting. Ultimately, our goal is to gain insight into the bidirectional and often complex processes that characterize family functioning and, undoubtedly, influence child development. As a first step in our explorations of such interdisciplinary terrain, we consider the developmental nature of the family itself.

THE FAMILY LIFE COURSE

Family researchers have written extensively about the cycle of events that typically occurs during the time between the marriage of a couple and the termination of the marriage through death of one of the spouses (Duvall, 1971). There are several attractive reasons for looking at the family in this way. One reason is that most families experience common events such as the birth of a first child, the child entering school, and the child leaving home. Since there may be some adjustments associated with these transitions that are similar from one family to the next, it can be useful to examine the dynamics of such transitions.

There are also some disadvantages to looking at families in this way, however, and criticisms of this approach have been increasing, as noted in the scientific literature (Spanier, Sauer, and Larzelere 1979). First, there is tremendous diversity in the ways in which families negotiate the life cycle. Some couples have children before they are married, some early in the marriage, and some later in the marriage, and some do not have children at all. Some couples move through the traditional life course events very quickly, and others do so at a much slower pace. The number and spacing of children may vary, and other historical and family circumstances may make the life course quite different, even for children within the same family.

Of course, death of a parent or sibling, divorce, remarriage, and other significant events and crises may make family life qualitatively different for a child. From both the parent's and child's viewpoint, then, the traditional life cycle of American families may be far from traditional. Indeed, studies have demonstrated this variability and diversity in life course events and timing (Spanier, Sauer, and Larzelere, 1979; Nock 1979), indicating that there is too much variation to attempt to characterize all or even most families by any one life cycle scheme.

Despite such limitations, it can be useful to consider one stratification scheme (Duvall, 1971) which gives us some insight into traditional families characterized by at least one child, born after the marriage, to two parents who live together until the death of one spouse sometime after retirement. Although this life cycle typology may not be characteristic of all or even most families today, it does apply to a significant number of families, and it may be considered the American ideal to many individuals. Further, such a typology is a standard against which other families are often judged.

This stratification scheme has nine phases. Each phase has associated with it certain *developmental tasks* that are thought to exist for the typical family (Duvall, 1971).

1. *The beginning family: establishment phase.* This stage starts with the wedding and continues until the first pregnancy. The developmental tasks of this stage include the establishment of a home and a pattern of living together as a couple and as members of an extended family and community.

2. *The beginning family: expectant phase.* This stage starts with the awareness of pregnancy and continues until the birth of the first child. The tasks of this stage include the reorganization of the home, the budget, the couple's various interpersonal relationships, and their philosophy of life to prepare for the arrival of the baby.

3. *The childbearing family.* This stage begins with the birth of the first child and continues until this child is thirty months old. Developmental tasks include adapting living arrangements to the needs of a young child. (Some refer to this process as "child-proofing" the home.) They also include meeting new expenses, reworking patterns of husband-wife responsibility, establishing new systems of communication and new interpersonal relationships with each other and with relatives, and fitting into the community as a young family.

4. *The family with preschool children.* This stage involves the couple learning to rear their children at the same time that they continue to develop as a couple, meeting new costs and new responsibilities.

5. *The family with school-age children.* This stage involves such developmental tasks as helping children to grow, providing for each family member's needs, learning to cooperate together as a family, and relating the family to a community.

6. *The family with teen-agers.* In this stage the needs of all members put new demands upon the family. Sometimes the needs of various members conflict. New patterns of money usage and communication must be worked out. Family responsibilities may be shared in a new way. The husband and wife, as well as each child, have need for continued development as persons. The parents also are called upon to develop a point of view consistent with teen-age values and activities.

7. *The family as a launching center.* This stage marks the beginning of family contraction. During this stage the children are prepared for leaving home to become independent and to establish new families. The parents must prepare themselves for this and for a renewal of their relationship as a couple.

8. *The family in the middle years.* In this stage the couple are called upon to readjust their living conditions, to adapt to the "empty nest," to develop new, or pursue already established, interests and friendships. During this stage many couples draw closer together.

9. *The aging family.* This stage involves making satisfactory living arrangements, learning to live on retirement income, maintaining meaningful contacts with friends, children, and grandchildren, providing for illness, developing a philosophy that will enable the individual to face bereavement, and finding new meanings and reaffirming old meanings in life.

CHILD EFFECTS ON MARRIAGE

Having given a brief overview of one framework for analyzing the changing nature of the family, we now turn attention to the effect of the child upon the marital relationship. In this regard, much attention has been paid to the effect of the first child on the marriage. Since it is with the birth of the first child that the child-rearing function of the family is initiated, we begin our examination of the effect of the child on the marital relationship with the transition to parenthood. Following consideration of this entry into parenthood, we consider briefly how marital quality changes across the entire family life course. Once we have examined the effect of the child on marital functioning, first by focusing in detail upon the transition to parenthood and then in more general terms on the entire family life course, we direct our attention to the manner in which marital relations may influence and be influenced by the parent-child relationship.

The Transition to Parenthood

The transition to parenthood is defined as the period of family life encompassed by the first pregnancy through the first year or two of the child's life. This period of family life, and especially the effect of the child on marital functioning, has received special attention from family sociologists on the assumption that

> the family is an integrated social system of roles and structures and that adding or removing members will force a major reorganization of the system. Simmel's role theory suggests that with the shift from dyad to triad, there is a *disruption* of affection and intimacy (Russell 1974, p. 294, emphasis added).

Given this point of departure, it is of little surprise that researchers interested in the "transition to parenthood" have concerned themselves primarily with the degree to which "crisis" is experienced by couples following the birth of the first child.

Adjustments to Be Made. Across the many investigations of the stress experienced by couples in adjusting to the transition to parenthood, four general classes of problems have been identified (Sollie and Miller 1980). The first of these involves the physical demands associated with caring for a child. More specifically, new parents routinely report an experience of stress caused by loss of sleep and constant fatigue which results from the extra work required in caring for a highly dependent child, especially that associated with caring for the baby in the middle of the night during normal sleeping hours. Mothers, not surprisingly, seem to be most susceptible to problems involving physical demands, as they are most likely to experience the "role strain" associated with adding to the pre-parenthood roles of spouse, homemaker, and employee, that of primary caregiver.

A second negative theme that emerges from investigations of the transition to parenthood focuses attention on strains in the husband-wife relationship. Frequent complaints of new parents highlight reductions in time spent together as a couple, changes in the sexual relationship, and the belief that the child's needs take priority over those of the spouse. Some of this stress, it should be evident, results from the physical demands of caregiving. As a case in point, consider how fatigue resulting from waking in the middle of the night to care for the infant might dampen one spouse's interest in sex.

A third negative theme that emerges from inquiries into the transition to parenthood centers around the emotional costs experienced by parents. One such source of emotional strain is having total responsibility for the care and well-being of the child, especially as parents come to realize, often quite slowly, that the responsibilities of parenthood last forever. Doubts regarding one's competence as a parent, which even the most skilled parents experience at one time or another, represent another source of emotional strain.

The final set of negative feelings experienced by parents adjusting to the addition of a child to the family involve opportunity costs and restrictions. Parents frequently comment about limits placed upon their social lives, particularly on their freedom to travel or to decide to do something on very short notice. Most new parents discover that doing things while they are responsible for young children is a far more complicated enterprise than ever imagined. Think for a moment about wanting to go to a movie but not being able to find a babysitter, or about the process of wrapping and unwrapping a baby in warm clothes in order to go shopping in the winter. In addition to such social costs and restrictions associated with parenting, there are also financial costs. The loss of income and career opportunities experienced when one parent remains home as primary caregiver can be very important. The sheer expenses of raising a young child are also economically significant.

A reader attending carefully to this description of the transition to parenthood might be understandably wary of becoming a parent someday. It would be a mistake, however, to conclude from this account of stresses associated with the transition to parenthood that there are no gratifications and rewards associated with parenthood. Indeed, there are, but these we will consider later. The purpose of this brief presentation of stresses has been to set the stage for a consideration of investigations dealing with the effect of having a baby upon marital functioning.

Despite the shared focus of many researchers upon the crisis that the transition to parenthood generates, it is difficult to draw definitive conclusions from the many investigations of this topic. Although some studies indicate that the arrival of the first child does indeed disrupt the marital relationship, resulting in stress often to the point of crisis (Dyer 1963; Feldman 1971; LeMasters 1957; Wainwright 1966), other data indicate that adjustment to parenthood is only mildly or moderately stressful (Hobbs 1965, 1968; Hobbs and Cole 1976; Meyerowitz and Feldman 1966; Russell 1974; Uhlenberg 1970; Beauchamp 1968; Feldman and Rogoff 1968; Waldron and Routh 1981).

A variety of explanations have been proposed to account for such divergent findings. One hypothesis is that initial levels of marital satisfaction mediate the subsequent influence of the baby on couples' transition to parenthood. But it is unclear whether high or low levels of initial satisfaction should predict subsequent crisis, and this theoretical confusion is mirrored in the available evidence. Whereas Feldman and Rogoff (1968) report that declines in marital satisfaction associated with the birth of the firstborn are greater for husbands and wives whose marital satisfaction was initially high, Dyer (1963) and Russell (1974) observe that high levels of initial adjustment to marriage are predictive of limited crisis scores. Ryder (1973) and LeMasters (1957), in contrast, fail to discern any systematic relationship between assessments of the marital relationship prior to and following the birth of the baby. Other inconsistencies are evident among reports examining the mediating influence that planned versus unplanned pregnancy (Dyer 1963; Hobbs and Wimbish 1977; Russell 1974; Tooke 1974), preparenthood employment status of mother (Dyer 1963; Hobbs 1965; LeMasters 1957; Russell 1974), and prior preparation for parenthood (Dyer 1963; Russell 1974; Touke 1974; Uhlenberg 1970) exert on degree of crisis experienced by marital couples.

Individual Differences in Experience. To a great extent, the inconsistency that is so evident in the transition-to-parenthood research may stem from the absence of conceptual frameworks in considering factors that might mediate the quality of adjustment to parenthood. That is, in study after study little or no rationale is provided as to why some variables are selected for consideration while others are not in efforts to account for variation in crisis experienced by couples. Yet, when the many measures included in these studies as mediating variables are clustered conceptually, greater consistency is evident between reports than when variables are considered singly. For example, the life-course perspective on human development, which "assumes that the consequences of events . . . vary according to their context and timing" (Elder and Rockwell 1979, p. 3), directs attention to data bearing on the timing and sequencing of parenthood. And here several studies indicate that adjustment to parenthood is easier the more normatively placed parenthood is in the life course. Specifically, crisis tends to be less severe when parents are older (Hobbs and Wimbish 1977; Russell 1974; Touke 1974), have been married for longer periods of time before conception (Dyer 1963; Russell 1974), and conceive after marriage (Russell 1974). The fact that a developmental perspective clarifies some of the confusion evident in research on the transition to parenthood underscores not only the need for a conceptual framework to guide inquiry but also the role that developmentalists can play in furthering understanding of this important domain of inquiry in family sociology.

A developmental, multidisciplinary perspective can contribute to understanding in other ways also. To date, the large majority of transition-to-parenthood studies have treated infants as if they were all alike, each presenting couples with exactly the same adjustment difficulties (Roberts and Miller 1978). The general failure of family sociologists to consider individual differences between infants is no doubt a function of the limited communication between disciplines, since developmental psychologists have long recognized that the effect the infant has is likely to be a function of his or her unique characteristics (e.g., temperament, health, physical appearance). It is interesting to note, however, that select findings from the transition-to-parenthood literature do highlight the importance of individual differences, even though they are rarely discussed in these terms. Hobbs (1965) reported, for example, that when infants required more than routine health checks, husbands tended to experience more crisis. Russell (1974) reported that babies who were more demanding (for example, cried frequently, were often "on the move," or had feeding problems) had parents who experienced more crisis than did those with less demanding infants (what Russell called "quiet" babies).

On the basis of findings such as these, it would appear that the temperamental difficulty of the infant or child can determine, at least in part, the degree to which the transition to parenthood is a stressful experience for couples. Thus, individual differences between children seem to affect not only the care they receive from parents (as documented in the previous chapter), but also the relationship that exists between parents as husband and wife. What we do not know at this point, given the general absence of interdisciplinary inquiry that focuses upon parenting and marital functioning simultaneously, is whether certain dimensions of infant functioning differentially influence marriage and parenting. Is it possible, for example, that the gender of the child has a greater impact upon parental behavior than marital functioning, whereas the reverse is true when we consider infant health?

While we currently lack the evidence to answer such questions of family process, recent studies do suggest that marital quality can be affected by child health. For example, Gath (1978) examined, in a longitudinal study, the effect of individual differences between infants on the marital functioning of their parents by comparing thirty families with mentally retarded Down's Syndrome infants with a matched sample of families with normal children. "The most striking difference between the families," Gath noted, was the greater "number of broken or disharmonious marriages in the mongol group" (p. 105). Moreover, marital interviews conducted in the second and third years of the child's life revealed greater sexual dissatisfaction, tension, hostility, and criticism in couples rearing a "special" child. Since an equal number of marriages in the two groups were noted as good (but not fair or poor), Gath reasonably concluded that the arrival of a baby with a congenital handicap may not so much mar a good marriage as "disrupt the balance of a moderate or more vulnerable marriage" (Gath 1978, p. 105). Indeed, the fact that a *greater* number of couples bearing a Down's Syndrome infant were rated as high on warmth displayed in the marital interviews suggests that under some circumstances the birth of an abnormal child can actually bring couples closer together.

Other factors besides individual differences between infants are likely to mediate or determine the effect that the transition to parenthood has on marital functioning. Consider, for example, the potentially disruptive effect of unfulfilled expectations. Many couples romanticize the manner in which becoming parents and having children will affect family life. The degree of real, and frequently stressful adaptation that goes on in a family when a new individual is added to the family, especially one as dependent as a new baby, is often unrecognized. As already noted, sleep routines are likely to be disrupted—and thus, sexual relations—as a result of the infant's night waking. The exhaustion mothers and fathers feel from such waking, and the lost sleep it occasions, can impair communication between spouses. The all-too-frequent advice that new parents often receive from well-meaning parents, in-laws, friends and neighbors is also stressful. When such quite possible effects of the baby are not anticipated, it seems quite probable that they will be experienced as even more stressful than they might otherwise be. In this regard, Kach and McGhee (1982) have recently reported that inaccurate expectations regarding how the transition to parenthood would affect family life were strongly and negatively predictive of the degree of difficulty mothers experienced in the transition to parenthood. More specifically, mothers who underestimated the stressful situations that might be encountered as the family was transformed from a dyad to a triad, and as husbands and wives adopted new roles as fathers and mothers, were more likely to feel stress following the birth of their first child.

An unexpected effect of the transition to parenthood for some couples will be the traditionalization of the household division of labor along sex-stereotyped lines. Available evidence indicates that with the adoption of parenting responsibilities, especially in households where mothers function as primary caregivers, women increasingly adopt traditional female responsibilities (cooking meals, doing laundry, changing diapers) and males adopt traditionally male responsibilities (caring for exterior of home, managing family finance) (Cowen et al. 1976; Feldman, Biringer, and Nash 1981; Lamb 1978). In many homes such a trend toward less egalitarian division of labor may pose little difficulty, but in households where liberated sex-role belief systems and expectations prevail, it is clear that such deviation from desired arrangements could be a cause of concern.

Quite likely, the relative contribution both parents make to the household division of labor will influence the degree to which the transition to parenthood is experienced as a crisis. In families in which becoming a parent simply adds to the mother's already burdensome responsibilities, conflict between husband and wife is probable. In fact, it seems reasonable to speculate that in homes in which fathers, even in their roles as secondary caregivers, make a considerable contribution to child care and assist their spouses in the completion of what may have been routine household tasks for their wives prior to the child's arrival, marital stress could be reduced. Essentially what is being proposed is that a division of labor in the marriage that reduces maternal role strain may very well have positive consequences for the marital relationship more generally. Some support for this contention can be found in a recent investigation which found that in families with high levels of shared child care responsibilities, marital warmth and affection, and spousal compatibility, were rated higher following observation of mother-father-infant interaction than in households in which fathers displayed little child care involvement (Dickie et al. 1981).

Even without such extra assistance, it would be inappropriate to conclude that the transition to parenthood is all problems. Miller and Sollie (1980) have identified several major positive themes that emerge from inquiry into the first parental experience. The first of these includes emotional benefits resulting from the love, joy, happiness, and fun that routinely accompanies certain dimensions of child care (e.g., play). Indeed, most parents regard these benefits as outweighing whatever costs are associated with the transition to parenthood. A second positive theme involves the self-enrichment and personal development that parents frequently report experiencing upon undertaking parental responsibilities and obligations. In this regard, parents often report feeling more like an adult, becoming less selfish and thinking more about the future. In sum, parenting seems to have a maturing effect upon individual development in adulthood (Gutman 1975). Evidence that such personal change can influence marital life comes from a recent study of marriage, parenting and infant development. In this investigation, Vincent, Cook-Illback, and Messerly (1980) found that husbands' evaluations of their wives as "good mothers" were an important dimension and determinant of their overall appraisal of their own marital happiness.

A sense of family cohesiveness is the third positive theme to emerge from studies. In many households children are viewed as a link that ties husband and wife together, possibly even more strongly than marriage vows, thereby adding to the sense of being a family. Strengthened relationships with extended families are also routinely reported. These positive effects of the first child invariably balance some of the stress experienced in many households. The exact extent to which the entire experience is viewed as more or less stressful will undoubtedly determine the effect of the first child on the marital relationship. What may be extremely important in influencing this effect is the general context in which parenthood is experienced.

Child Effects Across the Family Life Course

In a society like the contemporary United States, in which values often appear to be highly individualistic and hedonistic, and in which marital relations are expected to involve a high degree of emotional and sexual intimacy, as well as to serve as each spouse's primary source of companionship, it might be expected that the presence of children would undermine marital happiness and satisfaction. This expectation is based upon the assumption that children tend to interfere with marital companionship and to lessen the spontaneity of sexual relations. In addition, children's presence in the family creates the potential for jealousy and competition for affection, time, and attention (Glenn and McLanahan 1982).

The research evidence gathered to date provides general support for the preceding prediction, that is, that children, at least in contemporary U.S. society, exert a negative influence on marital functioning. Indeed, these negative effects appear quite pervasive, very likely outweighing positive effects among spouses of both sexes and all races, major religious groups, educational levels, and employment statuses (Glenn and McLanahan 1982). More specifically, when the results of a variety of investigations are considered together, a decline is evident in marital quality across the early years of the family life course, with satisfaction levels highest prior to the arrival of children and decreasing through the childbearing and early child-rearing years (e.g., Rollins and Feldman 1968; Rollins and Gannon 1974; Rollins and Galligan 1978; Deutsch 1964; Miller 1976).

In the early years of marriage, the findings of a general negative relationship between the presence of children and marital happiness may be a result of many couple's unwillingness to divorce or separate because they fear it will be bad for the children, even when the quality of the marital relationship is poor. The tendency to maintain a disharmonious marriage for the "sake of the children," which we will see in a subsequent chapter may not really be in the child's best interest, may tend to inflate the documented negative effect of children on marriages (Glenn and McLanahan 1982).

The actual impact of children on marital quality beyond these early years remains unknown (Spanier, Lewis, and Cole 1975). Reliance on data collected at one point in time on different individuals at different points in the life course makes comparisons potentially unreliable, since factors such as divorce eliminate couples from such samples, leaving only the more happily married for study. This selective attrition from study samples may explain why marital evaluations made during the empty nest period appear to highlight a beneficial effect on marriages of children leaving home. It may also be the case that those couples that do remain together through the empty nest stage report high levels of marital satisfaction due to their own needs to justify the long-term maintenance of their relationships.

Such potential social-psychological processes call into question the ultimate meaning of the decline in marital quality that appears to result from the rearing of children *and* the increase in marital quality that has been reported in conjunction with the child's departure from home. While caution thus seems warranted in interpreting cross-sectional, life-course data in terms of child effects on marital relations, the conclusion that the child's influence extends beyond making parents of a couple is most certainly sound.

MARRIAGE AND PARENTING

Historically, it has been the practice in studying parental influence upon child development to focus first upon the development of children who do not have a relationship with one of their parents. Thus, prior to undertaking detailed investigations of the manner in which mothers behave toward and influence their children, scientists studied the development of children without mothers, that is, children reared in orphanages and institutions. Similarly, prior to studying the behavior and influence of fathers, scientists studied the development of children whose fathers were absent from their home, either for reasons of death, employment (jobs away from home) or desertion. The assumption underlying most of this work was that if mother-deprived or father-absent children developed differently than age mates, the influence of mothering and fathering could be inferred.

Eventually, students of parent-child relations came to realize that there was no substitute for actually studying patterns of mothering and fathering in families in which parents were present. It took longer for investigators to focus upon the father, in part because of the assumed primacy of mother in influencing children's development. Focus upon the father in the preschool years preceded concern for his behavior and influence during the infancy years. In fact, fathers were neglected for such a long period of time that one critic was led to regard them as "forgotten contributors to child development" (Lamb 1978).

When fathers were eventually included in scientific formulations, attention was directed primarily upon how they were similar to and different from mothers. Indeed, only recently have investigators working from a multidisciplinary perspective come to realize that inclusion of the father in the study of parent-child relations does more than create an additional parent-child dyad. As Belsky (1981) has noted, it transforms the mother-child dyad into a family system comprised of husband-wife, in addition to parent-child, relations. With this realization came a theoretical imperative to inquire into the interrelations between marriage, parenting, and child development (Lerner and Spanier, 1978).

Scattered throughout the scientific literature are findings that suggest that the marital relationship does indeed influence child development. Much of this work focuses on the development of aggressive or antisocial behavior on the part of the child (e.g., Gibson 1969; Johnson and Lobitz 1974; Kimmel and Van der Veen 1974; Nye 1957; O'Leary and Emery 1983). Rutter (1971), for example, discovered that the association between parent-child separation and delinquency was mediated by the quality of the marital relationship. In fact, transient and permanent separations per se were found to be unrelated to the development of children's antisocial behavior when affectional relations between parents, marital dissatisfaction, shared leisure activities, husband-wife communication, and spousal quarreling (i.e., indices of marital quality) were considered. Only in those cases in which separation from parent was caused by marital discord and other household conflict was problematic child behavior observed.

In addition to the antisocial and delinquent behavior that Rutter's (1971) work highlights, there is suggestive evidence that the marital relationship can influence other domains of child functioning. Honzik (1967) reported, for example, that marital adjustment predicted daughter's, but not son's, mental test performance from twenty-one months through the school-age years. Working with the same data set from the Berkeley Growth Study, Bronson (1966) found that poor marital adjustment, marital hostility, and indifference during the toddler and preschool years were predictive of reactive-explosive, as opposed to placid-controlled, styles of emotional expression during the elementary and school-age years. And more recently, Goldberg (1982) and Solomon (1982) discerned positive associations between marital quality and quality of infant-parent attachment. In families in which infants displayed avoidance and resistance toward their parents, marital adjustment and emotional sharing between spouses was found to be low.

Process of Influence

Although these findings suggest that the influence of the marital relationship on cognitive and personality development may begin in infancy and be long-lasting, they shed no light on the actual processes of influence. That is, through what mechanisms or social-psychological processes does the marital relationship affect the child's cognitive and personality development? One possibility that comes to mind might be labeled a *direct* influence, whereby the atmosphere created by a loving or conflicted marital relationship fosters a sense of trust or anxiety within the child. Consider, for example, the tension which is probably generated within the child when parents fight openly with each other. Consider also the possibility of observational learning going on as the developing child observes his parents being friendly and considerate of one another in their roles as husband and wife. An intriguing question raised by consideration of these direct processes of influence involves what children learn about the nature of marriage and how such learning affects the kind of marriage they participate in as adults. Surprisingly, other than the fact that children from divorced homes are more likely to experience divorce in their own marriages (Mueller & Pope, 1977), we know surprisingly little about the transmission across generations of marital behavior and expectations. From a developmental perspective, socialization for marriage represents an area of inquiry that has gone virtually unexamined, what Lerner and Spanier (1978) refer to as an "omission of measurement" in the multidisciplinary study of marital and parent-child relations.

In addition to being influenced by the marital relationship directly, children can also be affected indirectly by their parent's relationship with each other. That is, the marital relationship can influence parenting which, as we know, can in turn influence child functioning. The fact that, as we have seen already, children can influence their parents' marriages suggests that a complex, bidirectional process may exist whereby children influence their own development: child behavior affects marriage, which influences parenting, which then affects child development. Of course, those very child behaviors that affect marital functioning may themselves be a function of the quality of care the child experienced.

It is such potential *indirect* effects of marriage on child development that will be the focus of the discussion that follows. Thus, we consider how marriage can influence parenting. Before initiating this discussion, two points are worth noting. First, virtually no investigation has focused simultaneously upon marital relations, parenting, and child development. Investigations have either measured marriage and child development (e.g., Porter and Laney 1980) or marriage and parenting (e.g., Wandersman 1980). We will therefore only be able to speculate upon the bidirectional processes whereby marriage influences parenting and parenting influences marriage.

A second point that needs to be made is that virtually all of the research concerning the interrelation of marriage and parenting is, like that concerning parental influences on child development, correlational in nature. Thus, actual cause and effect relations are quite difficult to identify. It is important to note, then, that although we speak in terms of marital influences upon parenting, the possibility must be entertained that the reverse process is at work, that is, parenting influences marital relations. This same comment applies to the earlier cited findings regarding marital discord and problematic child functioning. Rather than revealing marital effects on child behavior, it may be the case that disobedient and aggressive children foster marital conflict. As noted, however, such influential child functioning may itself be a function of the experiences the child has had in the family. Undoubtedly, a multiplicity of processes are at work since, as we have repeatedly stressed, pathways of influence in the family are bidirectional in nature.

Marital Effects

To understand how marital relations might affect parenting (and in turn child development), it helps to conceptualize the marriage as a parental support system. Marriages, like other support systems, provide two general types of support: emotional support and instrumental assistance. Emotional support communicates to the parent that he or she is loved, esteemed, and valued, and presumably affects the patience that a parent can bring to the caregiving role. Instrumental assistance involves the provision of goods and services and thereby frees up energy that the parent can use in the caregiving role (Belsky, Robins, and Gamble 1984). It is important to note that each of these forms of support can influence parenting in two ways—directly and indirectly. When a wife praises her husband for his skill in managing the children, we speak of direct influence, as the communication is focused at the parenting role. If a husband is involved in non-child related home maintenance tasks (e.g., vacuuming, grocery shopping), we speak of indirect influence, since although not directed specifically at his wife's parenting, mothering is nevertheless likely to be influenced.

With respect to the instrumental assistance that husbands can provide their spouses, it is of interest to note that most fathers make only a limited contribution to child care and family- or household-related tasks

(Lein 1979; Pleck 1979). Even when their wives are employed, husbands do not spend more time in housework or child care than do husbands of non-employed wives (Pleck 1979). A consequence of this is that employed women do double duty (Bernard 1974)—working outside the home and caring for children. Quite possibly, such women experience stress from role strain that may undermine their parental competence.

It has been suggested that during the infancy years the influence of fathers on child functioning may be primarily indirect, that is, mediated by the wife in her capacity as mother (Lewis and Weinraub 1976; Parke 1978; Pedersen, Anderson and Cain, 1979). And indeed, several studies highlight just such indirect effects. In one investigation of families during the infant's first month of life, Pedersen (1975; Pederson, Anderson, and Cain 1979) found that tension and conflict between husband and wife (as reported by fathers) strongly and negatively correlated with independent observational evaluations of maternal feeding competence. Husband's esteem for wife as mother (i.e., direct emotional support), on the other hand, was positively related to feeding skill. Price (1977) reported data remarkably consistent with Pedersen's observations linking marital support and maternal feeding ability. She was led to conclude, in fact, on the basis of her investigation of changes in mother-infant reciprocity across the first month of the baby's life, "that the mother's ability to enjoy her infant, and regard it with affection may be in part a function of the quality of her relationship with her husband" (p. 7).

Additional evidence supportive to this thesis has been reported in several investigations that examine relationships between parent-infant and husband-wife relations (Feiring and Taylor 1977; Donovan, Leavitt, and Balling 1975; Switzky, Vietze, and Switzky 1974; Wandersman 1980). For example, Belsky (1979a) observed that in families in which there was frequent marital communication about the baby, fathers were highly involved with their fifteen month olds, both when alone with them and while in their wives' presence. More recently, he and his colleagues have found that at one, three, and nine months of age, high levels of fathering and marital interaction go together (Belsky, Gilstrap, and Rovine 1983). These results are supported by data reported by a group of Stanford University researchers indicating that marital quality was one of the most consistently powerful predictors of fathering observed in free and structured laboratory play situations (Feldman, Nash, and Aschenbrenner 1982). These data suggest that wives may serve to interest their husbands in, and enhance their understanding of, the infant's development. And in a society that traditionally has not viewed men as "significant others" in the infant's world, it may be wives who are instrumental in encouraging paternal involvement in caregiving.

In the case of teenage mothers, "spousal" support may prove vital to the well-being of the mother-child relationship, even when mother and father are not married. Colletta (1981) discovered that the emotional support and instrumental assistance received from the infant's biological father predicted how teenage mothers felt and behaved toward their babies born out of wedlock. Mothers with high levels of support displayed less rejection, neglect, and aggression, and a more positive attitude toward child-rearing. Consistent with these findings are the results of a study of premature and full-term infants and their mothers. Crnic et al. (1981) found that mothers of four month olds who received lots of support from their spouses were more responsive to their infants and displayed more positively affectionate responses to them than did mothers who received less support. Since we know that it is just such parenting (e.g., affectionate, responsive) that facilitates optimal child development, there exist grounds for inferring from this research a marriage-to-parenting-to-child development pathway of influence.

Effects of marital relations on parenting, it must be recognized, may not always be positive. Pedersen, Anderson, and Cain (1977) found, for example, that the more husbands criticized and blamed their wives, the more these mothers were negatively oriented toward their five month olds. More recently, Vincent, Cook-Illback, and Messerly (1980; Cook 1979) reported that when the marital role is unsatisfying, individual parents (especially mothers) make compensatory investments in the parenting role, that is, they increase their parental involvement. Additional evidence of such a compensatory investment in child-rearing in the face of unsatisfactory marital relations comes from a study showing that in contrast to more maritally satisfied couples, parents with unhappy marriages were more likely to evaluate their children as one of their greatest or only source of satisfaction in family life. Since companionship between spouses was lower in unhappy marriages, it may be inferred that couples who find little in the way of interspousal companionship turn to their children for their primary satisfaction (Luckey and Bain 1970). Such compensatory involvement in children, however, may not be in the children's best interest.

The possibility that the effect of the marital relationship on parenting may ultimately extend to the infant's development is suggested by recent research on child abuse and parental visiting patterns in neonatal intensive care nurseries. Minde et al. (1977; Minde, Marton, Manning, and Hines, 1980) found that the quality of marriage predicted the frequency with which mothers visited their hospitalized premature infants. In an independent study, an empirical relationship was discerned between infrequent visits to hospitalized infants and subsequent parenting disorders such as child maltreatment (Farnhoff, Kennell, and Klaus, 1972). The fact that George and Main (1979) discovered that abused infants are impaired in their ability to engage peers and adults in social interchange suggests, when considered in light of the two just mentioned studies, that the marriage can influence parenting, which in turn can influence infant development. Furthermore, an earlier study by Leifer et al. (1972) linking prematurity and infant hospitalization with divorce, indicates that this complex process may be initiated by the infant who functions, inadvertently, as producer of his or her own development: infant development affects marital relations, which in turn affects parenting, which in turn influences infant development (Belsky and Tolan 1981).

The earlier discussion of parenting and infant development indicated that infants can directly influence their parents' behavior, whereas the preceding analysis of child abuse suggested that infant effects may "flow through" the marital relationship. Recent work by Vincent et al. (1979; Cook 1979) suggests that still another process of influence is possible, one in which infant characteristics and marital quality interact to jointly determine parenting. Disorganized infant functioning, these investigators discovered, predicted nonsynchronous patterns of mother-infant and father-infant interaction *only* when marriages were evaluated as low in marital satisfaction. These findings suggest that a well-functioning husband-wife relationship can serve to buffer or inhibit the negative impact of a difficult child on the parent-child relationship. When this buffer does not function, because the marriage is not very supportive, dysfunction in the parent-child relationship becomes more likely (Belsky, Robins, and Gamble 1984).

Almost all the work considered up to now has focused upon marriage-parenting relations during the infancy years. Very little work beyond this developmental period is available. That which is available, however, once again suggests that the marital relationship is an important support system for parenting and can be influenced by children and eventually influence their development.

In a recent study of mothers at risk for psychological depression, it was found that when mothers of preschoolers felt they could turn to their husbands for emotional support, they displayed less stress in the parental role and less depression. The same was true when fathers provided direct and indirect instrumental assistance in the form of help with child care and household tasks (Zur-Spiro and Longfellow 1981).

Processes of influence similar to these were reported over two decades ago in other work on parents and their preschool children. Bandura and Walters (1959) observed, for example, that mothers who were inclined to nag and scold their sons felt less warmth and affection toward their husbands. Since comparable findings were not discerned in the case of daughters, the possibility must be entertained that mothers were projecting their hostile feelings toward their husbands on the other males with whom they had a presumably close relationship. Complementing these findings are those of Sears, Maccoby, and Levin (1957) indicating that mothers' professed esteem for their husbands was systematically related to the praise they directed at their preschool children. Since it is just the kind of parenting observed in these two investigations that has been linked to less than optimal and competent child functioning, respectively, once again there are grounds for inferring a marriage-to-parenting-to-child development process of influence.

During the school-age years and during adolescence there is also evidence suggestive of a process whereby marital relations serve to support or undermine competent parenting. Santrock and his colleagues (1982) found that six- to eleven-year-old boys being raised in reconstituted families that consisted of a stepfather and biological mother were more socially competent than age mates reared in families composed of both biological parents. This surprising result, further inquiry revealed, was related to the more competent parenting displayed by the stepfathers. Most important to us here, though, was the observation that these more competent stepfathers, with more socially skilled stepsons, reported less marital conflict in their marriage than did the biological fathers whose parenting and sons' development appeared less competent.

Research has shown that parents of adolescents who employ disciplinary techniques that undermine competent child development (i.e., frequent use of punishment, infrequent use of reasoning) tend to be involved in marriages characterized by hostility and low satisfaction (Dielman, Barton, and Cattell 1977; Kemper and Reichler 1976). Indeed, Olweus (1980) reported that the quality of the emotional relationship between parents substantially predicted mothers' feelings of negativism toward their thirteen- and sixteen-year-old sons. These findings led him to conclude that a conflictual spousal relationship may increase mothers' negative feelings for their sons, which his research also indicated fosters an aggressive, antisocial orientation on the part of the child.

Parenting Effects

Attempts by family sociologists to account for the findings on the transition to parenthood that were summarized earlier are relevant to the issue of parental influences on marital relations. Repeatedly it has been suggested that much of the crisis that the first child purportedly fosters within the family system following its birth is a result of the role strain experienced by spouses (Rollins and Galligan 1978). With the arrival of the baby, husbands and wives must function not only as maintainers of a household, friends, and employees (at their places of work), but as parents as well (Nye and Berardo 1973). To the extent that the responsibilities of parenthood become a burden that overwhelms the mother and father, it is likely that these other roles are adversely affected. Indeed, the frequent finding that degree of crisis experienced by the marital couple following the birth of the child is systematically tied to wives' physical exhaustion and lack of interest in sexual relations illustrates quite nicely the potential for parenting (in this case mothering) to affect the marriage (Dyer 1963; Hobbs 1965; Hobbs and Wimbish 1977; LeMasters 1957).

This discussion of the potential influence of parenting on the marital dyad would be seriously flawed if only the negative were considered. Although it is doubtful that parenthood turns poor marriages into good ones, there is reason to believe that shared activities created by the care of the child (e.g., bathing, playing, picture-taking) can provide the opportunity for enjoyable marital interaction. Belsky (1979a) not only demonstrated that such incidents of shared pleasure do occur during the course of naturalistically observed family interaction, but also that frequent instances of such pleasure sharing between spouses in the course of parenting are systematically associated with high levels of maternal and paternal involvement. The fact that such patterns of parenting also correlated with infant exploratory competence, which was itself related to evaluations of spousal harmony, suggests, when interpreted in the context of the present framework, a process whereby parenting affects marital relations, which affect parenting and, thereby, infant development and, eventually, marital relations (Belsky 1981). This, of course, is not the only interpretation that could be applied to these correlational data. Nevertheless, it does highlight the utility of the proposed framework for guiding inquiry into indirect and complex pathways of influence within the three-person family system during infancy.

CONCLUSION: THE FAMILY AS A SYSTEM

Family sociologists as well as developmental psychologists have pursued the study of the child in the family. As we have seen, family sociologists have been intrigued by the transition to parenthood and have worked arduously to understand the effect of the child on the marriage. Developmental psychologists, of course, have pursued the characteristics and consequences of the parent-child relationship. To each discipline's detriment, little cross-fertilization has taken place, most probably because, as Aldous (1977) noted, social scientists have established "an unexpressed working arrangement" whereby they stay within these self-set confines. Thus, too often sociology remains largely ignorant of achievements in the developmental study of parent-child relations, while psychologists disregard studies of the effect of the child on the marriage.

What is so surprising in light of this failure to communicate is how nicely these two fields of inquiry complement each other. Indeed, when they are considered together, a better understanding of both parent-child relations and child effects on marriage is achieved. As we have tried to demonstrate, a means of integrating the disciplines of family sociology and developmental psychology, and thus advancing the study of the child in the family is suggested by coupling the respective concerns of each discipline. Figure 8.1 represents a graphic presentation of what this integrative conceptual framework looks like.

This organizational scheme, which highlights the possible reciprocal direct and indirect influences that marital relations, parenting, and child behavior/development may have on each other, has both uses and limitations. Foremost among its uses is its capacity to integrate disciplines while revealing interdisciplinary areas of inquiry in need of empirical attention. Specifically, the arrows linking parenting and child development represent developmental psychology's contribution to this perspective. The arrow depicting the child's effect on the marital relationship represents family sociology's contribution. And the arrow from the marital relationship to parenting represents the contribution of an emerging interdisciplinary literature. The remaining two arrows represent domains of study that have fallen between the cracks that separate the disciplines of family sociology and developmental psychology. They represent pathways of influence presumed to exist within the family system.

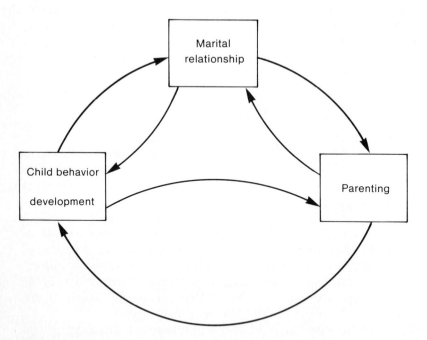

Figure 8.1 *A scheme for integrating the disciplines of family sociology and developmental psychology in the study of the child in the family.*

Source: Adapted from J. Belsky, "Early human experience: A family perspective," *Developmental Psychology*, 1981, *17*, pp. 3–23.

A serious limitation of this scheme is the manner in which it simplifies the experience of children in the family by focusing attention solely on a three-person (mother/wife, father/husband, child) system. Even though such social units are by no means universal, neither are they non-normative. Moreover, even though such families do not capture the experience of many children, they do succeed in capturing that of most parents during one period of family life. Of course, it should be recognized that most families involve more than three persons. Usually there are two or more children, and thus we are led to consider the topic of sibling relationships as an even more complex aspect of the mother-father-child system.

By highlighting linkages connecting related aspects of the family system, the conceptual scheme depicted in Figure 8.1 explicitly directs attention to the bidirectional pathways of influence within the family and to the complex ways in which the family may function. Direct feedback loops are represented, as when the parent influences the infant who, in return, affects parenting (Parke, Power, and Gottman 1979). Also represented in this graphic model are transitive influences (Lewis and Weinraub 1976) in which the actions and attitudes of one party (e.g., father) influence a second party (e.g., child) who in turn affects a third party (e.g., mother). Significantly, this conceptual model also subsumes transitive processes in which one party (e.g., child) affects the relationship that exists between spouses, which in turn influences parental functioning. Also depicted are circular processes (Parke, Power, and Gottman 1979) whereby this transitive process of influence completes a full circle to affect the child. In sum, the framework, and this chapter, document the fact that the family is a system of interdependent individuals (adults, children) and social roles (parent, spouse, child) in which parenting affects and is affected by the child, who both influences and is influenced by the marriage, which in turn both affects and is affected by parenting.

Families in Conflict

Divorce

W hen the bride and groom say "till death do us part," they almost always mean it. Virtually no one in America marries unless he or she fully expects to remain married for many, many years. Unfortunately, as documented in Chapter 3, the happiness of courtship, the joy of the wedding, and the novelty of early marriage vanish quickly for many couples. It is estimated that about half of all marriages begun in recent years will be terminated by divorce (National Center for Health Statistics 1980).

It is unrealistic to assume that all marriages will or should succeed. Yet this is an assumption that we are prone to make, an assumption made about few other human undertakings. It is important to realize that a divorce signifies the end of only a particular marriage, and not necessarily that marriage or the family as social institutions are in jeopardy. Rather, divorce tells us that a particular couple could no longer find satisfaction and love in their relationship. Divorce, then, usually involves the "rejection" of a partner or relationship, not a rejection of marriage as a meaningful lifestyle.

MARITAL QUALITY AND STABILITY

There is a not uncommon assumption that the high divorce rate in this country reflects the fact that marriages are poorer today than in earlier times. But is the divorce rate (an indication of *marital stability*) a fair indication of *marital quality*? Probably not. The liberalization of divorce laws, the tendency to divorce when things go wrong in a marriage, and society's greater tolerance of divorce and divorcing individuals have all inflated the American divorce rate in recent years. Thus, a marriage that might have remained intact but unhappy many years ago would be more likely to end in divorce today. No one knows how the *quality* of today's marriages compares to that of marriages of many years ago. We would speculate that the differences are not nearly as great as many are inclined to think. It is true, of course, that there are different pressures affecting modern marriages, many of which would tend to dissolve these unions. But there has really been no time in American history that was without imposing pressures.

In earlier times, too, standards of success and failure were different. Expectations and roles of husbands and wives were different. There was more emphasis on duty, a word unattractive to many contemporary Americans. Marital stability was considered to be a more reliable criterion of judgment than marital quality. In earlier days there was little for a couple to do about an unsuccessful marriage but "grin and bear it." Public opinion frowned upon divorce, and there was stigma attached to divorced persons. There were few ways for a wife to support herself if she left her husband. Laws governing divorce were less permissive than they are today. Hence, we might guess that many couples remained together in a marriage that many present-day couples would seek to escape. A generation ago, one sociologist (Goode 1956) made the observation that Americans at all times in history have expressed the idea that they wished we could return the family to the way it was "in the good old days," as if there were some time in history when the family was the way everyone thought it should be. He called this notion "the classical family of Western nostalgia."

When a group of unsuccessful marriages in which there is no divorce is compared with a group ending in divorce, all the elements characteristic of the latter are found in the former, with one exception: namely, the willingness to terminate the marriage in court. Some marriages hold together in spite of elements contributing to failure because the couples are not willing to resort to divorce. It is not true that the highest quality marriages always remain intact and the lowest quality marriages always end in divorce. In fact, it is possible to classify marriages in four ways to illustrate the relation between the quality of marriage and the stability of marriage (Lewis and Spanier 1982).

High-quality, high-stability marriages are the American dream; *low-quality, low-stability marriages* are part of the American nightmare. The first type, the "ideal marriage," describes only a minority of marriages in the United States today, considering the high divorce rate and the great number of marriages that are not very rewarding for the partners but remain intact anyway. The second type is the marriages that do not go well and end in divorce. We have already mentioned that this will be characteristic of a substantial proportion of marriages formed in recent years.

Two other forms of marriage have not received as much attention, but are important. *Low-quality, high-stability marriages*—those unhappy unions that continue despite the absence of love and harmony—have always been around. They undoubtedly will decrease as divorce becomes increasingly accepted and accessible as an alternative to an unhappy marriage. This is not to say that all low-quality marriage will some day end in divorce. Some individuals in these relationships continue to meet important needs of their partners and indeed may find that the threshold between being married and being separated or divorced is too burdensome to cross, no matter what the state of unhappiness.

Finally, *high-quality, low-stability marriages* are relatively few in number, but are likely to be noticed more in the future. These are marriages that are relatively happy, but end in divorce for reasons other than the quality of the marriage. An example might be a case of differing work and family opportunities. A husband and wife who are professionals might be offered jobs in opposite parts of the country, and may decide to end the marriage rather than interrupt their careers. As career/family conflicts grow in the future, so might this marriage type.

AMERICAN DIVORCE RATES

At the time of World War II the divorce rate took a sharp upward turn, owing to the breakup of many "war marriages" and the effect of the war on other unstable marriages. In 1946 the rate reached what was then an all-time high—a level Americans never thought would be reached again. The pattern settled down somewhat after the war but never again reached the lower prewar rates. Beginning in the 1960s and continuing through 1980, the divorce rate increased dramatically and steadily (National Center for Health Statistics 1981a). In 1975, for the first time in American history, more than one million divorces were granted in a single year (U.S. Bureau of the Census, *Statistical Abstract*, 1981). The divorce rate in the United States reached an all-time high by 1981. By 1981, more than 1.2 million divorces were granted.

The divorce rate may be expressed in various ways, some of which can be very misleading. One of the most common ways divorce rates are expressed is by calculating the ratio of divorces to weddings in a given year. In 1981, there were estimated to be 2,438,000 weddings and 1,219,000 divorces, a ratio of about one for every two weddings (National Center for Health Statistics 1982a). However, this is *not* equivalent to saying that one in two marriages ends in divorce, since the divorces granted in a given year represent marriages that, as a rule, began before that year. A better way of expressing the divorce rate is to look at the number of divorces per 1,000 married women 15 years of age and older or 1,000 total population. In 1980, for example, the divorce rate was 5.3 per 1,000 population (National Center for Health Statistics 1981a).

None of these figures are very helpful for determining the proportion of marriages that will ultimately fail. Since couples marrying in a given year may remain married for many years, may become widowed at any time, or may divorce early in the marriage or late in the marriage, it is very difficult to estimate how many of the marriages that are still intact may ultimately end in divorce. The problem is further complicated by the fact that the divorcing history of couples now marrying for the first time may turn out to be very different from that of couples who have married and divorced in the past. To estimate what proportion of marriages will ultimately end in divorce, we need to rely on methods of *demographic projection*, which allow social scientists to use mathematical formulas to predict, based on a series of assumptions, what *may* happen in the future.

Such an analysis (National Center for Health Statistics 1980), shown in Table 9.1, estimated that for persons first married in the early

Table 9.1
Divorce Projections

Year of Marriage	Number of Marriages in Given Year	Percent of Marriages Projected to End in Divorce
1977	2,178,367	...
1976	2,154,807	...
1975	2,152,662	...
1974	2,229,667	...
1973	2,284,108	49.2
1972	2,282,154	48.7
1971	2,190,481	48.0
1970	2,158,802	47.8
1969	2,145,000	47.1
1968	2,069,000	45.9
1967	1,927,000	45.3
1966	1,857,000	44.3
1965	1,800,000	43.7
1964	1,725,000	42.2
1963	1,654,000	41.0
1962	1,577,000	40.0
1961	1,548,000	39.1
1960	1,523,000	38.8
1959	1,494,000	37.6
1958	1,451,000	36.5
1957	1,518,000	35.4
1956	1,585,000	34.4
1955	1,531,000	34.4
1954	1,490,000	33.8
1953	1,546,000	32.3
1952	1,539,318	32.1
1951	1,594,694	30.9
1950	1,667,231	29.5

Source: Adapted from National Center for Health Statistics data (1980).

1950s, about three in ten marriages will ultimately end in divorce. For persons married in the early 1960s, about four in ten marriages will end in divorce. Nearly half of those persons married in the 1970s are likely to be divorced. Projections are not yet possible for persons married in the early 1980s, but it is likely that about half of the first marriages of these individuals will ultimately be disrupted by divorce.

Factors Affecting Divorce

The factors affecting the divorce rate are not necessarily the same as the ones that contribute to low marital quality. We have said that divorce is a symptom of failure in the individual marriage. The rate is also a symptom of social change. Much of this change has been in the direction of removing some of the outside props that used to keep marriages intact even when they were disintegrating on the inside. Modern marriage is like a tent that has had its stakes pulled out one by one, each time making it more vulnerable to wind and storm. In earlier times marriages were held together in part by coercion from without. Now, when they hold together, it is largely through cohesion from within.

Some of the elements in the social situation that may contribute to the high divorce rate are a decreased tolerance of poor marital quality, the higher status of women, new standards of marital success and new ideals of married life, a decline of religious authority, increased urbanization, the increased ability of women to support themselves following a divorce, the greater ease with which divorce may be obtained, the more widespread acceptance of divorce, and the mobility of the American population. In addition to these there are the following:

The Decline in the Death Rate. Since the death rate has declined and the average span of life has lengthened, some marriages that might have been broken by death end in divorce. A couple marrying in their early twenties and living until their early seventies are expected to remain married for over fifty years. It can whimsically be stated that marriage was never intended to last fifty years. Persons of previous generations and in previous eras were typically married for much shorter periods of time, simply because they did not live as long.

When a marriage ends in the death of one party, there is a not uncommon assumption that the marriage was at least passably successful. In some cases there might have been a divorce had the deceased spouse lived longer. When both death and divorce are considered, we find that there were actually more "prematurely" broken homes in earlier days in this country than there are today.

Not everyone agrees that the decline in the death rate plays a significant role. Says Weiss (1975), "We can quickly reject the theory that increased longevity is to blame [for the high divorce rate]." He points out that although there have been substantial gains in increasing the length of life, the divorce rate has risen faster than life expectancy. Nevertheless, there is still the possibility that some marriages might have ended in divorce had the couple, or one of them, lived longer. Life expectancy cannot be considered the only reason for the high divorce rate, but it is probably one reason.

American Attitudes Relating to Divorce. Generalizing broadly, we may describe Americans as comfort-loving. They are impatient with discomfort and inconvenience. They feel that whatever they do not like they have a right to change, either through established channels or by direct action. They are freedom-loving, and unhappy marriage may be interpreted as a form of restraint. "We have come . . . to regard the right of divorce as something like a civil liberty" (O'Neill, 1967). In spite of their sensitivity to group pressure, Americans are individualistic, and personal welfare is often given precedence over the welfare of the group. Americans are generally sympathetic with the "underdog," give help to someone in dire need, and lend support to a person or a group in time of unusual crisis or emergency. Such attitudes make us inclined to respond sympathetically to anyone who is the "victim" of a marital situation assumed to be caused largely by the other spouse.

Duration of Marriage before Divorce. There is great variability among divorcing couples in the length of time between the wedding and divorce. This variability suggests that the factors which influence marital instability operate throughout marriage and that they may take their greatest toll at different times for different couples. The fact that the *median* interval (middle point) has always been around seven years has led to the unfounded notion of a "seven-year itch." Actually, the *modal* (peak) interval between marriage and divorce is much shorter. The peak time of divorce action is between the second and fifth years of marriage. If we consider the fact that virtually all couples separate for at least a brief period before divorcing, the data are even more dramatic. An analysis conducted by the Division of Vital Statistics of the United States Bureau of the Census (Plateris 1973) found that more couples separate in the first year of marriage than in any other year. Since the average length of time between separation and divorce, depending on the state, varies from a few months to well over a year, marital disruption tends to occur earlier in marriage than most persons realize. The high incidence of separation leading to divorce in the early years of marriage indicates that *most marriages that fail show signs of this failure early in the relationship*. These data also indicate the lack of preparation for marriage that seems to characterize a great many couples.

What can we expect in the future? Projections for couples married in recent years indicate that about one in six first marriages will have already ended by divorce within five years of the wedding. By the tenth anniversary about three in ten couples will have obtained a divorce. After fifteen years of marriage, about two in five couples have ended their relationship (National Center for Health Statistics 1980). These figures support the notion that the greatest number of marriages fail early in the relationship, a time when children—if couples have them, are likely to be young, but that divorce is something that can happen any time in the marriage, even after twenty or thirty years of stability.

Although many divorces occur early in the marriage, there is no evidence to suggest that couples make hasty decisions. The overwhelming impression is the reverse; when divorce occurs, it typically comes as an "end of the rope" decision. As we will see in a subsequent section, the timing of divorce may be important from the perspective of the developing child.

DIFFERENTIALS IN DIVORCE RATES

Divorce rates vary widely by social, economic, and geographical characteristics.

Geographic Variation

Divorce rates tend to increase going from east to west. The lowest divorce rates are in the northeastern United States, whereas the highest are in the West. For example, in 1979 the divorce rate per 1,000 population was 3.6 in the Northeast and 6.6 in the West—almost double. The divorce rate in a given state is likely to be influenced by the stringency of requirements for divorce in that state, the rural-urban balance, the religious affiliations of its residents, the proportion of young couples in the state, as well as by the length of residency required for divorce. Massachusetts has the lowest divorce rate, Nevada the highest (National Center for Health Statistics 1981c).

Racial Variation

Blacks have higher divorce rates than do whites. In 1980, the proportion of black men and women who were divorced was about double that of white men and women, and this was an even greater gap than it was in 1970. The proportion for persons of Spanish origin more nearly resembled those of whites in 1980 (U.S. Bureau of the Census, P-20, No. 371, 1982). Since blacks tend to be of lower socioeconomic standing, part of the higher black divorce rate can be attributed to lesser economic resources. There is also geographical variation involved; southern blacks have lower divorce rates than southern whites, whereas blacks in the North have higher divorce rates than whites in the North (Plateris 1973).

Educational Variation

There is an overall inverse relationship between divorce and educational level. In other words, the higher the educational level, the lower the divorce rate. There is, however, one interesting exception to this rule (Houseknecht and Spanier 1980). Women with graduate training significantly increase their probability of divorce over women with just a bachelor's degree. Whereas the divorce rate among women declines as educational level increases up to the bachelor's degree, it almost doubles for that portion of the female population that ventures on to graduate school. Furthermore, higher levels of graduate training involve even higher divorce rates. This exception to the general inverse relationship is related to the greater financial and social independence of these women, their greater participation in the labor force, and perhaps additional pressures that are encountered in a dual-career marriage.

Social Class Variation

There is an inverse relationship between social class and divorce rates. Those couples at the lower end of the socioeconomic ladder have the highest divorce rates, while persons in the upper middle and upper classes have significantly lower divorce rates. Perhaps more than any other social factor, financial hardship may cause severe strain on a marital relationship. Couples in the lowest socioeconomic strata often struggle to meet their day-to-day needs, and such a struggle can take a great toll. With greater income, a couple is more likely to be able to structure life in such a way as to avoid marital disruption. In addition to a higher divorce rate among persons of low social standing, separation and desertion rates are also higher. Everything considered, then, there is a greater amount of marital instability in the lower social strata.

Rural-Urban Variation

Divorce rates are traditionally higher in urban areas, but the differences in recent years appear to be small (Bumpass and Sweet 1972). The difference may be due partially to the complexities and pressures of urban life, but also urban areas may attract persons who are more prone to divorce. Furthermore, possibly persons who will soon divorce occasionally migrate to urban areas, where their adjustment to post-divorce life may be made more easily.

Variation in Family Stability

Individuals whose parents have been divorced are considerably more likely to divorce than individuals whose parents had an intact marriage (Bumpass and Sweet 1972). This relationship has led some sociologists to remark that "divorce runs in families." While it would be oversimplifying to state than an individual is a likely candidate for divorce simply because his or her parents divorced, it appears that the tendency for divorce to occur from generation to generation exists even when other social factors are taken into account (Bumpass and Sweet 1972). Thus, we must look for explanations for this occurrence. Tolerant attitudes toward divorce may be transmitted from parent to child. The child of a divorce may have a model of family life which defines divorce as a permissible remedy for an unhappy marriage. Or a number of others, as yet unanalyzed, social factors associated with divorce may simultaneously operate in conjunction with social class and family background variables (which are transmitted through families) to make such an individual a more likely divorce candidate.

Age at Marriage

About one-fifth of the males and two-fifths of the females in the United States have married by their twentieth birthday. Early marriage is now more common than it was at the turn of the century, but the numbers and proportions of teenage marriages declined in the 1970s. Nevertheless, more than 800,000 males and females marry while still in their teens each year, more than 200,000 of them under age eighteen (U.S. Bureau of the Census 1978). Of course, there is nothing magical about a particular birthday, and many eighteen- or nineteen-year-olds are as well or better suited for marriage than some persons much older.

Studies show that the younger people are when they marry, the greater the likelihood of both poor adjustment in marriage and subsequent divorce (Bumpass and Sweet 1972; Lewis and Spanier 1979; National Center for Health Statistics 1978). Males who marry in their teens are more than twice as likely to divorce as males married in their early twenties, and more than three times as likely to divorce as males married in their late twenties. Females married before their eighteenth birthday are more than twice as likely to divorce as females married at age eighteen or nineteen, who in turn are twice as likely to divorce as females married in their early twenties. Thus, women married between ages fourteen and seventeen are more than four times as likely to divorce as women married in their early to mid-twenties (Lewis and Spanier 1979). Age is related to social and emotional development, and thus individuals marrying at especially early ages may find it difficult to cope with the adjustments to early marriage (Burchinal 1959; deLissovoy 1973; Eshleman 1965; Martinson 1955, 1959). Persons who marry young are more likely than those marrying later to be confronted with the responsibilities of parenthood early in the marriage. Their educational attainment at the time of marriage is not likely to be as great, and consequently their occupational status and income may not be as high. These factors collectively may result in a poor economic situation for the couple, making marital adjustment more difficult.

DIVORCE AND CHILDREN

Approximately 60 percent of divorces are granted to couples with children under eighteen years of age (Spanier and Glick 1981). Does the presence of children contribute to the stability of marriage? Statistical answers to this question must be interpreted with caution. The divorce rate for couples without children is higher than the rate for couples with children. Also, divorce rates tend to decline as the number of children increases. But the likelihood of divorce also declines with increasing age and with the duration of the marriage. Available data do not permit separating the effects of these three variables.

In many cases in which there are no children the divorce occurred rather early in the marriage, when there was insufficient time to have offspring. There is no way of determining whether such couples would have had children or not. In some cases there is no doubt that children are the reason for a couple's continuing to live together after their marriage has failed. In others, too, children serve as a very absorbing common interest, one which binds the couple together and may counteract some of the factors operating to force them apart.

Figure 9.1 shows that more and more children are involved in divorces every year. However, the number of children per decree has declined in recent years, to an average of one child for each divorce. Actually, since just over half of divorcing couples have children, there is an average of about two children in each of the divorces where any children are present.

Should a couple remain married "for the sake of the children"? There are no conclusive answers, since every case is different. It is generally agreed, however, that children are likely to be better adjusted if they grow up in a peaceful home with one loving parent than if they grow up in a home filled with the turmoil created by two parents who do not love each other and who are constantly quarrelling. Scholars agree that couples should not consider having a child to prevent a failing marriage from ending in divorce. Children are not a remedy for marital ills.

Joint and Split Custody

Although we hear much in the media about innovations in child custody arrangements, data show that most children are still awarded to their mothers in custody determinations. In the United States, about nine in ten children live with their mothers following divorce (Spanier and Glick,

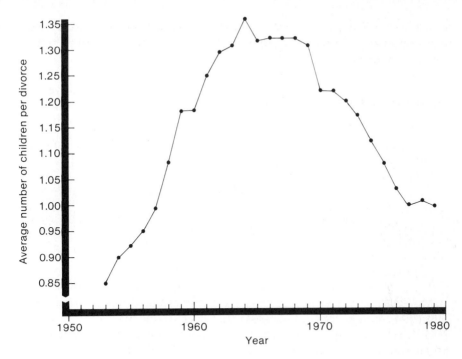

Figure 9.1 *Estimated average number of children involved per divorce decree, 1953–1979.*

Source: National Center for Health Statistics, *Monthly Vital Statistics Reports*, 29(4) Supplement, "Advance Report: Final Divorce Statistics, 1978."

1981). It is interesting to note that among all children in the United States under the age of eighteen, there are actually more living with neither parent (but with relatives, in foster home, institutions, and so forth) than with their fathers only (U.S. Bureau of the Census 1980). This may be changing somewhat, and attitudes are certainly becoming more open to children living with their fathers, but a clear-cut trend has yet to be established.

Fathers are more likely to obtain custody of the children if the children are all boys and least likely to obtain custody if the children are all girls. They are also more likely to have custody if the mothers have remarried. Roughly half of the fathers with custody of any children appear to have custody of all the children. In other words, in about half the cases, the father has custody of only some of the children (Spanier and Glick 1981). Such an arrangement is known as *split custody.*

Joint custody is a legal determination that both the mother and father have custody of the children and are legally entitled to participate in decisions about the children, even though the child lives with one parent at a time. The child may alternate weeks, may split the week between the residences of the parents, or may spend different parts of the year with each parent. The time-sharing is not always equal. The concept of joint custody implies a certain equality of child rearing, but in practical terms this may be difficult to obtain.

Across the country, some state legislatures have considered bills to require that joint custody be awarded as the preferred alternative. The burden is then on the judge to *not* award joint custody. There is widespread controversy, however, among professionals who work with divorcing couples about the wisdom of such arrangements, and most states have been reluctant to take this step. Some persons argue that a couple who can not manage a marriage relationship will not be able to manage joint child-raising responsibilities after the divorce. Others argue that it is in the best interests of both children and parents to encourage joint custody, since a parent-child relationship can never truly be terminated by divorce. Time and future research will tell how well joint custody meets the needs of the parents and children involved.

Developmental Effects of Various Custody Arrangements

Although father custody remains a relatively unusual post-divorce family situation, recent research suggests that such an arrangement may be in the developmental best interest of boys. Indeed, several investigations indicate that sons and daughters alike function better when reared in the home of their same-sex parent. Warshak and Santrock (1983) discovered, for example, that middle-class six to eleven year olds not only had a preference for the same-sex parent-child custodial arrangement over the opposite-sex arrangement but, possibly as a consequence, that girls in father custody were more likely to express separation anxiety. Further study of these same children revealed, moreover, that boys whose fathers had custody were less demanding than girls in this type of family structure, whereas girls were less demanding than boys in mother-custody families. Finally, children being cared for by their same-sexed parents were evaluated as more mature, more sociable, more independent, and higher in self-esteem than girls being reared by fathers and boys being reared by mothers (Santrock, Warshak and Elliot 1982). Consistent with these findings regarding the development of children in mother-custody and father-custody families are studies that include only mother-custody families and demonstrate that daughters do better than sons in such post-divorce family situations (Kurdek and Berg 1983; Hetherington, Cox, and Cox 1978; Santrock & Warshak, 1979).

Child Support

All states have some provision for the support of children whose parents are divorcing. *Child support* refers to monetary payment made by the parent who does not have custody of the children to the parent who does have custody. The money is intended to be used for the support of the children. Most women are awarded custody of their children. Although this is changing somewhat, it is likely to continue to be the rule rather than the exception for some time. Husbands, therefore, usually pay child support. Fathers usually will be given privileges of visitation or custody during parts of the year. The amount of child support is determined by the husband's income, the number of children, and the ability of the wife to contribute to the support of the children. The amount will be determined by the judge presiding over the divorce, but the judge will accept a reasonable recommendation by the couple and their attorney(s).

THE PROCESS OF DIVORCE

It is important to recognize that from the child's perspective divorce is more of a process than an event. Indeed, divorce should be conceptualized as

> a sequence of experiences involving a transition in the lives of children. This transition involves a shift from the predivorce family situation to the disequilibrium and disorganization associated with separation and divorce, through a period when family members are experimenting with a wide variety of coping mechanisms, some successful, some unsuccessful, in dealing with a new life situation. This is followed by the reorganization and eventual attainment of a new pattern of equilibrium in a single parent household (Hetherington 1980, p. 5).

For most children, the initial response to divorce involves anger, fear, depression, and guilt. And it is not until after the first year following divorce that reductions in tension and an increased sense of well-being emerge (Hetherington 1980).

One study indicates that both mothers' and fathers' parenting practices tend to deteriorate in the first year following divorce, but make a marked recovery in the second post-divorce year. Immediately following divorce, mothers and fathers alike tend to be less consistent and affectionate, and lacking in control over their children (Hetherington, Cox, and Cox 1978). Fathers whose eventual relationships with their children may improve or deteriorate following separation, frequently behave in a way that suggests "every day is Christmas," at least in the period immediately following separation. Being particularly concerned about losing the love of their children, they begin by being indulgent and permissive. With time, however, their restrictiveness and use of negative sanctions increase. This trend reverses, however, during the second year, at least in middle-class homes with preschool children (Hetherington, Cox, and Cox 1978).

In the early postdivorce months, fathers tend to spend the same amount of, and sometimes more, time with their children as they did prior to divorce. This maintenance of predivorce relations tends to be short-lived, though, with fathers becoming rapidly less available over time, especially in the case of daughters (Hess and Camera 1979). Visits with sons are not only more frequent, but tend to last longer (Hetherington, Cox, and Cox 1978). Fathers who maintain frequent contact and involvement with their children have more impact on their children's development than do fathers who are less available.

Recent national data on parental contact with children after divorce shows that only one father in six in the United States sees his children at least once a week. Two of every three fathers see their children less than once a month. In fact, the majority of fathers who do not have custody of their children have either had no contact with their children in the last five years or at best have had their last contact between one and five years ago. The greater the amount of child support the father provides, the more likely he is to visit his children (Furstenburg and Nord 1982).

In most divorcing families, the first year following separation is a period in which mothers are likely to be depressed, self-involved, erratic, nonsupportive, and ineffectually authoritarian in dealing with their children. Male offspring and their mothers are especially likely to get involved in conflicted relationships. While daughters tend to whine and to complain, sons are likely to be oppositional, disobedient, and aggressive. Such familial processes led Hetherington (1980) to conclude that divorced, single-parent mothers are harassed by their children, especially by their sons. One year following divorce, a time that marked the peak of parent-child conflict in this two-year longitudinal study, mothers described their relationships with their children as "declared war," "a struggle for survival," "the old Chinese water torture," and "like getting bitten to death by ducks." By the end of the second year following divorce, parent-child relations have improved markedly, though problems continue and remain more frequent than in intact nuclear families (Hetherington, Cox, and Cox 1978).

The child of divorced parents is in a position somewhat akin to that of the middle horse in a three-horse team, pulled now in one direction, now in another as it attempts to accommodate itself to the movements of the other two horses. The child is torn between conflicting loyalties. It is difficult to cooperate with and understand two persons who are at odds and do not understand each other. If the child lives with each parent at different times, neither home may provide preparation for living in the other. If there is a leaning in the direction of one parent, and especially if there is an inclination to blame the other, there may be conflict and disappointment. The child may feel insecure and exhibit compensatory behavior. On the other hand, many children of divorced parents are well-adjusted. "The evidence now available does not warrant the conclusion that children whose parents divorce are more likely later in their lives to have emotional problems than children whose parents do not divorce" (Weiss 1975). There is much to be said for a child living in security and harmony with one parent rather than in an atmosphere of insecurity and conflict with two.

THE DEVELOPMENTAL EFFECTS OF DIVORCE

It has been suggested that a crisis model of divorce is most appropriate in thinking about the short-term effects of this significant life event on children. In the initial period following divorce, the child is responding to a variety of stressors—the loss of a parent, marital discord, family disorganization, and alterations in parent-child relations. Available evidence indicates that most children can cope with and adapt to the relatively brief crisis associated with divorce. When the crisis is compounded by other stressors, though, developmental impairment is likely (Hetherington 1980).

The well-being and adjustment of the child over the longer term seems to be determined more by the conditions associated with growing up in a one-parent home than with the divorce event per se. As we will see, most significant are the quality of parent-child relations and postdivorce spousal relations. Also important are the fewer adults in the home to contribute to decision-making and to household maintenance and child care, to serve as role models, disciplinarians, or as a source of nurturance. "Divorce, then, should be viewed as having two phases: one phase involving the crisis of divorce, and a subsequent phase involving developing in a one parent family where changing developmental tasks and changing competencies of the child are interacting with factors associated with life in a one parent family" (Hetherington 1980, p. 7).

Mediators of Divorce Effects

The child's age, gender, and temperament are likely to determine, at least in part, the experience and effects of divorce. With respect to temperament, some evidence suggests that difficult children are at increased risk when confronting marital breakup. In their study of preschoolers, for example, Hetherington, Cox, and Cox (1978) found that those children displaying the most problems (a) were described by their mothers as having had, during their infancies, a prevalence of negative mood, including extremes of fussiness and crying; (b) showed distress and slow adaptability in response to new situations; and (c) had biological irregularities in sleeping, feeding, and eliminating. Similarly, Kelly (1978) found, in a study of children one to twenty-two years of age, that extended histories of maladjustment preceding divorce forecasted more long-lasting emotional disturbance in response to divorce.

In light of these patterns, it is reasonable to ask a question for which no firm answer is presently available: Could such difficult children actually contribute to the likelihood of divorce? Findings reported in an earlier chapter on marriage, parenting, and child development certainly suggest this could be the case, especially when such temperamental difficulty co-occurs with an already at-risk marriage. Recall that in an investigation of mentally retarded children, the birth of such a handicapped infant was likely to exert a particularly negative impact in homes in which a marriage could already be regarded as vulnerable (Gath 1978).

In addition to temperamental differences between children, the developmental capacities of the child and the developmental tasks she or he faces are important mediators of the divorce experience. Consider, for example, the fact that younger children experiencing divorce not only have fewer experiences outside the home as a result of their greater dependency on their parents, but also have limited cognitive and social competencies for understanding and dealing with the dissolution of their parents' marital relationship. It is also important to recognize that the preschooler, unlike the school-age child or adolescent, confronts the important developmental task of establishing a sex-role identity. The absence of a father, who we have noted is extremely important to both sons and daughters in this arena of development, would be expected to have quite a different effect on a three to five year old than on a nine or ten year old as a result (Hetherington 1980).

Available evidence indicates that the coping styles of children of different ages, and the patterns of adjustment they display, vary as a function of their development competencies. While feelings of sadness, loneliness, anger, anxiety, and rejection, as well as grieving for the lost paent, are common to most children whose parents separate (Wallerstein and Kelly 1980), the intensity and duration of these feelings vary depending on the child's developmental status. As a result of their egocentrism and limited cognitive and social skills, preschoolers are relatively unable to evaluate the divorce situation accurately, particularly the child's own role in the situation and the experiences of his/her parent. Indeed, young children, because of their limits, are likely to blame themselves for causing the separation and to exaggerate the possibility of their parents getting together again (Wallerstein and Kelly 1975; Hetherington 1980). In a clinical study of forty-four children whose parents had separated, Neal (1983) chronicled the common belief among preschool children that they must have done something "bad" to make the parent go away. Indeed, in a doll play situation one three-year-old boy responded to the question "Do you know why the daddy left?" with the response "Cause the little boy was naughty" (Neal 1983, p. 8).

Possibly even more problematical than such a perception is the tendency which Neal (1983) also observed for preschoolers to assume that if a parent physically moved away from him then the parent no longer likes him. Consider, in this regard, the following exchange which took place between Neal and a three-year-old boy who was experiencing nightmares, difficulties with separation from father, and an intense fear of monsters at bedtime (Neal 1983, pp. 7–8):

Clinician: Can I tell you a story about mommy and daddy?
Boy: Yeah.
Clinician: This mommy was sad, and so she moved to a different house and this . . .
Boy: I know a different story.
Clinician: Will you tell me your story?
Boy: Somebody stole the daddy.
Clinician: Somebody stole the daddy?
Boy: Yeah, someone took him away.
Clinician: Why did they do that?
Boy: So the boy would feel bad. The daddy doesn't love the boy.
Clinician: Why doesn't the daddy love the boy?
Boy: Cause he went away.

A striking difference exists between preschoolers' and early elementary school-age children's reactions to divorce. Indeed, Neal (1983) discovered, in this clinical study, that while five to eight year olds also evaluated divorce egocentrically and personally, they were aware that conflicts existed between their parents. Rather than believing that their own "badness" caused the parent to leave, they believed that their actions resulted in difficulties between spouses, which *in turn* resulted in marital dissolution. Consider the following exchange with a five-year-old girl in this regard (Neal 1983, p. 9):

Clinician: So you think that their arguments were the reason that made them get the divorce?
Girl: No, because you know what? I think I can remember more than my mom and my dad and my brother. But they think that's not true. But it is.
Clinician: What do you remember that they don't?
Girl: When I fell off the slide and bumped my head. My mom thinks that I really got hurt badly and my dad says that I'm just cranky. And then they got a divorce after they argued about it. And it's true!

Older school-age children, Neal (1983) discovered, were more aware of the inner feelings of parents as spouses. Nine to twelve year olds "often believed that their parents divorced when they no longer cared about each other 'on the inside,' or when feelings had changed" (p. 10). And while the children often did not understand why parental feelings had changed, they frequently believed that this process could be reversed if parents would "try hard enough" or "really wanted" it (Neal 1983, p. 11):

Clinician: Do you know why your mom and dad decided to get a divorce?

Girl: Not really. They said that they didn't love each other anymore.

Clinician: Do you know what they mean by that?

Girl: Not really.

Clinician: What do you think it might mean?

Girl: That they just lost interest in each other.

Clinician: Do you think they could have prevented it?

Girl: Yeah, if they really wanted to.

Children of school age appear more capable of being sympathetic and concerned in response to the stress that their parents experience. Since they are more able than preschoolers to consider the point of view of others, divorce is likely to heighten their concern for how others think about their families. With further development this concern for others can translate into using anger as a defense against depression and feelings of loss of love. Indeed, explosive outbursts and temper tantrums have been noted to be characteristic of nine- and ten-year-old boys from divorced homes (Hetherington 1980).

Adolescents are more capable than younger children of evaluating the causes of divorce and of handling the conflicting loyalty to parents which children frequently experience following separation (Wallerstein and Kelly 1975). As noted earlier, since adolescents are less restricted to the home, they are freer to seek gratification outside the family and, thereby, disengage themselves from the conflict that exists between their parents. The risk here, of course, is that the still dependent adolescent may prematurely detach from the family in a way that is dysfunctional over the long term. Nevertheless, the availability of support systems (e.g., peers, schools, church) beyond the confines of the home can serve to buffer the older child from the stresses of living in a pre- and postdivorce family (Hetherington 1980).

The preceding analysis of children's perceptions of divorce as a function of their developmental status raises the very real possibility that the effects of divorce will depend upon how old the child is who experiences marital separation (Hetherington 1979; Longfellow 1979; Wallerstein and Kelly 1980). Empirical support for this contention exists in research by Kurdek and Berg (1983) who found that older children were better adjusted to their parents' divorces than were younger children. The reason for such effects undoubtedly lies in the varying cognitive and emotional maturity of children. And, in this regard, it has been found that possessing an internal locus of control and high level of interpersonal understanding, both of which are more characteristic of older children, are related to experiencing a less difficult time adjusting to divorce (Kurdek, Blisk, and Siesky 1981; Kurdek and Berg 1983).

Having noted that parental separation and divorce are better conceptualized as a process than as discrete events, and that the effects of divorce on child functioning are likely to be mediated by individual characteristics of children such as their temperaments and developmental capacities, we consider next the general developmental effects of divorce. Specifically, we focus upon the cognitive, sex-role, and social development of children from divorced families, qualifying our conclusions, where appropriate, in terms of characteristics of individuality of the children studied.

Cognitive Development

It has frequently been asserted that, in general, children growing up in father-absent or single-parent homes perform less well on tests of intelligence and in school (Shinn, 1977). Methodological problems with much of this research make the interpretation of these results difficult, however. For example, evaluations of the effects of father absence frequently fail to distinguish between homes in which fathers are absent as a result of death, divorce, or desertion; yet there is some evidence that the *cause* of father absence may be more important in explaining the effects of growing up in a mother-headed family than is father absence itself. Additionally, single-parent homes are grossly different from two-parent families in ways beyond the mere absence of the father. Most important in this regard is the lower socioeconomic status of many single-parent families. Thus, it is likely that many of the deficits frequently attributed to growing up with only one parent may be the result of growing up in a poorer neighborhood or in a home in which financial resources are relatively limited (Bane 1976; Herzog and Sudia 1973).

When evaulations of the effects of divorce are made, and social class differences between children are controlled, the evidence reveals that IQ and school performance of school-age children are adversely affected by divorce. One investigation comparing children from intact and disrupted homes living in Connecticut revealed that children of divorce scored lower on school achievement tests. This was true at both one and two years following marital dissolution, suggesting that the negative effects of family disruption are not limited to the immediate postdivorce period (Crescimbeni 1965). Similar results were reported by Santrock (1972) for both IQ and achievement test scores for a sample of mostly lower-class third through sixth graders and in an investigation of a large national sample of children. Children between six and seventeen years of age during the years 1963 to 1970, Levin and his colleagues (1978) found, performed significantly poorer on measures of cognitive achievement if they came from divorced households than from intact nuclear families. It is possible that these results were a function of the performance of the school-age children in this large sample, rather than that of the adolescents, since most reports indicate few, if any, differences between high school students from divorced and intact homes on measures of cognitive functioning (Bales 1979; Bane 1976; Burchinal 1964; Nye 1957; Walters and Stinnett 1971).

Sex-Role Development

When divorce, or father absence more generally, occurs prior to the child's fifth birthday, some disruption in sex-role typing is likely. The reason for this is that sex-role typing, for which father appears so important, is largely established by this age. Thus, if divorce occurs after this "sensitive" period, this domain of social development appears relatively impervious to disruption. This is not to say that the effects of divorce are not evident after the age of five. As we will see, the effects of divorce on sex-role functioning appear to be long-lasting.

Preschool boys, as well as boys in elementary school, who are reared in single-parent, mother-headed homes display more dependent, less masculine, and less aggressive patterns of behavior than do boys reared in two-parent homes. When sons of divorce engage in aggressive behavior, it is more likely to take the form of traditionally feminine as opposed to masculine aggressive styles, that is, it is more likely to involve words (e.g., name calling) than physical actions (e.g., hitting) (Hetherington, Cox, and Cox 1978). In an attempt to explain these effects, it has been suggested that boys whose fathers leave home prior to their fifth birthday identify primarily with their mothers and therefore adopt patterns of functioning more characteristic of daughters than of sons.

In certain cases, father absence—often due to divorce—has been linked to an exaggerated, super-masculine style of behaving in older boys. Indeed, preadolescent and adolescent males who grow up without fathers can show both excessively assertive and aggressive forms of behavior and more traditionally feminine dependency. Efforts to explain such "compensatory" masculinity suggest that hyper-masculine behavior results from father-absent boys' desperate attempts to establish and maintain a male identity when no appropriate sex-role model is available. Such boys, it appears, have developed only a set of loosely integrated responses that functions as almost a caricature of the stereotyped male role, rather than a stable male identification (Hetherington, Cox, and Cox 1978).

Girls, in contrast to boys, appear to be relatively unaffected by divorce or father absence—until adolescence, that is. Those effects that do emerge during the period of "transition to adulthood" appear restricted to relations with male peers and adult men. The disruption of relations with males which manifests itself during adolescence takes the form of sexually precocious and inappropriately assertive behavior with male age mates and adults (Hetherington 1972). In fact, observations at recreation center dances of adolescent girls whose parents were divorced revealed that, in contrast to girls from intact families, these daughters of divorce spent much more time at the end of the dance hall where the boys congregated. Moreover, these assertive girls more frequently initiated encounters with boys (by asking them to dance, for example) and, more often than girls from intact homes, established physical contact with their male peers. Furthermore, when these same girls were interviewed by an adult male, they were more likely to choose seats close to the interviewer and to adopt more open body positions, i.e., sitting with arm slung over the back of the chair and legs not crossed, as opposed to arms folded on lap, with legs crossed (Hetherington, Cox, and Cox 1978).

Interestingly, when these sexually precocious and assertive females from divorced homes were studied in young adulthood, the effects of divorce were still evident. Daughters of divorce, in contrast to a control group, not only married younger, but were more likely to be premaritally pregnant at the time of their weddings. Additionally, in comparison to daughters from nondivorced homes, the women whose parents had divorced reported less satisfaction in their sexual relations, and married men with less stable employment records and with a greater frequency of trouble with the police. Finally, the husbands of these daughters of divorce felt more ambivalent or hostile toward their wives and infants, and were less emotionally mature, and more impulsive and self-centered (Hetherington, Cox, and Cox 1978). The fact that the husbands of these women were such "bad catches" may be one reason why, as noted in Chapter 5, children who grow up in homes in which parents divorced or separated are at greater risk of having their own marriages end in divorce (Mueller and Pope 1977).

Social Development

Self-control is the area of social development that seems most affected by the divorce experience. And it is boys whose development seems most adversely influenced. In general, boys from single-parent, mother-headed households tend to be more antisocial and impulsive, less self-controlled, and less able to delay immediate gratification. They also tend to be more rebellious against adult authority (Hetherington, Cox, and Cox 1978).

Such developmental effects of divorce are especially apparent in preadolescent boys (Hoffman 1970). Santrock (1977) compared a group of ten to twelve year olds from divorced homes with a control group of boys matched to the sons of divorce on the potentially important factors of IQ, school, and age. Comparisons revealed that the sons of divorce were more physically aggressive and disobedient. Similar findings come from a large scale study of 2,258 seven to eleven year olds (Zill 1978). Higher levels of aggression were found for children reared in homes in which parents were divorced, separated, or involved in an unhappy, but intact marriage. This last piece of information, showing that the effect of growing up in a household where the marriage is poor, yet intact, is the same as growing up in a single-parent home is important to note; as we will soon see, it appears to be the case that the day-to-day experiences children have, be it in a one- or two-parent home, are of primary importance in determining how children develop. In divorced households certain experiences simply have a higher probability of occurrence.

One explanation offered to account for these deleterious effects of divorce on the self-control of boys is that the child "adopts the predominant behavior exhibited by his parents during a crisis and that this becomes a guiding framework for his later behavior and coping. In the case of divorce, particularly in one that has been preceded by considerable acrimony and conflict, anger, aggression and hostility are the behaviors displayed by parents and adopted by the child" (Hetherington, Cox, and Cox 1978, pp. 27–28). The stigma associated with divorce, anger at being abandoned by the father, and the negative image of father likely to be conveyed by the mother responsible for caring for the child are also likely to fuel antisocial behavior. These factors probably all contribute to the duress and frustration experienced by children in divorced households and to their acting-out behavior (Hetherington, Cox, and Cox 1978).

Processes of Influence

Popular reports in the media, as well as our discussion of the effects of divorce through this point, are likely to leave the reader with the impression that there is something inevitable about marital separation disrupting child development, particularly in the preschool and early elementary school years. Serious consideration of the social interactional processes by which divorce affects the child suggests not only that this is not the case, but that when certain conditions are met the separation of parents need *not* impair children's social, emotional, and cognitive functioning. In fact, under certain circumstances, the dissolution of marriage may be in the best interests of the child.

The work of Hetherington and her associates reveals that divorce frequently results in disorganized household functioning. Indeed, in her sample of middle-class families with preschoolers, this disorganization was manifested in children in single-parent homes in such ways as less frequently eating with their mothers, going to bed at irregular times, being read to less at bedtime, and being more likely to arrive late at school. Furthermore, divorce marked a breakdown in the use of appropriate and consistent control, the placement of fewer demands for mature and independent behavior on the preschool child, and less parent-child communication, especially that involving explanation and reasoning (Hetherington 1980).

It is especially interesting that it was primarily in families in which household organization was disrupted in the manner just described, and in which quality of parenting was severely undermined by the stress of divorce, that children tended to display high distractibility, impulsiveness, short attention span, and lack of persistence in tasks, all of which were associated with declines in cognitive performance over the two-year course of this study. In fact, children with divorced mothers who were available and responsive to their offspring, who remained firm but sensitive disciplinarians, and who communicated effectively with their preschoolers and encouraged independent mature behavior displayed *no* cognitive deficits as a result of the divorce experience (Hetherington 1980).

Similar findings regarding processes of influence have been noted with respect to social development. Indeed, the quality of care divorced parents provide their children seems to explain why it is that children reared by their same-sexed parents develop better than girls reared by fathers and boys reared by mothers. That is, Santrock, Warshak, and Elliot (1982) found that in same-sexed custodial arrangements, mothers and fathers are more likely to engage in authoritative parenting (warmth, clear-set rules and regulations, and extensive verbal give-and-take) than authoritarian or permissive parenting, and this is probably why sons cared for by fathers and girls cared for by mothers display higher self-esteem, maturity, sociability, and independence. In fact, these same investigators observed that, regardless of type of custodial arrangements, when parents were authoritative their children looked more socially competent. In contrast, permissive rearing in mother-custody homes was associated with poor adjustment in girls, whereas authoritarian rearing in father-custody homes was associated with poorer adjustment in boys.

In addition to general social competence and emotional adjustment, the effects of divorce on sex-role development also appear to be mediated by the quality of care children experience in postdivorce families. Although, as already observed, nontraditional sex-role development has been linked with father absence, this outcome also does not appear to be a necessary byproduct of parental separation. In the previously noted study of preschoolers from divorced homes, Hetherington found that when mothers encouraged independent, mature behavior, positive masculine behavior, and had a positive attitude toward males and toward their ex-husbands, boys in divorced homes did not differ in sex-role development from age mates reared in intact, nuclear families (Hetherington, Cox, and Cox 1978). What we observe here, then, is that although mothers exert generally little influence on sons' masculinity in two-parent households, when the male identification figure is absent, mothers can indeed exert an influence.

It would seem that the negative effects of divorce chronicled earlier are not inevitable. Rather, they appear to be the direct result of parenting practices which, following divorce, are likely to break down in their consistency and effectiveness. When sensitive parenting is maintained, even in the face of divorce, the child's well-being is not adversely affected. Thus, it does not appear to be divorce per se but the parenting that is often disrupted by divorce that disrupts child development (Hess and Camera 1979; Hetherington 1980).

Interestingly, the breakdown of parenting seems to be directly related to the quality of the relationship between ex-spouses (Raschke and Raschke 1979; Wallerstein and Kelly 1980; Kurdek and Berg 1983). In the Hetherington study, for example, it was found that when ex-spouse relationships were harmonious, as revealed by high agreement on child-rearing, positive attitude toward ex-mate, and low conflict following divorce, the quality of mothering was less likely to break down and, as a result, child functioning was less likely to be undermined (Hetherington 1980).

This set of family processes suggests that divorce does not so much have a direct as an indirect effect on the child. Stress in the marital relationship negatively influences parental functioning and, thereby, adversely affects the child. To the extent that this process-of-influence model is accurate, one would expect to find, and indeed Hetherington did discover, that if divorce leads to an *improvement* in relations between parents, children benefit, since their parents' caregiving is not undermined by the stress emanating from the marital relationship. Unfortunately, these investigators also found that when conflict characterized the marital relationship in intact, two-parent households, parenting and child development tended to be negatively affected. Children from such families differed little from those raised by divorcees still in conflict with their ex-mates.

This analysis suggests once again that the marital relationship is an important, though generally indirect influence on child development, and highlights one way in which the family functions as a set of interdependent social relationships. Such a perspective on the family serves to enhance our understanding of child development by making us aware that what occurs within the parent-child relationship can be influenced importantly by forces beyond the relationship itself. In the case of divorce we discover that it is marital, or ex-marital, relations that indirectly exerts an influence on the child's development.

THE BROADER CONTEXT

The degree to which family processes are undermined by divorce, thereby negatively influencing parental competence and child functioning, is likely to be largely determined by the broader context in which marital separation takes place. Indeed, the negative effects of divorce, for parents and children alike, seem to be compounded when stresses other than divorce exist for the parent. One unfortunate aspect of the divorce situation is that such additional stress often results from the divorce itself. Consider, for example, the financial strain experienced by single parents in trying to support a home, especially when relying on child support payments (Bane 1976), or the loss of contact with friends and relatives that frequently results from the divorce experience (Hetherington 1980).

As noted in Chapter 8, a spouse serves as a primary support system, hopefully providing instrumental assistance as well as emotional support. In the case of divorce, it is quite likely that such support has long been absent prior to the actual marital separation and termination. When alternative sources of support are not available, both before and after separation, the responsibilities of home maintenance and child-rearing are especially burdensome. Quite likely, this is one reason why single-parent support groups are springing up in communities all over the nation. Evidence indicating that divorce-related stress is reduced by turning to friends, counselors, and self-help groups (Kurdek 1981; Spanier and Casto 1979) suggests that the challenge which the socially isolated and unassisted single parent confronts is especially great. The implications of this stress for the child is highlighted by Kurdek and Berg's (1983) finding that social support was also related to the children's functioning, particularly their adjustment to divorce.

In addition to the absence of social supports, maternal employment can also exacerbate the stress of divorce for the child. When mothers begin work at the time of divorce or shortly thereafter, preschool children experience heightened adjustment problems, probably resulting from the double loss they experience—mother working, father leaving home (Hetherington, Cox, and Cox 1978). A poor-paying job which burdens the single parent without providing sufficient income to provide material resources to make the task of parenting easier is also likely to make coping with divorce problematical.

If the single parent does work, the availability and utilization of quality supplementary child care, especially for preschoolers, may determine the actual effect of divorce on the child. This would seem to be especially the case for young children whose home lives has been rendered disorganized and stress-producing by divorce. When a day care arrangement provides the child with the daily routine and consistent care that postdivorce family life is likely to be lacking, opportunity to attain a sense of control in one's life is probably enhanced and, with it, general psychological functioning.

CONCLUSION

Divorce, as we have seen, is becoming increasingly an experience large numbers of children in the United States face. While certain subgroups of the population are more at risk for divorce than others, it would be erroneous to conclude that divorce is something other than a broadly distributed fact of family life in America. No ethnic, socioeconomic, or age group seems to be immune from the reality of dissolving marital bonds.

From the perspective of the child, divorce is stressful. The probability of being adversely affected by divorce seems to far outweigh the prospects of experiencing only beneficial consequences. While it is true that the effects of divorce are mediated by the developmental status of the child, and his or her gender, it is fair to conclude that divorce is usually a negative experience.

This is not to say, however, that deleterious consequences of divorce for the child are inevitable. As has been pointed out, the effects of divorce can only be understood when family processes are examined. If divorce reduces marital conflict, and thereby lessens stress on the parenting system, then sensitive parenting and optimal child functioning is likely to be promoted. In such cases, divorce is in the child's best interest.

In many divorce families, unfortunately, the marital discord that led to marital dissolution is not reduced, and, in fact, may even increase following parental separation. When children are confronted with one parent's negative sentiment toward their other parent, loyalty ties are strained, resulting in an experience likely to be anxiety-provoking to even the most mature child or adolescent. Further, it seems that it is just such spousal conflict that continues to undermine parental competence and, thereby, child development.

But even when such inner-family processes are stressful, the potential for crisis resolution and continued development exists. If support systems function to lessen such stress, the child's development trajectory is far more positive than when such support systems are nonexistent (e.g., social isolation) or actually function to place further stress on the family (e.g., angry relatives). As we have said repeatedly, the context of child and family functioning is critical to understanding the processes of development—and the case of divorce is no exception.

Child Maltreatment

In recent years the abuse and neglect of children in the United States have become social problems attracting a great deal of attention—from scientists, policy-makers, and concerned citizens alike. While hard and fast definitions of child maltreatment are difficult to come by, and engender a great deal of debate, it is useful to think of child abuse and neglect as those cases in which a child "receives nonaccidental physical injury (or injuries) as a result of acts of commission (or omission) on the part of his parents or guardians that violate the community standards concerning the treatment of children" (Parke and Collmer 1975, p. 3).

Several aspects of this definition are noteworthy. First, acts of commission, as when a child is hit, are included, as well as acts of omission, as when a certain minimum standard of care is absent. Most child neglect would be subsumed under the notion of acts of omission, that is, what is *not* done for the child. Consider, for example, the neglecting nature of a parent who fails to attend to the physical needs of a sick child. A second noteworthy feature of this definition is the absence of the requirement that abusive or neglectful care be perpetrated with intent. Thus, as defined here, parents can be considered to maltreat their child whether or not they intend to do so. Finally, this definition recognizes that child maltreatment is a community-defined phenomenon which must be viewed in terms of community norms and standards governing the appropriate conduct of adults in caring for children.

This contextual nature of child abuse becomes most apparent when we recognize that although child abuse, as currently defined, has gone on through the ages, it is only recently that hostile, punitive child care has come to be labeled as abusive. Consider, for example, the fact that Roman law permitted fathers to sell, abandon, kill, or offer in sacrifice all their children, or the Greek philosopher Aristotle's contention that "the justice of a mother or a father is a different thing from that of a citizen, for a son or a slave is property, and there can be no injustice to one's own property" (Radbill 1974). Even the Bible can be read as permitting, if not encouraging, mistreatment: ". . . foolishness is bound in the heart of the child; but the rod of correction shall drive it far from him" (Proverbs 22:15); "Withhold not correction from the child, for if thou beatest him with the rod, he shall not die" (Proverbs 13:13). And, of course, the history of child labor in this country, as well as around the world, clearly documents that the mistreatment of children is not a modern phenomenon (Radbill 1974).

Child abuse was "discovered" as a result of changing attitudes regarding the rights of children and the responsibilities of parents. Also important was medical technology, as X rays enabled physicians to identify multiple injuries to children in various stages of healing which indicated that an injurious incident that brought the child to the attention of doctors was not an isolated event. But it was not until Kempe coined the phrase, "the battered child syndrome" to call attention to the seriousness of mistreatment that child abuse was formally declared to exist (Kempe et al. 1962). Since that time three basic issues have occupied the attention of scientists studying child abuse — its prevalence, its causes, and its developmental consequences for the child. Each of these issues will be discussed in turn.

PREVALENCE

Despite the considerable attention that has been devoted to child abuse and neglect, valid and reliable data regarding the incidence and prevalence of the use of violence and aggression on children by their parents are almost nonexistent. Those statistics that are available are flawed in a variety of ways. Most significantly, it is probably the case, in spite of recent laws requiring teachers, physicians, and other community personnel to report suspected cases of child mistreatment, that a great deal of abuse and neglect goes uncounted because it does not come to the formal attention of authorities. Information based upon official statistics must be qualified by the fact that they represent only "caught" cases of abuse. A second problem that plagues current estimates of child abuse is that states and localities that keep records do not employ uniform definitions of child abuse. In point of fact, the definition of abuse frequently varies in order to magnify or lessen concern for this social problem. Although some scientists and policy-makers use the term to cover a wide spectrum of phenomena that hinder proper development of a child's potential, others use the term to focus attention only on the specific case of severely injured children.

In an effort to improve knowledge of the incidence of abuse, a 1965 survey was conducted on 1,520 individuals. Three percent of this nationally representative sample reported knowledge of forty-eight different incidents of child abuse. Extrapolations from this sample to the national population resulted in the estimate that between 2.5 and 4.1 million adults knew of families involved in child abuse incidences (Gil 1970). When corrective adjustments were applied to these data, it was estimated that 500,000 children in this country were abused in the survey year (Light 1973).

Despite this apparently scientific evaluation and analysis, it might be emphasized that opinion on the actual frequency of child abuse in the United States is quite varied. A report to the United States Senate in 1973 estimated that there were only between 30,000 and 40,000 instances of "truly battered children" each year, whereas Fontana (1973) proposed a figure of 1.5 million. Perhaps the most accurate summary of our knowledge regarding the prevalence of abuse was provided by Cohen and Sussman (1975) who argued that "the only conclusion which can be made fairly is that information indicating the incidence of child abuse in the United States simply does not exist."

In fact, it has been the case until very recently that most projections of incidence have actually been little more than educated guesses. In an effort to correct this sorry state of affairs, a national survey was undertaken in 1975 to estimate the amount of violence directed against children in their own homes. For purposes of the study, violence was defined as "an act carried out with the intention, or perceived intention, of physically injuring another person," and injury could range from slight pain, as in a slap, to murder. A broad definition of violence, which would include spanking as a form of violent behavior, was employed to estimate the frequency with which children are hit in their families. A national probability sample yielded 2,143 completed interviews with 960 men and 1,183 women focused upon tactics employed in dealing with family disputes (Gelles 1978; Straus 1979; Straus, Gelles, and Steinmetz 1980).

Sixty-three percent of the respondents who had children between the ages of three and seventeen living at home cited at least one violent episode during the survey year (1975), with 73 percent of the survey sample reporting at least one violent occurrence in the course of raising children. As expected, milder forms of violence were reported more frequently. Slaps or spankings were mentioned by 58 percent of the respondents as having occurred in the previous year and by 71 percent of the parents as having ever taken place. During the survey year, 41 percent of the parents admitted pushing or shoving a child, while 13 percent admitted to hitting the child with something. Throwing an object was less common, but still occurred in 5 percent of the families surveyed.

Even though the smallest percentage of parents reported exposing a child to the more dangerous types of violence, 3 percent still admitted to kicking, biting, or hitting a child with a fist in 1975. Slightly more than 1 percent of the respondents reported "beating up" a child in the survey year. Finally, one-tenth of 1 percent, or one in a thousand parents, claimed to have threatened their child with a gun or a knife in 1975, and the same number actually admitted using a gun or a knife.

When these rates of violence are extrapolated to the total population of children three to seventeen years of age living with both parents, an astoundingly large number of children appear to have been kicked, bitten, punched, beaten, threatened with a gun or a knife, or actually had a gun or a knife used upon them. There were nearly 46 million children between three and seventeen years old who lived with their parents in 1975. Of these children, we may estimate that between 3.1 and 4 million have been kicked, bitten or punched by parents at some time in their lives, while between 1 and 1.9 million were kicked, bitten, or punched in 1975. Between 1.4 and 2.3 million children may have been "beat up" while growing up. Lastly, the data suggests that between 900,000 and 1.8 million American children between three and seventeen have ever had their parents use a gun or knife on them!

When these data were summarized in the form of a child abuse index, measuring whether a parent had ever kicked, bit, punched, hit with an object, beaten up, or used a knife or gun upon a child, it was estimated that fourteen out of every one hundred American parents of chidren three through seventeen treated their children violently enough to be considered abusive. This means that of the 46 million children of these age groups in the United States who live with both parents, approximately 6.5 million are abused each year. Even when the abuse index is recalculated to consider only incidents as severe as, or more severe than, hitting the child with an object, abuse rates drop to three or four out of every hundred parents—1.7 million children per year. Clearly, child mistreatment, however defined, is not as isolated a phenomenon as most of us believe or would like to be.

ETIOLOGY OF CHILD MALTREATMENT

According to their disciplinary biases, sociologists, psychologists, psychiatrists, and physicians have proposed various explanations of the causes of child maltreatment. Some have argued that child abuse is elicited by the child, whereas others have contended that disturbances in the parents' psychological makeup, patterns of family interaction, societal stresses and supports, or cultural attitudes and values are primarily responsible for abuse and neglect. To a certain extent, these divergent viewpoints have generated healthy debate among those concerned with this disturbing problem. In ever-increasing numbers, though, persons working in the field are coming to recognize the complex and multi-faceted nature of the etiology of child maltreatment. In what follows we detail the multiple causes of child maltreatment that have been identified and highlight processes by which they interact to increase the likelihood that children will be mistreated. First we focus upon the developmental history of the parent, then upon the role of the child, then upon the community context of child abuse, and finally a societal perspective is adopted before presenting an ecological integration of these distinct, yet complementary viewpoints.

Parent's Developmental History

One major characteristic that child abusers repeatedly have been found to share is a history of maltreatment in their own childhoods (Belsky 1980; Kempe et al. 1962; Spinetta and Rigler 1972; Steele and Pollack 1968). Such consensus should not be equated with established fact, however, as many scholars have highlighted the weaknesses inherent in the reports supportive of the intergenerational-transmission explanation of child abuse and neglect (Belsky, 1978b; Jayarante 1977; Parke and Collmer 1975). Nevertheless, observations in support of this proposition have been made so frequently, even if only by clinicians not engaged in systematic data collection, that to disregard them entirely (as some have suggested) would be to deny the legitimacy of information gleaned through our senses, outside the confines of hard, objective, scientific methods.

The fact that several recent prospective studies do document an association between the rearing of individuals and their subsequent parenting provides additional support, moreover, to claims that a parent's socialization history can be a causative agent in the process of child abuse or neglect. Especially noteworthy is a Tennessee study indicating that the nurturance mothers reported receiving during their own childhood was one of the most consistent predictors of their children's nonorganic failure-to-thrive (i.e., neglect) in a sample of almost 500 mothers studied longitudinally from their pregnancies into their children's second year of life (O'Connor et al. 1979).

There is a need to recognize that a parent's own rearing need not be characterized as abusive or neglectful to contribute to mistreatment of his or her own children. A voluminous literature on the effects of observing aggression (e.g., Bandura 1973) and of being rewarded for antisocial behavior (Patterson 1976; Patterson and Cobb 1971) would seem to justify the conclusion that exposure to, and experience with, violence as a child might result in the adoption of aggressive strategies for coping with parent-child conflict as an adult. Further, cross-cultural data suggest that the developmental roots of punitive (i.e., abusive) and insensitive (i.e., neglectful) child rearing may lie not solely in exposure or subjection to violence and aggression per se, but in the more general experience of parental rejection (Rohner 1975).

Since so many parents who were mistreated in their own childhoods do not mistreat their offspring, it is doubtful that a parent's experience as a child is sufficient, by itself, to account for the occurrence of abusive or neglectful behavior as an adult. Most probably, parents' developmental histories play a role in the abuse and neglect process by predisposing them, as adults, to respond to certain situations in aggressive (abusive) and insensitive (neglectful) ways. The results of a recent investigation provide evidence in support of this claim, indicating that it is primarily when parents are subject to rapid life changes that a punitive childhood history predicts abusive or neglectful behavior in adulthood (Conger, Burgess, and Barrett 1979). It would be mistaken, though, to regard these data as evidence that childhood rearing is associated with later child maltreatment only when coupled with high levels of stress resulting from excessive demands for coping with life change. The more general lesson to be gleaned from this study should be that this or any other attribute identified as characteristic of child abusers most likely interacts with additional personal, social-situational, and cultural factors in fostering abusive and neglectful parenting. Although much more research is required to identify the exact nature of these interactions, several possibilities are suggested in the course of this discussion.

The Role of the Child and Family Interaction

Many of the additional influences that may stimulate maltreatment through some catalytic interaction with a parent's developmental history are to be found within the family itself. Traditionally, examination of the family system in the study of child maltreatment has focused attention on parents. More recently, however, we have come to recognize that within the family, abused children have to be considered as potential contributors to their own maltreatment; available models no longer view the child exclusively as an unwitting victim but also as a causative agent in the abuse process (Belsky 1978b; Friedrich and Boriskin 1976; Parke and Collmer 1975). The emergence of this relatively new perspective on child abuse can be traced back to repeated observations indicating that a disproportionate number of mistreated children were born prematurely, as well as to the attempts of developmental psychologists to reconceptualize the traditional, unidirectional theories of socialization that had dominated the study of parent-child relations (Bell 1968; Sameroff 1975). Furthermore, recognition of the fact that children influence their parents' behavior while simultaneously being influenced by it has encouraged theorists and researchers alike to search for processes that might mediate the relation between prematurity (or other characteristics of children) and abuse or neglect by parents.

Over the past several years the investigation of such processes has been productive in expanding the list of abuse-eliciting characteristics of young children. Recent observational studies, for example, have revealed a lack of social responsiveness on the part of premature and maltreated infants (Egeland and Brunnquell 1979; Goldberg 1978). Moreover, experimental investigations have highlighted the role that the premature infant's aversive cry and appearance, as well as the older child's lack of physical attractiveness, may play in the abuse process (Dion 1974; Frodi et al. 1978). At a more general level, it has been pointed out that the young child's temperament may also be influential in child maltreatment (Parke and Collmer 1975). While it may be easy to see how a parent's inability to cope with a colicky baby or hyperactive child might lead to abuse, it may be less obvious that a passive, lethargic infant can also encourage mistreatment—especially in the form of neglect—simply by not demanding attention. Any serious evaluation of the role of child characteristics, however, must take into account the match between parent and child; characteristics of the child make sense as elicitors of maltreatment only when considered vis-à-vis the caregiver's attributes (Belsky 1978b; Parke and Collmer 1975).

Ultimately, child maltreatment must be considered an interactive process; although children may play a role in their own abuse or neglect, they cannot cause it by themselves. Indeed, in one intensive investigation of family interaction patterns, Burgess found that in certified abusive and neglectful families there was less interaction between family members than there was in matched control families (Burgess and Conger 1978). Mothers from maltreating families, moreover, displayed 40 percent less positive interaction (i.e., affectionate and supportive behavior) and 60 percent more negative behavior (i.e., threats and complaints) than control mothers did. Most intriguing, however, are the findings concerning child behavior, since they provide some indirect support for the role of childhood experiences in the development of abusive behavior. Children from abusive households, Burgess and Conger reported, displayed almost 50 percent more negative behavior than did their counterparts from control families. Although these data certainly suggest that these children may be developing social skills that might predispose them, as adults, to engage in aberrant parenting styles, it must be recognized that on the basis of this investigation alone, it is impossible to determine whether parental behavior fostered negative behavior on the child's part or whether it was the child's negative manner that elicited parental hostility.

In a series of investigations of family interaction, Patterson and his associates (Patterson, 1976, 1977; Patterson, Littman and Bricker, 1967) have found that aggressive and coercive (negatively controlling) behaviors tend to occur in bursts. In fact, parental punishment tends to accelerate ongoing coercive behaviors on the part of the child. Child maltreatment may be the eventual (and possibly predictable) consequence of an escalating cycle of parent-child conflict and aggression. Interestingly, a simulation study demonstrating that adult punitiveness increases following defiant child behavior in response to disciplinary action provides additional support for this interactional model (Parke 1974).

In addition to defiance on the part of the child, other factors or incidents probably also serve as instigators of an abusive episode—for example, a colicky outburst that does not respond to soothing, a report card that indicates unsatisfactory performance in school, or the discovery that one's child has wrecked the family car, broken a cherished possession, or beaten up a sibling. By themselves, it is doubtful that any of these potential stimuli would result in an abusive outburst. In concert with each other or with other factors (e.g., if a parent is prone to responding to stress with violence), however, they might be sufficient to provoke an excessive response—possibly in the name of discipline.

This last point cannot be overemphasized. Child abuse is caused by no single factor. And especially when it comes to the role of the child, it must be recognized that children do not really cause mistreatment. It may be the case that some aspect of their functioning makes parenting especially difficult for particular parents. The very same characteristics of a child, in another household, would not be likely to lead to abuse or neglect. Only in certain homes and with certain parents would such behavior on the part of a child stress the parent to the breaking point of abusing the child. The child's contribution can only be understood—indeed, can only be conceptualized as a contribution—by taking into consideration certain aspects of the parent or the family more generally. To say that children cause their own mistreatment, then, is misleading; to say that they contribute to parent-child relations which may be dysfunctional for many other reasons is more accurate. And, finally, we must note the fact that those very aspects of child functioning that prove irritating to parents and thereby contribute to child abuse may themselves be products of the care children have experienced at the hands of their parents. In some sense, then, families are likely to create the difficulties they encounter in caring for their offspring which, in certain instances, lead to child abuse and neglect.

The major assumption underlying a contextual explanation of child maltreatment, such as that being described, is that its causes are ecologically nested within one another (Belsky 1980). Thus, a full understanding of the conditions under which characteristics of children increase the likelihood of abuse or neglect can be achieved only by examining other aspects of the family. Since the parent-child system (the crucible of child maltreatment) is typically nested within the marital relationship, what happens between husbands and wives—from an ecological point of view—has implications for what happens between parents and their children. Evidence for such a linkage between these two dyadic systems within the family comes from the frequent observation that marital conflict and discord run high in abusive households (Clark 1976; Elmer 1967; Green 1976). In fact, Steinmetz (1977) found that families that use aggressive tactics (both physical and verbal) to resolve spousal disputes tend to adopt similar strategies in disciplining their children. To the extent that physical punishment of children is considered more socially acceptable than the exercise of physical force against one's spouse, child abuse may result from displaced aggression. Alternatively, stress and conflict resulting from marital discord may simply spill over into the parent-child relationship and contaminate the socialization process.

The fact that abuse also has been reported to occur with disproportionate frequency in large families, as well as in families in which children are closely spaced (Gil 1970; Light 1973), suggests that to the extent that economic and human resources become overextended in large families with many dependent offspring, it is likely that abuse results as tolerable levels of stress are surpassed. Household disorganization has also been frequently cited as a causative agent in the abuse and neglect process (Elmer 1967; Young 1964), and it is likely that tolerance of stress is as much a function of a family's skill in effectively marshalling its resources to cope with adversity as it is a function of the absolute levels of stress to which a family is subjected. If correct, this analysis would partially explain why it is that among families facing equivalent levels of social and economic privation, maltreatment occurs in some families but not in others.

The Community Context

An understanding of the ecological approach to human development is basic to an appreciation of the embeddedness of the individual and the family within larger social units (Bronfenbrenner 1979). Operationally, this requires that the family be considered from the vantage point of formal and informal social structures that do not themselves contain the developing person but nevertheless exert an impact upon his or her development. Sociologically based investigations of the etiology of child abuse and neglect have identified two extrafamilial factors that may play a role in the abuse process through the influence they exert on the family: the world of work and the neighborhood.

The most direct evidence linking the world of work with maltreatment comes from research on unemployment (Gelles 1975; Young 1964). Gil (1971) has shown, for example, that nearly half of the fathers of the 13,000 cases of abuse he analyzed in his national survey experienced joblessness in the year that immediately preceded the abusive incident. Light's (1973) reanalysis of these data revealed, moreover, that unemployment was the single factor that most frequently differentiated abusive and nonabusive families—even after controlling for biased reporting evident in Gil's survey.

The processes through which unemployment may eventuate in or, to use Gil's (1977) term, "trigger" maltreatment are likely to be varied. The mere fact that joblessness is associated with frustrating circumstances such as lack of monetary resources may account for this relationship (Parke and Collmer 1975). Additionally, the sense of powerlessness resulting from being dethroned as family provider might fuel intrafamily violence (Gelles 1976), especially when status can be regained by exercising one's force against defenseless children (Polansky, Hally, and Polansky 1975). Or maltreatment may simply be a consequence of the increased parent-child contact (and thus conflict) that results from unemployed parents spending more time at home (Belsky 1978b).

The influence that the neighborhood exerts in the etiology of child maltreatment is demonstrated most clearly by the repeated observations that child-abusing families are isolated from formal and informal support systems. As Garbarino (1977) has pointed out, every investigation that has examined social isolation as an etiological variable has discerned an association between it and child maltreatment. In point of fact, this relation clearly illustrates why embeddedness is a concept critical to the ecological perspective on child maltreatment. As Kempe (1973) noted, what abusive families lack is a "lifeline," so that during particularly stressful times they have no means of escape, no friends or relatives to whom to turn for help. The significance of emotional and material assistance (including child-care services) in promoting the healthy functioning of all families should not be underestimated (Cochran and Brassard 1979).

The absence of support systems, it must be noted, may be in part a situation of the family's own making. After all, such isolation frequently results from a person's inability or lack of inclination to establish and maintain friendships. Moreover, this tendency to become isolated may itself be a function of a parent's failure or lack of opportunity to acquire, while growing up, the interpersonal skills necessary for friendly social relations (cf. Polansky and colleagues, 1975). Some indirect support for this contention comes from a study indicating that by the ripe old age of two or three, abused children are socially isolating themselves by responding less positively to friendly overtures and displaying more avoidance of peers and adults than nonabused age mates (George and Main 1979).

In addition to Kempe's explanation of the linkage between social isolation and maltreatment, which focuses on the crucial assistance that members of one's social network can provide in times of stress, a process which emphasizes social conformity has also been proposed to account for this frequently observed association. Specifically, it has been argued that since there are few persons entering the home, there is little opportunity for anyone to informally scrutinize caregiving patterns and provide instructive feedback when they violate community standards (Belsky, 1978b; Garbarino, 1977). In commenting more generally on the role of social conformity, Caplan (1976) describes the function of support systems in the following terms: "They tell him [the individual] what is expected of him and guide him in what to do. They watch what he does and judge his performance" (pp. 5–6). Interpersonal supports, he further notes, provide assistance in the handling of emotions and in the controlling of impulses. Finally, social networks also provide parents with role models (Cochran and Brassard 1979).

Whatever process actually accounts for the association between maltreatment and isolation, it is clear that child abuse or neglect may result when a parent's developmental history conspires to keep him or her from establishing contacts with those very persons whose support can help prevent such abnormal parenting. Here again, then, is an illustration of the way in which the various etiological factors interact in causing child maltreatment.

In evaluating the role played by extrafamilial forces in causing child maltreatment, it is necessary to emphasize two important points. The first is that these influences are most likely to stimulate abuse and neglect because of the pressures they place on the family and the consequent stress they create. To the extent then that stress within the family is already high (due to such factors as overcrowding, spousal conflict, a colicky baby), the likelihood of maltreatment increases if the family is isolated or a parent loses a job. If a parent's developmental history predisposes him or her, moreover, to respond to such stress in an aggressive manner or to use corporal punishment as a means of socializing the child, then the probability of maltreatment increases still further.

The second point to be made regarding extrafamilial influences is that they themselves are often the by-product of changes taking place in the larger social environment. The best examples of this are unemployment resulting from a global energy crisis and social isolation stemming from the increased social mobility of the population. It should be evident on the basis of these two illustrations alone that to truly understand the multifaceted nature of the etiology of child maltreatment, our analysis must move beyond the individual, the family, and even the community in which they are embedded.

The Cultural Context

By examining the larger cultural fabric in which the individual, the family, and the community are inextricably interwoven, we can analyze the role of the macrosystem in child maltreatment (Belsky 1980). In so doing, we can shed still more light on the complex web of causative agents that conspire against the child and the family by fostering child abuse and neglect. Most evident in this role are society's attitudes toward violence, corporal punishment, and children.

Compared to other Western nations, the level of violence in America can only be characterized as high. Indeed, one expert on family violence has concluded that "the United States is a country that practices and approves violence" (Straus 1974, p. 53). Basic to the ecological model of maltreatment is the assumption that societal willingness to tolerate such high levels of violence sets the stage for the occurrence of family violence, one form of which is child abuse (Gelles 1976; Gil 1971; Straus 1974; Zigler 1978).

Even more clearly implicated in the abuse process is the general acceptance, if not sanctioning, of physical punishment as a means of controlling children's behavior. Not only is such punishment practiced with extraordinary frequency in this country (Gelles 1978), but it is explicitly condoned by many would-be sources of influence on parenting behavior. Viano (1974) reports, for example, that two out of every three educators, police officers, and clerics who were questioned condoned physical discipline (in the form of spanking with the hand), while more than 10 percent of those queried believed that the use of belts, straps, and brushes was acceptable for maintaining control. More recently, the Supreme Court (in *Ingraham v. Wright*) ruled that schools have the right to corporally punish disobedient children (Zigler 1977). When the highest court in the land passes such a judgment, it is difficult to argue with those who contend that child maltreatment is simply behavior that departs from social norms in intensity and appropriateness. Indeed, some indirect evidence in support of the cultural explanation of child abuse can be found in several cross-cultural reports; in countries in which physical punishment is infrequently practiced as a disciplinary strategy, child maltreatment is rare (Levy 1969; Sidell 1972; Korbin 1978).

Society's general attitude toward children is also implicated in this cultural analysis of the etiology of child abuse. The belief that children are property to be handled as parents choose may be particularly important (Garbarino, 1977; Gil 1976). It is worth pointing out that the historic roots of such a belief system, as well as evidence of its potential role in the maltreatment process, can be traced back to antiquity (Bakan 1971; Radbill 1974). Although some critics might debate the significance of such cultural history for understanding contemporary child maltreatment, Zigler (1977) has pointed out that the previously mentioned Supreme Court decision was based on the very assumption that children's rights are distinct from those of others. Indeed, he noted that although criminals are protected by the Eighth Amendment from cruel and unusual punishment, the majority opinion of the Court ruled that school children have little need for such protection.

Despite the fact that advances are being made in the fight for children's rights, it is doubtful that maltreatment can be eliminated so long as parents rear their offspring in a society in which violence is rampant, corporal punishment is condoned as a child-rearing technique, and parenthood itself is construed in terms of ownership. It is likely, moreover, that recent cultural developments, such as the denigration of the role of child care, stimulated in part by the most radical segments of women's movement (cf. Zigler 1978), and the narcissistic "me first" approach to life that seems to be rapidly enveloping contemporary American society (cf. Lasch 1978), work against efforts to prevent child maltreatment by devaluing the responsibilities of parenthood. Historically, the passage of child labor laws and compulsory school attendance were responses to the devaluation of children that was exacerbated by the rise of industrialization (cf. Elder 1974). The point here is simply that what happens within and beyond the family is invariably influenced by prevailing cultural attitudes and values, as well as by historical changes.

Ecological Integration

To summarize this analysis of the multifaceted nature of the etiology of child maltreatment, parents bring to the family and to their roles as parents developmental histories that may predispose them to treat their offspring in an abusive/neglectful manner. Stress-promoting social forces both within the family (e.g., handicapped child, marital conflict) and beyond (e.g., social isolation, unemployment) increase the likelihood that parent-child conflict will occur. The fact that a parent's response to such conflict takes the form of maltreatment is considered to be a consequence of both the parent's own prior experience as a child and the prevailing values and child-rearing practices that characterize the society, subculture, or community in which the child, the family, and the community are embedded (Belsky, 1980). Once we recognize that child abuse is not simply a problem of a disturbed parent, we can move beyond traditional interventions that focus upon parental disturbance alone, to propose efforts to attack the child abuse problem at several levels simultaneously (e.g., parent, child, family, community, society) (Belsky 1978b, 1980; Parke and Collmer 1975).

DEVELOPMENTAL CONSEQUENCES

Until recently, virtually all attention paid to child abuse has been devoted to understanding its causes. This, in and of itself, should not be surprising. Concern for etiology stems from concern for treatment. Given the general expectation that child abuse is bad for children, and that abuse and neglect need to be remediated, if not prevented, it stands to reason that more attention has been paid to cause than consequence. What though is the current state of our knowledge regarding the consequences of mistreatment for the developing child?

Until the mid 1970s most of what was known about the development of mistreated children was based upon the clinical impressions and evaluations of practitioners dealing with abused and neglected children. What was lacking, as a consequence, were firm grounds for drawing strong conclusions. Without adequate groups of nonmistreated children with whom to compare abused and neglected children, it was difficult to determine whether dysfunctional behavior displayed by the mistreated child was a contributing agent to or consequence of the hostile or indifferent care they received at the hands of their parents. Consider, for example, the reports of child care workers who characterized a group of abused children as "whiny, fussy, listless, chronically crying, demanding, stubborn, resistive, negativistic, pallid, sickly, emaciated, fearful, panicky, unsmily" and difficult to manage (Johnson and Morse 1968). Given what we have already seen regarding the role children can play in the abuse process, there are certainly grounds for contending that, under certain contextual conditions, such characteristics of children are as likely to contribute to, as result from, child abuse and neglect.

On the basis of more recent inquiry, especially studies using control groups of nonmistreated children, it is possible to draw a tentative picture of the developmental consequences of child maltreatment. During the infancy years, abused children tend to display, not surprisingly, disturbances in affective expression, emotional maladjustment, and insecurity in the quality of their attachment relations to their mothers. In one recent investigation, abused and neglected infants between the ages of twelve and twenty-six months were observed in a laboratory setting to determine how they reacted to their parents and to strangers in a variety of social situations. Some of these situations involved the gradual and friendly approach of a strange adult that culminated in picking the baby up, a free play session involving mother and baby, the administration of standardized infant assessments, and a brief separation from and reunion with mother and stranger. As predicted, the emotional responses of abused babies were characteristically different from those of normal infants. In general, the abused infants appeared sad, fearful, distressed, and often angry. Moreover, their play behavior tended to be aimless, disorganized, and inhibited (Gaensbauer, Mrazek, and Harmon 1981).

In a follow-up investigation aimed at refining the clinical description of distorted affective communication as reflected in social interaction, abused children were observed in interaction with strange adults while playing with inanimate objects (Gaensbauer & Sands, 1979). The primary interaction pattern observed in the mistreated children involved social and emotional withdrawal. Abused and neglected infants not only failed to initiate social contact, but also failed to respond to pleasurable interactions; in fact, they tended to isolate themselves to prevent social interchange. In addition to such disturbed social patterns, affective communications were distorted, inconsistent, and unpredictable, with those emotional expressions that did emerge from these children being notably shallow.

The results of two studies, one focused upon the quality of infant-mother attachment and the other on behavior in a day care program, complement these investigations of the effects of child maltreatment. Abused one year olds, Egeland and Stroufe (1981) found, were significantly more likely to be classified as avoidantly attached to their mothers—a style of relating to caregiver that has been linked to subsequent developmental incompetence (see Chapter 4). In the day care study, although abused and nonabused control toddlers were similar in the number of approaches they made to peers, children with a history of mistreatment approached caregivers only half as often as the control children. Moreover, in response to a friendly advance by caregiver, abused toddlers were more likely to terminate social contact and to respond to such friendly overtures by moving to the side of the individual or by backing up when approaching them. In fact, avoidance constituted 25 percent of the abused children's responses to encounters with peers and caregivers, but only 6 percent of controls'. Many of the abused children wriggled or pushed away from situations involving physical contact, as when a caregiver went to sit a child on her lap during story time (George & Main, 1979).

These findings, and other clinical impressions suggesting that abused children tend to be inhibited and overly compliant, and to rarely express pain or distress, most certainly convey a picture of psychological disturbance—a picture which, upon reflection, does not appear all that surprising. If the quality of care one receives is hostile and rejecting, the tendency to avoid others for fear that similar experiences may be encountered appears both reasonable and potentially adaptive. After all, how does the child know for certain that the pain experienced at the hands of her abusive caregiver is not a routine cost of engaging in social interchange?

The other primary pattern of response to abuse chronicled by clinicians and scientists, particularly in older children, involves aggression. In many cases, severe temper tantrums and angry outbursts, including self-destructive behavior (e.g., head-banging, self-biting), have been noted among mistreated children (Galdston 1975; Green 1978; Martin 1976). In the George and Main (1979) observational study of abused and nonabused toddlers in a therapeutic day care center, they found that acts of aggression against friendly caregivers occurred on the average of six times per two-hour observation; in contrast, nonabused control children engaged in similar aggressive acts only once per two-hour period. The incidence of aggression against age mates, it is interesting to note, was similar across groups in this study.

The findings just summarized have been extended in investigations of preschoolers and school-age children. Observation of three-to-five-year-old children engaged in free play with peers reveals greater aggression amongst children identified as mistreated and less tolerance for situations in which they could not have their own way (Herrenkohl and Herrenkohl, 1981). Reidy (1977) also found that abused children, these averaging 6.4 years of age, displayed more aggression than nonmistreated peers across a variety of situations, including fantasy, free play, and in school. Violence, then, seems to be a consistent pattern displayed by abused children, many of whom are otherwise characterized by an emotional unresponsiveness.

In terms of causation, a variety of underlying processes may account for the aggression that is repeatedly observed in abused children. One possibility that might account for the greater aggression observed amongst mistreated children is that they simply are modeling the hostile interpersonal exchanges they have experienced. Complementing this notion is the observation that maltreated children are "hypervigalant" (Martin and Breezely 1976). That is, they appear to be constantly on the alert for danger, scanning the environment for signs of impending attack. To the extent that this is indeed the case, such children may be quick to interpret any interruption or obstacle as such a sign of danger and, as a result, respond aggressively because they perceive frustrating circumstances as a threat to them. Alternatively, mistreated children may simply have failed to learn and develop the social skills required to engage others in harmonious interaction, because of the poor quality care they have experienced. Aggression may simply be a response to the frustration caused when one cannot effectively communcate with, and thereby influence, another.

Whatever the exact process by which avoidance and aggression are promoted, mistreated children run an increased risk of developing disturbed patterns of functioning. From the standpoint of earlier discussions of parental influence on child development this situation is not surprising. Child abuse can be viewed as an extreme case of hostile, punitive rearing. And we have seen already that such care undermines, rather than supports, the well-being of the developing human being.

CONCLUSION

Certainly child abuse and neglect are disturbing social realities worthy of great concern and attention. As we have shown in this chapter, the mistreatment of children undermines optimal development. To the extent that children are, as many advocates proclaim, our best hope for the future, then parental dysfunction that takes the form of child mistreatment must be treated seriously.

But, as this chapter also suggests, in order to successfully prevent or treat child mistreatment, an understanding of its etiology is essential, as strategies of prevention and remediation derive from causal explanations. Thus, if one adapts a psychological frame of reference, treatment is directed at the individual disturbances of the abusive or neglectful parent. In contrast, a sociological perspective dictates a need for community- and society-based social change. Finally, a point of view that underscores the role the child plays, either intentionally or inadvertently, in contributing to his or her own mistreatment directs intervention efforts to the aversive characteristics of the child.

Since these vantage points are by no means mutually exclusive, probably the most effective prevention and treatment strategies will be ecological in nature and will take into consideration the behavior, personality, and developmental history of the individual parent, the characteristics of the child, and the familial, community, and societal context in which parent and child are embedded. Only by addressing these multiple determinants of child abuse and neglect can we expect the efforts to reduce the incidence of this multifaceted social problem to be effective.

Contemporary Issues

The Dual Worker Family

In Chapter 3 we pointed out that the rising rate of women in the work force represents one of the most pronounced changes in the American family since the turn of the century. As noted, too, this change has been most dramatic since World War II. Indeed, by 1980 more than half of all women in the United States were working. When this figure is broken down in terms of marital status, we find that 60 percent of the never-married women were in the work force and 50 percent of those married and living with their husbands were employed. The highest rates of labor force participation, though, are found amongst divorced women, where 75 percent were employed in 1980 (Waite 1981).

Consideration of women with children reveals that mothers are more likely to work than are women without children. For example, 57 percent of all women in the United States with children under eighteen were working in 1980, compared with 48 percent of women with no children under eighteen. Those who had children ages six to seventeen only were the most likely to be working, with 64 percent in the labor force. However, even women with younger children are found increasingly in the labor force, with 42 percent of women with children under the age of three working in 1980. This represents a notable increase during the last thirty years. Figure 11.1 graphically displays the changes that have taken place in women's participation in the labor force between 1968 and 1979 as a function of the age of their offspring. Clearly, the employment of mothers is no small issue to those concerned with the child in the family. Employment outside of the home is now, and is likely to continue to be, a part of a woman's role for a majority of American mothers.

The increase in working mothers is indicative of the desire of many women to establish careers early in life. It may also indicate a willingness on the part of men and women to enhance a family's standard of living by having two incomes. Apparently, many couples see this as a worthwhile sacrifice. However, many women value work because of the rewards it brings. In a national sample of working women studied in 1976, 76 percent said they would continue to work even if they did not have to (Dubnoff, Veroff, and Kulka 1978). This percentage represents a considerable increase over the percentage of working women responding similarly to the same question asked in a 1957 survey (Hoffman 1979).

Such changing attitudes and behavior of American women illustrate the importance of the wider social context in understanding how children develop, because the long-term growth of mothers working outside the home while their children are still young can be traced to the changing role of women and the national economy. While contemporary ideology

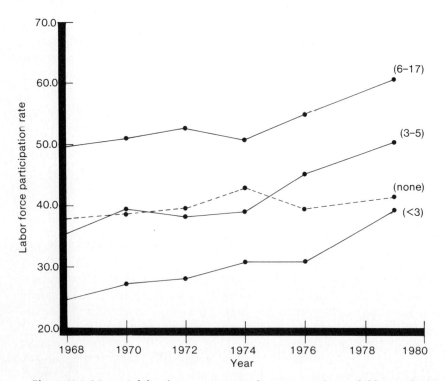

Figure 11.1 *Women's labor force participation by presence of own children under 18, 1968–1979.*

Source: Bureau of Labor Statistics, Special Labor Force Reports "Marital and Family Characteristics of the Labor Force" (various nos.).

regarding the role of women in society has encouraged many mothers to pursue careers and educational goals, economic forces have driven other women to work, as two incomes become necessary to maintain the standard of living in an inflationary economy. The reduced family sizes that we have witnessed in recent years and the fact that child bearing and child rearing take up a declining portion of the average indivdual's life span also contribute to this increase in maternal employment. And, because less energy is required to rear two children than four or five, the child-rearing years themselves are likely to be less demanding today than they were in the past (Lamb 1982). The fact that labor saving appliances like dishwashers, self-cleaning stoves, and microwave ovens make homemaking less time-consuming than it has been traditionally is also significant.

Still another factor affecting rates of maternal employment is the fact that families are formed later in the life course today than in the past. With couples deferring child bearing, married women become accustomed to being employed and their spouses come to rely on their incomes. As a result, many women are not ready to leave the labor force because they have become mothers (Lamb 1982).

With this increase in maternal employment has come a change in attitudes toward women working during the child-rearing years and toward the use of nonmaternal child care, that is, day care. As Lamb (1982, p. 2) has noted, "Just a generation ago ... the working mother (especially one with young children) was considered selfishly derelict in her maternal responsibilities. ... By contrast, popular attitudes toward maternal employment are much more accepting today." This issue of historical change cannot be stressed enough. Only a generation ago mothers who went to work when their infants were young often experienced severe condemnation from their friends and relatives. This criticism of the "neglectful" mother was in part a function of both child development theory and research. Classical psychoanalytic theory placed special emphasis upon the mother-child tie and its role in character development. Thus, any deviation from the consistent availability and responsiveness of mother was presumed to be detrimental for the child. This view received some empirical support from research that indicated that children growing up in institutions without special relationships with their mothers developed in a less-than-optimal manner (e.g., Spitz 1945). While the understimulation of many of these institutions no doubt was responsible for the deficits children displayed, the prevailing ethos led many to interpret such dysfunction as caused by the absence of mother love. Maternal employment was, therefore, often construed in similar terms. Even today, contemporary critics of day care call into question the routine practice of rearing children away from their mothers during the infant and preschool years (Fraiberg 1977).

The historical change that has taken place with respect to maternal employment and day care is important because it may well affect the impact that mothers' working has on children's development. This would seem to be especially likely if it is not maternal employment per se that influences children, but rather parents' attitudes and style of interacting with their offspring. To the extent that mothers felt guilty in the past about leaving their children in the care of others, the possibility arises that such an emotional orientation could affect parenting, which, as we have seen already, influences child development. Conversely, if mother's working in contemporary society enhances her feelings of self-esteem and provides personal fulfillment, quality of parenting and, thereby, child functioning, could be enhanced.

Interestingly, there exist some data that substantiate this speculation. Lamb (1982) reported, in a study of one year olds, that while mothers who were employed (especially full time) were more likely to have infants who were insecurely attached to them than were unemployed mothers, this apparent effect of employment on child development was qualified when mothers' attitudes toward parenthood and work were considered. Specifically, when employed mothers valued both work and parenthood highly, their infants tended to develop secure attachments. These data suggest that insecure attachment is not necessarily the result of maternal employment per se, but rather of mothers' attitudes and, presumably, their manner of interacting with their children. Given the importance placed on maternal sensitivity in Chapter 4 when considering parental influences on infant development, we can reasonably speculate that parents' dissatisfaction with their roles—as either parents, workers, or homemakers—undermines parental sensitivity and, thereby, optimal infant and child functioning.

Support for this analysis has been found in several studies. In one recent investigation of preschoolers, Stuckey and her colleagues (1982) discovered that when parental attitudes toward dual worker roles did not match actual employment status, patterns of mother-child and father-child interaction were disrupted. More specifically, in households in which mothers worked but in which parents felt it better that they stay home, and in homes in which mothers did not work and parents wanted them to, parents were more likely to communicate negative feelings toward their children. This process of family dynamics may explain why, in three separate investigations, researchers found that when mothers desired to be employed but were not (Farel 1980), or when they were working and desired not to be (Hoffman, 1963b), their children have been reported to be poorly adjusted, yet when mothers were working and had positive attitudes towards employment, their children have been found to be well adjusted (Woods 1972).

Clearly, mothers who are satisfied with their lives, be they primarily employees or homemakers, seem to have children who function most optimally (Etaugh 1974). Most likely this effect results because satisfaction with one's life serves to support one's effectiveness as a parent (Hoffman 1974; Gold and Andres 1978b; Lamb 1982). It should be clear on the basis of this discussion that a world of difference is likely in the experiences of children and parents when a woman works *or* remains home and does not want to, and when she works *or* remains home and this is what she desires to do.

This discussion highlights the fact that the conditions of maternal employment are not the same for all families. In some households the employment of both parents (or only one if it is a single-parent family) is an economic necessity if the family is to be able to afford their chosen standard of living. In other households maternal employment is likely to be primarily a function of a woman's personal desires—be they her interest in a career or daily contact with adults in situations not related to child care. One survey revealed that the most common reason provided for the desire noted earlier to remain employed even if one did not have to was "to fill the time"; in fact, only 10 percent of the women interviewed as a part of this national survey claimed to work to fulfill achievement aspirations (Dubnoff, Veroff, and Kulka 1978).

Unfortunately, in most studies of maternal employment, the reasons for employment and mothers' satisfactions with their current situations, be they working or not working, have not been investigated. As a consequence, in reviewing research in this area, we will not be able to stress processes of influence as much as we think they need to be. This limit is an important one since it must be recognized that in and of itself maternal employment is a status variable with little explanatory value unless the conditions of employment, both within and beyond the family, are detailed (Bronfenbrenner and Crouter 1980; Crouter, Belsky, and Spanier 1983; Lamb 1982).

One important environmental circumstance likely to play a major role in determining the effects of maternal employment, especially during the infancy and preschool years, is the kind of nonmaternal, supplementary child care the child receives. Like mothers' attitudes toward their jobs and the nature of their employment, this factor also has been neglected in the study of maternal employment. Surprisingly, investigation of the effects of such supplementary child care has proceeded independent of the study of maternal employment—this despite the fact that the primary reason families rely on day care is because mothers are employed. Although maternal employment and supplementary nonmaternal child care are causally linked in this manner, we consider separately the effects that each has on child development. While this strategy is by no means ideal, it is dictated by the rather distinct approaches researchers have adopted in studying children in families in which both parents are working.

MATERNAL EMPLOYMENT

Examination of the effects of maternal employment reveals that the influence of a mother's working on child functioning varies as a function of the developmental status of the child. The reason for this variation, no doubt, is that the mother plays a different role in the child's life during infancy, childhood, and adolescence and because children make different demands on their parents during these distinct developmental periods. During infancy, for example, the physiological, psychological, and behavioral dependency of the child on its mother is greatest. After all, in the earliest months of life infants rely totally on their parents (or some other caregiver) for nutrition; and toward the end of the first year and the period of focused attachments, the child is especially oriented toward the physical location of parents, often being very wary of being separated or being left with someone else.

During the preschool years children still require love, guidance, and a supportive home base, but, as a result of their ever-increasing ability to function autonomously, also need independence and the opportunity to cope on their own, plus the chance to develop a sense of responsibility and feelings of competence (Hoffman 1979). From this perspective, maternal employment may well serve the developmental needs of preschoolers by providing children with opportunities to exercise their developing skills away from the watchful eye of the parent and beyond the familiar confines of the home.

If this is true during the preschool years, it is even more likely to be the case during the elementary school and adolescent years. As Hoffman (1979, p. 863) has remarked:

> The adolescent is coping with problems of identity, autonomy, and sexuality. The self-esteem obtained in middle childhood may be challenged by new standards of the teenage peer group or the greater proximity of adult roles. Parenting may require a further distancing from the child and an indication of confidence in his or her independent judgment, even though there is much in this situation to make the parent want to hang on or even increase the controls.

Having demonstrated in these few comments, as well as in Chapter 7, how the child changes over time and how such development places different demands upon parents, we show that maternal employment may mean different things to children at different ages and, consequently, may differentially affect them as a function of their developmental status. In what follows, we review the effects of maternal employment during early childhood (infancy and preschool), the elementary school years, and adolescence.

Early Childhood

It is during the infancy years that the issue of maternal employment is most sensitive for many parents. The utter dependency of the child on its caregiver, coupled with concern that the child will develop closer ties with individuals other than parents if cared for by persons not in the family, are the main reasons why so many mothers experience difficulty in deciding to seek employment during this time. Most investigations of the effects of maternal employment during infancy have been conceptualized as studies of day care and are reviewed in the second half of this chapter. In preview, it is worth noting that in most cases few differences have been discerned in the emotional bonds infants develop toward their mothers as a result of their day care experience (Belsky, Steinberg and Walker 1982). While infants with employed mothers do form attachment bonds to their caregivers, it is not the case that such bonds weaken emotional ties to mother. In fact, in every investigation of the subject to date, mothers remain preferred sources of security when contrasted with familiar day care providers (Farran and Ramey 1977; Kagan, Kearsley and Zelazo 1978).

Although the actual effects of maternal employment on child development have not been well studied during infancy, several investigations have recently focused upon processes of family functioning, specifically parent-child interaction. Focusing solely upon the mother-infant dyad during structured laboratory tasks, Cohen (1978) found no differences in the manner in which employed and nonemployed mothers of premature infants interacted with their babies during the first year, but more positive interactions were observed at twenty-one months on the part of mother-child dyads in which mother was not employed. The fact, however, that a greater proportion of employed mothers were single parents, and thus likely to be under more stress generally, may have accounted for these differences more than did maternal employment per se.

Although most research on mother's working focuses upon the child's development or the mother-child relationship, a recent study of five-month-old infants in a family setting indicates how maternal employment can influence the father-child relationship. Pedersen and his colleagues (1980) discovered that fathers whose wives worked during the day interacted less with their infants when observed on weekday evenings under everyday home conditions than did fathers who were sole breadwinners in their families. Consideration of mothers' behavior revealed the likely cause of this apparent effect of maternal employment on fathering. Working mothers interacted with their infants more than nonworking mothers, suggesting to Pedersen and his collaborators that working mothers were compensating for their time away from their babies during the day. Such compensatory involvement served to limit fathers' access to their children. Unfortunately, no developmental follow-up of these families was conducted to permit assessment of the effects of such compensatory mothering on infant development.

The fact that most other investigators have found few effects of maternal employment on patterns of parent-child relations means that we must be cautious in generalizing the results of the Pedersen study despite the common-sense explanation that may be used to account for his data. Goldberg (1977), for example, found that in middle-class homes employed and nonworking mothers spent equivalent amounts of time in high quality one-to-one interaction with their children. The results of a larger study of how parents spend their time suggest that it is only in the case of more educated and, presumably, economically well-off families, however, that maternal employment does not cut into time spent with children (Hill and Stafford 1978). Less educated mothers, Hill and Stafford (1978) discovered, spent less time with their children as the time they spent working increased.

During the preschool years themselves, most investigations of the effects of maternal employment reveal few differences between children whose mothers are employed and those whose mothers are not employed (Nye, Perry, and Ogles 1963; Siegel et al. 1963; Hensseler and Borduin 1981). Despite this trend in the data, recent work in Canada and in the United States suggests not only that maternal employment can have an impact on child development during the preschool years but, in addition, processes of family interaction may be principally responsible for this influence. In a Canadian study of 110 nursery school children, Gold and Andres (1978) found that both male and female children whose mothers worked had more egalitarian sex-role concepts than did age mates whose mothers were full-time homemakers. That is, children with working mothers were less inclined to view certain behaviors, roles, and occupations as being principally the province of one gender or another. Thus, for these children both men and women were regarded as candidates for occupations such as policeman and physician. With respect to intellectual functioning, this same investigation revealed that boys from families in which mothers were employed scored lowest on intelligence tests when compared to boys whose mothers did not work and to girls whose mothers either worked or did not work. Finally, sons of working mothers also perceived their fathers more negatively than sons of women who were homemakers.

Although this investigation, in and of itself, does not enable us to draw firm conclusions regarding the effects of maternal employment in general, it is especially interesting as it foreshadows effects that have been documented more consistently in studies of older children. In fact, on the basis of these and other findings, it is often argued that daughters benefit more than sons from maternal employment. Why might this be so? One reason is that while girls gain a competent role model (in the working mother), boys' role model (i.e., father) tends to lose some status (since mother has to work). Another basis for a differential effect of maternal employment on boys and girls which will be chronicled even more consistently in our discussion of older age children has to do with the differential rearing sons and daughters may experience in their families. In this regard, the results of Stuckey, McGhee, and Bell (1982) comparative analysis of parent-preschooler interaction patterns in dual-worker and single-worker families is especially illuminating. Working with families from the southwest United States, these researchers observed that daughters of employed women received increased parental attention during the preschool years, whereas sons received decreased parental attention.

When considered in the context of the Canadian study documenting effects upon children rather than effects on family functioning, these findings suggest that maternal employment may influence patterns of parent-child interaction as well as children's development. Indeed, it may well be the case that it is the effects of maternal employment on parenting that mediates any discerned effects on children themselves. To the extent that this is the case, the implications for intervention are profound. If the influence of mother's working on child development is dependent upon its effect on patterns of parent-child interaction, then by intervening to affect processes of family functioning one should be able to modify the impact of maternal employment on the child. Especially in the case of sons such intervention efforts may be extremely important.

Childhood

In order to develop further understanding of how maternal employment affects child development during the elementary school years, several aspects of family functioning must be considered. In households in which mothers are employed, fathers have been found to participate more in housework and child care (Blood and Hamblin 1958; Pleck 1979; Pleck and Rustad 1980; Walker 1970). This is not to say, however, that homemaker responsibilities are evenly divided, as working women still perform the large majority of home maintenance tasks. Nevertheless, household division of labor is still less traditional than in homes in which only father is the sole breadwinner (Hoffman 1979; Lamb 1982).

In addition to fathers' contribution to household functioning, children in families in which mothers are employed are more likely to have household responsibilities during the later part of middle childhood and during adolescence (Hoffman 1979; Walker 1970; Douvan 1963; Yarrow et al. 1962). Furthermore, families in which both parents work, or in which the single parent is employed, are more likely to have structured rules for their children (Hoffman 1974). As Hoffman (1979) suggests, such increased independence training and reliance on rules in families in which mothers are employed are likely to represent adaptive responses to living with such a family structure. Simply put, the household functions more smoothly in mother's absence under these conditions.

The independence training that daughters receive apparently contributes positively to academic and occupational competence and, more generally, to positive adjustment (Hoffman 1979). Like sons with employed mothers, daughters whose mothers work show less sex role-stereotyped attitudes and expectations regarding what are appropriate behaviors and careers for boys and girls and for men and women (Hoffman 1963, 1979; Romer and Cherry 1978; Lamb 1982). For example, Bacon and Lerner (1975) found, in their study of second, fourth, and sixth grade girls, that those whose mothers were employed outside the home had vocational role perceptions that were more egalitarian than were those of age mates whose mothers did not work. In another study, this one of 223 Canadian ten-year-olds, children whose mothers worked were found to have the most egalitarian sex-role concepts (Gold and Andres 1978a). Consistent with the argument advanced in the introduction to this chapter, these apparent effects of maternal employment were primarily a function of working mothers' greater satisfaction with their roles than they were of working per se.

Although female development seems to benefit from maternal employment, the same does not always appear to be the case for boys during childhood. Interestingly, the specific effects that working has on sons seems to be mediated by social class (Hoffman 1979; Lamb 1982), thereby highlighting the importance of considering the broader social and cultural context in which children and their families reside. In the case of boys in lower-class homes, the diminishment in sex stereotypes already noted as a general effect of maternal employment, is less pronounced (Hoffman 1979). Moreover, there is evidence that in such families the mother's working undermines the father-son relationship (Gold and Andres, 1978b; Hoffman, 1974; Romer and Cherry 1978). More specifically, boys from lower-class homes whose mothers work appear to respect and admire their fathers less than boys from similar homes whose mothers do not work (Hoffman, 1974; Hoffman 1979; Lamb 1982). In all likelihood, this negative effect reflects the more conservative and traditional sex-role attitudes of lower-class families (Komarovsky, 1962). Given the traditional view that men are responsible for providing economic support for their wives and children, the father-son difficulty observed in lower-class homes "may reflect a perception that maternal employment implies a failure on the part of the father" (Hoffman 1979, p. 863), thereby undermining his status in the family (Elder 1974).

In middle-class homes, comparable strain in the father-son relationship is not evident (Hoffman 1979). There is some evidence, however, that mothers' working is related to poor school achievement and lower scores on tests of intelligence (Gold and Andres 1978a; Rees and Palmer 1976; Hoffman 1979). This is not a consistent finding, however, and since most research has discerned no such effect, it should be cautiously interpreted (Hoffman 1979).

Adolescence

The task of being a full-time mother during adolescence is a difficult one. As children become increasingly independent, there is less for the parent to do but often more to be concerned about (e.g., drugs, delinquent behavior). Furthermore, as Hoffman (1979) pointed out, it is likely to be a time when parents confront their own developmental status, with concerns of aging as well as anticipation of the empty nest emerging. When families were composed of five or six children, not only were the parenting years more spread out, they also tended to end less abruptly than they do when fewer children are involved.

In view of this situation, the fact that nonemployed mothers have a more difficult time should not be that surprising. Birnbaum (1975) found, for example, that full-time mothers experienced a lower sense of competence, felt less attractive, had lower self esteem, and indicated greater feelings of loneliness than other middle-class mothers employed full time. Indeed, these nonworking mothers expressed more concern about their adolescent children and more regret about their increasing independence. Similar results were reported by Gold and Andres (1978a, b) in their study of Canadian ten year olds and adolescents.

Since, as we have argued, parents' feelings about self are likely to affect their parenting, the psychological status we have just described of nonemployed mothers during their children's adolescence suggests that certain benefits will accrue from having one's mother employed during this developmental period. Further support for this contention comes from the fact that the role strain which mothers of younger children are likely to experience as employees and homemakers is reduced as their children reach adolescence (Hoffman 1979). Those studies of adolescence which have been carried out reveal few negative effects of maternal employment and some positive ones—such as the foregoing theorizing would suggest.

In the case of daughters, maternal employment during adolescence appears especially beneficial. As one authoritative source put it, "The daughters of working mothers are more outgoing, independent, active, highly motivated, score higher on a variety of indices of achievement, and appear better adjusted on social and personality measures" (Hoffman

1979, p. 864). Moreover, when females are raised within a family in which their mother is employed (1) they have less stereotyped views of female roles than do daughters of nonworking mothers; (2) they have a broader definition of the female role, often including attributes that are traditionally male ones (e.g., assertiveness); and (3) they are more likely to emulate their mothers; that is, they more often name their mother as the person they aspire to be like than is the case with daughters of nonworking mothers (Huston-Stein and Higgins-Trenk, 1978). Presumably these developmental effects of maternal employment are the result of the less traditional sex-role models working mothers provide their daughters.

Consistent with this interpretation is the fact that some of the most striking effects of maternal employment concern the child's own vocational aspirations and expectations. Once again, these effects are most pronounced in regard to the daughters of employed mothers. As summarized by Huston-Stein and Higgins-Trenk (1978, pp. 279–280):

> The most consistent and well-documented correlate of career orientation and departure from traditional feminine roles is maternal employment during childhood and adolescence. Daughters of employed mothers (i.e., mothers who were employed during some period of the daughter's childhood or adolesence) more often aspire to a career outside the home (Almquist and Almquist 1971; Hoffman 1974; Stein 1973), get better grades in college (Nichols and Schaffer, 1975), and aspire to more advanced education (Hoffman 1974; Stein 1973). College women who have chosen a traditionally masculine occupation more often had employed mothers than those preparing for feminine occupations (Almquist 1974; Tangri 1972).

Summary

There can be little doubt that maternal employment is characteristic of much contemporary family life. Not only does it appear to meet family financial needs and, under some circumstances, the personal needs of women, but the evidence we have reviewed also indicates that, when conditions are appropriate, the developmental needs of children are also positively influenced. As we have seen, the older children get, the more their increased desire for autonomy and independence are in harmony with the realities of working motherhood. It is important to recognize, though, that mothers' own attitudes toward working, or remaining home, are critical to understanding how maternal employment exerts its impact.

Daughters seem to benefit the most from mothers' working as it liberates them from the traditional sex-role stereotypes that for so long constrained the dreams and aspirations of girls in American society. Boys seem to be adversely affected primarily when, as in lower-class homes, maternal employment is regarded as a sign of paternal failure. Such social and familial atmospheres would appear to be in the best interests of no one—neither the husband who works but requires a wife's income to keep up with inflation, nor the women who is likely to experience the marital stress that such undermining of the traditional male role is likely to occasion, nor the son who distances himself from his tie to his father, which we have seen can be so important to masculine development.

All of this is not to say that those concerned with children can give maternal employment a "clean bill of health." As we will see shortly in the case of day care, it is the *conditions* under which maternal employment is experienced, and the familial processes it sets in motion or inhibits, that determine its developmental impact. Only when such conditions are supportive of both individual and family well-being is maternal employment, or any other social force for that matter, likely to be in the child's best interest.

SUPPLEMENTARY NONMATERNAL CHILD CARE

One major consequence for children of increasing numbers of women entering the labor force, either for reasons of personal fulfillment or economic need, is that increasing numbers of children are being cared for by individuals other than their parents. Until recently, such nonparental care was viewed as a necessary evil, to be employed by the working poor or to be called upon by the nation in times of national emergency (e.g., World War II industrial mobilization). But, as the women's movement has gained increased acceptance, and as economic pressures have made middle-class lifestyles all the more difficult to achieve and maintain, the utilization and acceptance of day care has grown. In this second section of this chapter on dual-worker families we consider the use, nature, and effects of supplementary child care.

It is worth noting before considering these issues that day care, at its best, is a family support system. As such, day care is a supplement to, not a substitute for, parental care. Thus, it must be recognized that it is children's family experience, and the interrelation of day care and in-home experiences, that undoubtedly determine the development of day care-reared children.

Day Care Today

Rates of Use. According to the most recent data gathered by the United States Department of Health, Education, and Welfare, as of June 1978, 11 million children under fourteen years of age spent a substantial part of their week in supplementary child-care arrangements. When broken down by age, these data indicate that 2.5 million infants and toddlers, 3.7 million preschoolers, and 4.9 million school-age children spend a sizable amount of their waking day being cared for by someone other than their parents (Office of Assistant for Planning and Evaluation, 1978). When these data are considered in terms of the type of supplementary care used, we find that about 2.6 million families use in-home care for more than ten hours per week, 3.4 million rely on family day care, and 1.3 million rely on center care. What we see here, then, is that the type of care that is most publicly visible (day care centers) is the least used. And, as we will see when we consider the effects of day care, we know most about this kind of care, which we have least of, and far less about the kinds of care that are most widely employed.

Which families use day care? As a group, they can be distinguished from the general population on several dimensions. While most children enrolled in day care centers are white, minorities (especially blacks) are disproportionately represented. Although minorities account for only 17 percent of the U.S. population under fifteen years of age, 37 percent of children in day care centers are from minority households. Single-parent and low-income families are also disproportionately represented among users of center care. In 1977, fewer than one in five families with children under eighteen years of age could be considered single-parent families, yet one of every three center users came from such families. Analogously, while approximately 50 percent of U.S. families with one or more children had annual incomes below $15,000, 73 percent of center users experienced such low earnings. These figures highlight the fact that many families that use day care, and virtually all who receive public subsidy, are either low-income single parents struggling to stay off welfare and to remain self-sufficient, or dual-worker households in which a second parent's income keeps the family above the poverty line. Thus, millions of American parents have essentially no choice but to share the rearing of their children with others for extended periods of time each week (Ruopp and Travers 1982).

Recent census bureau projections, which estimate an average 2.1 children per family, suggest that the demographic pressures which affect the demand for supplementary child care will increase greatly in the 1980s (Hofferth 1979). This is because the children of the post-World-War-II baby-boom era (1946–1964) will, as parents, produce a sizable increase in the number of preschoolers in the American population. Specifically, the population of children five years of age and under is expected to rise from a low of 17.1 million in 1977 to a high of 23.3 million in 1990; about one-half of the mothers, projections indicate, will return to work prior to the sixth birthday of these preschoolers, thereby increasing the use of day care beyond even its current high levels (Hofferth 1979).

Variation in Day Care. Day care is considered in relatively global terms when the effects of nonparental child care are examined. Yet, we must recognize that there is tremendous diversity in the day care market and, thus, in the kinds of experiences that children have when away from their parents. Appreciation of this diversity is extremely important because the effects of day care, as we will point out, are likely to be determined more by the day-to-day quality of care children experience than by the simple fact that they are being cared for by persons other than their parents. In order to facilitate understanding of the variation that exists we briefly compare three types of day care: center-based day care (CDC), family day care (FDC) and home care (HC). As its name implies, CDC is provided in a center, such as a church basement or community recreation facility, and usually serves twelve or more children. FDC is provided in a private family home and, by federal regulation, cannot serve more than six children. Finally, HC defines what is often referred to as babysitting—a person coming into the child's home to provide care.

Child care in centers has received the most systematic attention. The greatest advantages of such care arrangements involves stability and predictable hours of operation. But such strengths, it must be noticed, can also present problems for families, as centers tend to have fixed hours of operation that may limit their ability to respond flexibly to the individual and special needs of working parents. Few centers, for example, are capable of responding on short notice to parental needs when overtime at work is required by one's employer.

As additional advantages, day care centers tend to offer a wide variety of formal learning experiences; are always licensed and thus publicly evaluated; and are most likely to employ at least some trained professional staff. Centers also tend to have reasonable, if not high quality, play materials, equipment, and space. By offering children a wide variety of playmates, and by providing caregivers with other caregivers to work with who can serve as support systems, day care centers are frequently regarded as attractive contexts by children, parents, and child-care workers alike.

As already noted, family day care constitutes the single largest system of out-of-home care in this country, both in terms of the number of families using care and the number of children served. As of 1980, an estimated 1.3 million day care homes served an estimated 2.4 million full-time children (for periods of thirty hours or more per week), 2.8 million part-time children (ten to twenty-nine hours per week), and 16.7 million children in occasional care (less than ten hours per week). More than half of the full-time children are under six years of age, with the greatest proportion of these under three. FDC, it should be noted, also represents the most prevalent mode of after-school care for 5 million school children between six and thirteen years of age whose parents work (Fosburg 1980).

Two advantages of FDC relative to CDC are the daily and close contact it affords children with mixed-age peer groups (in contrast to the segregated age grouping in centers) and its more flexible hours, as parents are more free to establish individual arrangements with care providers of their choosing. FDC also tends to be cheaper than CDC. Of course, FDC has its own unique disadvantages, most notably the tendency for such informal care arrangements to be unstable, thereby making this kind of arrangement unreliable over the longer term. As we will see when we discuss the effects of day care, it is just such unreliability of these informal arrangements that has been linked to poor developmental outcomes for infants experiencing such informal care.

In-home care is the least studied of the three types of nonparental child care arrangements under consideration. Its primary advantages are flexible scheduling, a single caregiver who is well-known to the child (like FDC) and who can perform functions other than child care (e.g., housework), and a setting that is familiar to the child (i.e., his own home). Its most obvious disadvantages are expense, the relative absence of experience with peers (other than siblings), and the great variability in caregiver competence.

Just as it would be inappropriate to consider all different forms of day care arrangements (i.e., CDC, FDC, and HC) alike, it would be similarly mistaken to regard all centers, all family day care homes, and all babysitting arrangements as being equivalent in the experiences they afford children and the quality of care they provide. We stress again the fact that consideration of such variation is essential to understanding the effects of day care, be it center, family, or home based, because it is likely to be the experiences children have on a day-to-day basis, and not the type of program they are in, that will influence development. Type of program simply represents a statement of probability regarding the kinds of experiences that are more or less likely. For example, while it is more likely that children will be exposed to a wider variety of play things in CDC, it is more likely that they will be exposed to children of more varied ages in FDC. Given that these are only statements of probability, it will certainly be the case that in some particular centers and homes just the reverse will be true.

Some of the most important dimensions upon which centers vary are group size, ratio of adults-to-children, and the degree to which staff has background in child development. In several recent investigations the significance of variation across these dimensions has been highlighted. More specifically, it has been shown that in large as opposed to smaller groups more emphasis is placed upon control and children are less likely to display pleasure, wonder, and delight. Group sizes greater than fifteen to eighteen children have also been linked to less embellished caregiver involvement (i.e., questioning, responding, praising, comforting, more simple monitoring of children, and more caregiver-to-caregiver interaction). And, interestingly, children in these larger groups are less actively involved in classroom activities (i.e., considering and contemplating). The presence of caregiving staff who have educational training in early childhood has also been found to increase the likelihood of high quality experiences (Travers & Ruopp, 1978).

Another way in which centers vary is in terms of their explicit or implicit "curricula." Some programs are clearly preacademic, stressing reading readiness, counting, and the like, whereas others are built more around a traditional free-play preschool model. Prescott (1973) distinguished between "closed" and "open" structure programs. Closed programs are more likely to set clear limits, lack opportunities for the exercise of autonomy and initiative, and provide less positively affective adult-child interaction. Open structure programs, in contrast, encourage autonomy and warm relations with caregivers, but provide less frequent intellectually stimulating activities. On the basis of cmparisons such as these, it should be evident that all CDC programs are not alike (Belsky, Steinberg, and Walker 1982).

With respect to variation in FDC, three different types of homes can be identified. *Unregulated* homes are those not licensed or registered by a public agency. Unregulated care, although illegal in many cases, is the most prevalent form of FDC. Indeed, a 1971 survey estimated that unlicensed care constituted 90 percent of all day-care arrangements (Westinghouse/Westat 1971). In regulated or *licensed* care, the provider has been licensed by a state, county, or local government agency (e.g., department of human resources, county board of health). Across the nation there is considerable variation in licensing standards, but most deal with group composition (i.e., staff-child ratio) and basic health and safety measures. Licensed homes are visited (often irregularly) by local officials who review the health and safety of the environment. Finally, sponsored or *supervised* homes are part of networks or organizations of child-care providers. These networks are groups of licensed caregivers whose organization provides them with referrals and training or other child support services (e.g., play material). Such networks are founded on the assumption that provision of training and assistance to caregivers improves the quality of care provided.

A recent study of forty-one sponsored (i.e., supervised), thirty-five licensed, and twenty-three unlicensed FDC homes indicates that this assumption is indeed valid. On the basis of lengthy, naturalistic observations, Hawkins and her colleagues (Carew 1979; Hawkins et al. 1979) found that sponsored caregivers were most involved with their children (e.g., teaching, helping, offering direction), whereas providers in unlicensed homes were least involved. Moreover, these sponsored homes were found to offer safer physical environments (Stallings and Porter 1980). Probably as a consequence of such differences between types of FDC homes, toddlers in the unlicensed homes were more likely to spend time on their own, not interacting with anyone; were most frequently unhappy; and were most inclined to engage in antisocial behavior (Carew 1979). Such differences in caregiving environments and children's experiences in FDC are probably a function, at least in part, of the fact that unlicensed homes tend to have less favorable adult-child ratios than do licensed and supervised homes (Emlen 1977; Hall and Weiner 1977). On the basis of these data it should be clear that, under certain circumstances, variations within a single type of care can be as great as that between CDC, FDC, and HC (Prescott 1973).

The Developmental Effects of Day Care

Before examining the effects of day care on child development, a few comments are in order regarding limitations of available research. First and foremost, most day care research has been carried out on children enrolled in university-sponsored, high-quality day care programs that should not be considered entirely representative of the kind of care most American children receive. This trend, we should note, is gradually changing, as community-sponsored day care becomes more widely available and as social scientists become encouraged to move beyond the controlled environments that university-based programs provide. Although sampling restrictions in day care research may limit the degree to which results can be generalized, this limitation does not necessarily mean that available studies are without significance. Where the evidence indicates that high quality day care is not detrimental to development, there is good scientific reason to refute the claim that daily separation of young children from mother *necessarily* impairs the child's psychological functioning (Fraiberg 1977).

The second limitation of much day care research is its restriction to immediate effects. Since we know little if anything about the long-range impact of day care, we have reason to be cautious in drawing any conclusions, positive or negative, about the effects of day care.

The third and final limitation of day care research to be considered concerns the comparability of samples. The assumption that day-care and home-reared children are comparable is, in all likelihood, invalid, since families that place their children in day care differ in important respects from those that do not (e.g., attitudes toward maternal role) (Hock 1976; Sibbison, 1973). Moreover, as Roopnarine and Lamb (1980) have recently discovered, home-care/group-care differences between children may actually precede enrollment in child care programs. Consequently, except under unusual circumstances (e.g., random assignment of day-care and home-care groups), we can not presume that observed home-care/day-care differences are the result of rearing environment per se.

Having made these cautionary comments, we proceed to consider the effects of day care upon the intellectual, emotional, and social development of young children. In each subsection we will orient the reader to the perspective that American psychologists have brought to each area of study, as we believe that available day care research can be best understood in the context of American culture.

Intellectual Development. Ever since the Soviet Union beat the United States into space with the launching of Sputnik in the 1950s, Americans have displayed great concern for the intellectual development of their children. In point of fact, this concern is one reason why the theories of Piaget and the cognitive perspective in general have come to dominate the American psychological scene over the past two decades. Concern for the effects of day care on intellectual functioning merely reflects this historical influence.

An overwhelming majority of studies of the effects of day care on subsequent intellectual development of children from middle-class households have indicated no differences between day care-reared children and matched home-reared controls (Belsky, Steinberg, and Walker 1982). Although a number of these investigators had found initial gains in one or many test subscales, all significant differences between day-care children and matched controls disappeared during the program or soon after termination. In the only long-term follow-up study in this area, 102 of 120 Swedish children initially investigated by Cochran (1977) during infancy were found at five-and-a-half years of age to be equal in intelligence regardless of whether they had been continuously reared in a day care center, family day care home, or in their own homes by their parents (Gunnarson 1978). For children from relatively advantaged families, then, exposure to day care, even to high-quality, cognitively enriched programs, does not appear to result in any long-term gains in IQ test performance. Neither, though, does it seem that any losses in intellectual performance result from enrollment in day care.

In contrast to this conclusion regarding children from advantaged families, it is significant that positive effects of the day care experience on performance on standardized tests of intellectual development have been reported by a handful of investigators for those children who have been categorized as higher risk than the average middle-class child. We should note, however, that most of the programs in which these economically disadvantaged children were enrolled were specifically designed to provide cognitive enrichment, although they varied widely in the type and degree of special enrichment provided for the children and families involved (Belsky and Steinberg 1978). Lally (1973), for example, found that while 29 percent of a low-level-of-parent education, home-reared group obtained an IQ below 90 on the Stanford-Binet test, only 7 percent of a day-care group from a similar parental background did so. On the basis of these results, it would appear that an enriching day-care experience may reduce some of the adverse affects typically associated with high-risk environments.

Further support for this conclusion comes from a longitudinal study of day care rearing beginning in early infancy (Ramey, Dorval, and Baker-Ward, 1981). In this work, three groups of children were compared: (1) a high-risk experimental group enrolled in a specially designed, cognitive enrichment day-care program; (2) a high-risk, home-reared control group matched to the experimentals on a number of important variables (e.g., social class, age, sex, race); and (3) a general population contrast group reared at home in more economically advantaged households. During the period between six and eighteen months, performance on the mental developmental subscale of the Bayley Infant Test declined for the high-risk controls (from 104 to 86), while it remained stable (near 104) for the high-risk experimentals (who were *randomly* assigned to the day-care rearing group). In addition, motor development subscale scores on this same test revealed significant differences between these two groups favoring the day-care-reared children.

Follow-up comparisons demonstrate that these patterns of decline in the level of functioning for the home-reared, economically disadvantaged children and of stability for their day-care-reared counterparts continue into the child's third, fourth, and fifth years of life. In fact, while only 11 percent of the day-care-reared children are scoring in the range of cognitive-educational handicap (i.e., IQ $\leq$ 85) at age five, a full 35 percent of the home-reared controls are scoring below this level of functioning. Whether such group differences will remain once the experimental day care children enter the public schools is presently being investigated.

The overall picture of evidence, duly qualified, suggests that the day-care experience has neither beneficial nor adverse effects on the intellectual development (as measured by standardized tests) of most children. For economically disadvantaged children, however, day care may have an enduring positive effect, for it appears that such day-care experience may *reduce the declines in test scores* typically associated with high-risk populations after eighteen months of age (Belsky and Steinberg 1978; Belsky, Steinberg and Walker 1982).

Emotional Development. Historically, the mother-child bond has been of prime concern to those interested in the influence of early experience upon emotional development. Psychoanalytic theory and early research on institutionalized children (e.g., Bowlby 1951; Spitz 1945) suggested that any arrangement which deprived the child of continuous access to the mother would impair the development of a strong maternal attachment and thereby adversely affect the child's emotional security.

Since day care, by its very nature, entails the daily separation of mother from child, a good deal of attention has been devoted to discovering whether child care outside the home does indeed disrupt the child's emotional tie to his mother. The major strategy for making such an appraisal has been to observe young children's responses to separation from and reunion with their mothers (usually in an unfamiliar laboratory playroom), and to see whether children prefer to interact with their mothers, their caregivers, or a stranger in free play situations.

In a very early, and therefore noteworthy study, Blehar (1974) observed disturbances in the attachment relationships that children thirty and forty months of age, and enrolled in day care for five months, had developed with their mothers. Specifically, while the thirty-month-old children were more likely to show "anxious-avoidant" attachments to their mothers (more resistance and avoidance behavior and less proximity-seeking during reunion) than were their home-reared counterparts, the forty-month-old children manifested "anxious-ambivalent" attachments (less exploration prior to separation, more crying and searching during separation, and more proximity-seeking *and* resistance behavior to mother during reunion). In each age group, the home-reared comparison subjects were more likely to greet their mothers positively following the stressful separation experience, a behavioral style that is considered to index a secure emotional attachment (Sroufe 1979). Much criticism has been leveled against this study (Belsky and Steinberg 1978), and a recent attempt to replicate Blehar's forty-month results, using many more methodological controls, failed to find the home-care/day-care differences she discerned (Moskowitz, Schwarz, and Corsini 1977).

Results from several other investigations are contradictory in showing that either day care (Cochran 1977; Ricciuti 1974) or home-reared children (Doyle and Somers 1977) are more likely to be distressed upon separation from caregiver. It seems ill-advised, however, to interpret group differences on a single measure as indicative of a meaningful and functionally significant difference in psychological development (Belsky and Steinberg 1978). This would seem especially true in the case of a measure of distress following separation from mother, since Kagan and his colleagues (1976) have observed that distress upon separation shows virtually the same developmental course in children reared in markedly different contexts around the world, suggesting that it may be more maturationally programmed than experientially influenced. This is probably the reason why Kagan, Kearsley, and Zelazo (1978) found, in the most comprehensive and controlled study to date, that between three and a half and thirty months of age day care and home-reared infants did not differ in their emotional responses to separation from mother.

Further evidence of similar patterns of emotional development in day care and home-reared children comes from a series of recent studies of ten to twelve month olds (Brookhart and Hock 1976), five to thirty month olds (Doyle 1975), thirty-six month olds (Roopnarine and Lamb 1980), and forty-one to forty-five month olds (Portnoy and Simmons 1978). In each investigation response to separation from and reunion with mother were generally equivalent between groups that varied in early rearing experience. Why then do Blehar's (1974) previous results differ so markedly? Two explanations come to mind—one historical, the other developmental.

It is important to note that Blehar's children were enrolled in day care in the early 1970s, a time when day care, especially for very young children, was still looked upon negatively by many. Possibly, then, the guilt that parents may have experienced in violating cultural standards, or even the quality of care that was offered when day care was such a relatively new phenomenon, could have adversely influenced the Blehar subjects. Thus, a cohort effect, emphasizing the historical timing of day care enrollment, might be responsible for her divergent results.

Additionally, it needs to be noted that Blehar's children were only in day care for five months when evaluated. Recent evidence indicates that a "transient distress reaction" may be associated with initial adaptation to daily separation from parents and thus may account for Blehar's data. Support for this possibility comes from several sources. First, Portnoy and Simmons (1978), who originally proposed this explanation, were unable to replicate Blehar's results, but studied children who averaged nine and a half months of day care experience prior to assessment. And, in an entirely independent study, Blanchard and Main (1979) found that avoidance of mother, both during daily pick-up from day care and in a structured laboratory situation, decreased the longer that child had been in day care. These findings suggest, then, that young children may go through a period of *stressful adaptation* to supplementary child care. But once they come to understand that regular separation from parent need not imply loss of the attachment figure, adaptation is achieved and problematic behavior is reduced.

We should emphasize that beyond the transient-distress reaction we have just discussed, negative effects of day care may be absent primarily when supplementary child care arrangements are reasonably stable and care is of a reasonable quality. In fact, a recent study of infants enrolled prior to their first birthday in unstable (i.e., frequently changing) day care arrangements reveals that children in such poor quality care arrangements are at risk for developing anxious-avoidant attachment relations with their mothers (Vaughn, Gove, and Egeland 1980). Such attachment relations, it is important to note, have been found to predict problems in adjusting to peers during the preschool years (Arend, Gove, and Sroufe 1979).

Apparently, then, supplementary child care exerts little influence on the child's emotional ties to his or her mother (other than *transient distress*) except when children are from high-risk environments and are enrolled in unstable day care arrangements prior to their first birthday. Under such conditions, infants will be more likely to develop a particular kind of disturbance in their relations with their primary attachment figure: They will be likely to avoid her. Since this avoidance is presumed to result from mother's psychological unavailability, we can reasonably speculate that even under the conditions described above, disturbed attachment relations with mother are not inevitable *if* the quality of maternal care is not compromised during those periods of the day when she is with the infant. Indirect support for this hypothesis comes from the Vaughn, Gove, and Egeland (1980) study, since a full 50 percent of the infants whose mothers went to work prior to their first birthday had established secure attachments to their mothers by the time they were eighteen months of age.

Social Development. Earlier we noted that both economics and ideology play a major role in the utilization of day care in the United States, as increasing numbers of mothers with young children are working outside the home—either for reasons of financial necessity or personal fulfillment. To understand fully such early reliance on group rearing, one also needs to recognize the value that American culture places on independence. In marked contrast to the Japanese, for example, who view their newborn children as independent and thus in great need of developing dependency relations with parents, family, and community, Americans view the newborn child as exceedingly dependent, needing to be weaned from his excessive reliance on others if he is to succeed in a society as competitive and individualistic as the United States (Caudill and Weinstein 1969; Kagan, Kearsley, and Zalazo 1978). Thus, we should not be surprised that one important reason American families place their children in group rearing situations is to give them opportunity to be independent of their families and to learn how to get along with others, most especially their peers. When it comes to assessing the effects of day care on social development, then, primary attention has been directed toward children's behavior toward peers and nonparental adults.

With respect to peer relations, available evidence indicates that day care has both positive and negative effects. On the positive side, Ricciuti (1974) and Kagan and colleagues (1978) have shown that one to two year olds with group experience during infancy are more willing to approach a strange peer or continue their play in the presence of an unfamiliar age mate, and Clarke-Stewart (1979) has reported that two and three year olds cared for in day care centers, nursery schools, or family day care homes display more cooperation while playing with a strange peer and are better able to appraise the perspective of another than are age mates reared by their mother or a babysitter at home. (But note that in the Clarke-Stewart investigation children had been reared at home for their first two years of life.) Data such as these clearly suggest that day care rearing may enhance certain social competencies, probably by providing children with early and increased opportunities to relate to peers. That these effects may be enduring is suggested by Moore's (1975) study of adolescents: Boys who had experienced group rearing prior to the age of five reported higher concern for social activities and were also observed to be more sociable with peers and found to be chosen more regularly by peers as likeable than were boys who were home reared during their preschool years.

On the negative side, Moore (1964) observed that when these children were preschoolers, those in supplementary child care arrangements were more prone to toilet lapses and were more self-assertive. Schwarz et al. (1974) found that preschoolers with day care experience in infancy were more aggressive (both physically and verbally) toward peers than a group of home-reared children who were enrolled in day care for the first time when three to four years old. Finally, researchers have recently reported that the children we mentioned previously (Ramey, Dorval, and Baker-Ward 1981) who were enrolled in a day care/early intervention program since infancy were rated as more hostile by their kindergarten teachers during their first term in public school than were their home-reared counterparts (Ramey, MacPhee & Yeats, 1982). In sum, day care rearing can have negative as well as positive effects on social relations with peers.

When it comes to relations with adults, and the socialization of adultlike behaviors, the available evidence also raises concern. In the Schwarz et al. investigation cited above, observations and teacher reports revealed that preschoolers with extensive day care experience were less cooperative with adults, more physically and verbally aggressive toward them, and somewhat less tolerant of frustration. Results consistent with these data were reported a decade earlier by Ralph et al. (1964) who found that negative interactions between middle- and upper-class first graders and their teachers varied directly with the amount of group rearing the children experienced prior to first grade. Paralleling these results are recent findings from a retrospective analysis of five and six year olds who were reared at home or in day care during the preschool period. Robertson (1982) observed that boys with day care histories were rated by their teachers as substantially and significantly more troublesome than peers cared for at home. Specifically, these day-care-reared boys were more likely to be rated as having little respect for other children and as being quarrelsome, disobedient, and uncooperative.

Additional evidence also indicates that day-care-reared children may orient to peers more than to adults. Schwarz et al. (1974) found, for example, that while preschoolers with prior day care experience interacted more with peers than teachers, the opposite was true of the home-reared children who were having their first group experience at age three to four (Lay and Meyer 1973). Similar results have been reported by McCutcheon and Calhoun (1976) who observed that increased interaction with peers was accompanied by decreased interaction with adults in day care. The implications of this trend are supported by several results from Moore's (1964) initial study that indicate that day-care-reared preschoolers are less conforming and less impressed by punishment.

Given these potentially disturbing effects of day care on social development, several comments are in order. Lest these data be taken as a sweeping indictment of day care rearing, we should note that

> . . . like all social and educational efforts, day-care programs are likely to reflect, and in some measure achieve, the values held explicitly or implicitly by their sponsors and, through them, by the community at large.
>
> From this perspective, the tendency we have observed for all-day group care to predispose children toward greater aggressiveness, impulsivity and egocentricism may represent a phenomenon specific to American society, for these outcomes have been identified as characteristic of socialization in age-segregated peer groups in America generally . . . That the phenomena may indeed be culturebound is indicated by . . . comparative studies of peer group socialization in the United States, the USSR, Israel, and other contemporary societies, which show that, depending on the goals and methods involved, group upbringing can lead to a variety of consequences, ranging from delinquency and violence at one extreme to unquestioning conformity at the other (Belsky and Steinberg 1978, p. 942).

Ambron's (1980) recent suggestion that day care staff are more permissive, more tolerant of disobedience and aggression, and less inclined to set behavior standards than parents is consistent with these conclusions. So too is McCrae and Herbert-Jackson's (1975) claim that the effects of day care may be program-specific. Empirical support for these speculations can be found in Gunnarson's (1978) Swedish day care study, the findings of which contradict much of the data reviewed above. Specifically, naturalistic observations of five year olds reared since infancy in day care centers, family day care homes, or their own homes, revealed no rearing-group differences in children's compliance and cooperation with, and positive affect expressed toward, adults. Moreover, structured doll play assessments of these five year olds revealed that day care children were no more likely than home-reared children to transgress against adult wishes in the face of peer pressures to do so. However, children reared in Swedish day care centers, in comparison to those reared in homes (by family day care providers or mothers), did engage more freqently in information-sharing, compliance, and cooperation with peers. These data demonstrate not only that day care can promote positive peer skills, but that negative interactions with peers and adults need not be more frequent in any rearing environment. This finding leads us to reaffirm the conclusion quoted earlier: The effect of day care on social development is likely to depend on the community and cultural context in which day care is employed as well as the particular practices of the day care program.

Processes of Influence

The simple documentation of group differences between day care- and home-reared children permits us only to speculate on the causes of such differences. Group comparisons offer limited guidance for designing (or redesigning) programs to enhance positive developmental outcomes and minimize the negative consequences of group rearing. Only in the last several years have investigators moved beyond the group-comparison stage of day care evaluation research in an effort to understand the mechanisms that influence differences discerned between day care- and family-reared children.

In the large-scale National Day Care Study, group size and training of caregivers were found to be the most important determinants of variation in preschoolers development across fifty-seven day-care centers in three cities (Travers and Ruopp 1978). Specifically, children cared for in small groups (which we have already noted are characterized by more active teacher involvement and less aimless wandering by children) showed greater improvement across testing periods on examinations designed to measure kindergarten and first-grade reading readiness. Specialized training of staff in subject areas pertinent to child care were related not only to positive classroom caregiver behavior (e.g., social interaction with children, less adult-adult interaction, less management-oriented activities), but also to child achievement. Apparently, then, small group size and caregiver training enhance children's daily experiences in day care, which in turn facilitates cognitive-motivational development.

During the infancy years the ratio of adults to children seems to be another important factor in the development of day-care-reared infants. The National Infant Day Care study revealed this (Ruopp and Travers 1982), as did a recent investigation of two year olds reared in day care centers on the island of Bermuda during their infancy (Schwarz et al., 1981). Having sufficient number of caregivers to rear a group of infants, like having a small group, probably enhances development by assuring quality care. The developmental importance of such quality care is itself highlighted in a large-scale investigation of all kinds of infant day care arrangements in New York City. Specifically, those children who experienced high levels of cognitive stimulation from and social interaction with their caregivers scored higher on measures of social competence and language comprehension when they were three (Golden et al. 1978). Note how these aspects of quality day care mirror the very patterns of sensitive mothering found in Chapter 4 to promote optimal development in home-reared infants and preschoolers.

Quality can characterize both the interpersonal environment and the physical environment. Which is more important? Recent evidence from a study of three to five year olds on the island of Bermuda indicate that what goes on between caregiver and child is most important. Not only were children in centers characterized by high quality on both interpersonal and physical dimensions able to perform better on measures of language development and to be more considerate and sociable than age mates cared for in poor quality centers, but children from centers in which adult-child interaction was frequent and physical plant was poor developed better than those cared for in which physical, but not interpersonal, quality was high (McCartney et al. 1982).

Stability of care is another dimension of quality that needs to be considered in examining process of influence. Unfortunately, and surprisingly, very little work exists on this important topic. Rubenstein and Howes's (1979) recent study of experiences at home and in day care suggests that in addition to the frequent claim that a low turnover rate among staff is in the child's best interest, so too is a stable peer group. Stability has also been implicated as an important dimension of quality care in Cummings's (1980) recent investigation of behavior during separation from mother during daily morning drop-offs at day care. Children averaging twenty-two months of age were more likely to be distressed when left with a caregiver identified as unstable than when left with one with whom the child was very familiar. Finally, the Vaughn, Gove and Egeland (1980) findings reviewed earlier regarding the effect of day care on infant-mother attachment when supplementary care is unstable also underscore the importance of this dimension of the day-care experience.

The significance of stable rearing is likely to be most pronounced when home environment is relatively unstable; for example, when parents are either inconsistent in their own caregiving demands or when there is frequent change in persons moving in or out of the home. In her review of the effects of divorce, Hetherington (1980) makes a similar argument: Constructive relationships with teachers and peers in school, and a relatively structured and predictable environment can reduce the negative effects of a stressful home experience. Because many day care centers and family day care homes create just such an atmosphere via regularly scheduled routines and activities, it is likely that a quality day care experience may be especially important in offsetting the negative effects of divorce.

Summary

As we have shown, supplementary child care is employed today by a large number of families as a strategy for caring for their children. To date, little evidence exists that day care negatively influences intellectual or emotional development. Indeed, under certain circumstances (i.e., center-based rearing of children from impoverished homes) day care can positively influence intellectual functioning, and it appears that only when child care arrangements are unstable and of low quality will emotional development be undermined. The data regarding social relations with peers and adults raises more concern, but, as we have observed, these potentially detrimental effects are probably more a result of the way day care programs have been designed than they are necessary effects of day care.

This should come as no surprise, since, as we have seen, supplementary child care programs very immensely (just like parental care) and this variation seems to determine the day-to-day experiences children have in day care and, as a consequence, the effects of such nonparental care. To summarize, small size groups (less than fifteen to eighteen children) and caregiver training in child development and child care tend to promote active teacher involvement, less aimless wandering by children, infrequent negative interactions, and frequent positive and cognitively stimulating interactions and, thereby, positive developmental outcomes.

CONCLUSION

Despite the evidence that has been reviewed in this chapter concerning the effects of maternal employment and day-care rearing on family functioning and child development, many still regard a mother's working and day care as bad for children. In large measure this is likely to be a function of the fact that traditions die hard; and by tradition, at least in middle-class homes, mothers remained home to rear their children while fathers went to work to "bring home the bacon." This is not to say, however, that there should be no cause for concern in the large numbers of children cared for outside of their homes because both parents are, or their only parent is, employed. When mothers are dissatisfied with a stressful employment situation or when quality of care provided by a day care environment is poor, or when both occur, family functioning and child development are likely to be compromised.

The debate should no longer hinge on whether maternal employment or day care is good or bad for children. The fact of the matter is that mothers work and children are cared for by persons other than their parents. Since it is unlikely that mothers will return in large numbers to the role of full-time homemakers, and that day care will go away, the task is to assure that children experience optimal rearing experiences. The critical issue is the *conditions of care*. We have seen not only that many of the conditions that promote optimal development have been identified, but that they are consistent with what was observed with respect to the care provided by parents in their own homes. These findings should serve to orient those concerned with the well-being of children and their families to the fact that increased attention has to be devoted to insuring that quality rearing experiences are provided wherever a child is placed.

CHAPTER 12

Teenage Pregnancy and Parenthood

A n interesting aspect of the study of children and their parents is the transition from childhood to adolescence to adulthood. Although there are many ways of defining when one period of the life course ends and another begins, this issue is perhaps most perplexing when one considers the case of teenagers who become parents. Such young men and women are likely to find that role definitions change very quickly when one has a child. They are defined as adults and as parents when they otherwise might still be seen as children. Before examining the consequences of teenage parenthood, we consider sexual activity, pregnancy, and the social context surrounding them.

TEENAGE SEXUALITY TODAY

Sex is a great concern of teenagers and of the adults who are responsible for them. It is not difficult to imagine why this is so. Although sexual development begins in childhood, not until adolescence does sexuality become an important focus in the lives of most individuals. The teenagers hormonal balance changes throughout this period of life. As a consequence, the genitals develop to their nearly adult form. And both males and females begin to experience new feelings, including new bodily functions such as menstruation for females and ejaculation for males. Perhaps more important than these physical changes, however, are the social and psychological changes that accompany adolescence. Sexual behavior and sexual interaction take on meaning as the teenager begins to think about social events in school, parties outside of school, love, and dating.

Society has taken a special interest in the topic of teenage sexuality in recent years, undoubtedly because of the vast changes that have taken place in the extent of sexual behavior among young persons. In addition, concern about the potential consequences of sexual involvement during the teen years is growing. Not only is sexuality sometimes a source of anxiety for the individuals who must negotiate adolescence, but it is also the source of some of our society's most troublesome social problems. Indeed, pregnancy outside of marriage is an increasingly prominent feature of the teen years for a sizable segment of American youth. The consequences of pregnancy—abortion, illegitimacy, and early marriage—are all significant social issues. Moreover, many topics pertaining to sexual development, such as homosexuality and incestual relations, are of considerable interest and controversy. Finally, some of our most fervent religious and moral debates revolve around issues such as the acceptability of teenage sexual behavior and contraception.

Incidence of Teenage Sexuality

The number of teenagers who are sexually experienced increased by two-thirds during the 1970s. The increases in sexual activity seen during the 1970s are *not* accounted for primarily by younger teens, although by age fifteen, 18 percent of the boys and 6 percent of the girls have already had sexual intercourse. In the United States today, seven million teenage men and five million teenage women are sexually experienced (Alan Guttmacher Institute, 1981). In other words, twelve million of the nation's twenty-nine million teenagers have had sexual intercourse. In fact, by the time they are nineteen, only a minority of individuals in contemporary America have not had sexual intercourse. A national survey conducted in 1978 (Zelnik and Kantner 1978a, b) found that eight in ten men and seven in ten women had coitus by this age.

The increase in sexual activity over the past decade is attributed mostly to whites, particularly those in the fifteen to seventeen age range. Although age for age the proportion of black teenagers who are sexually active has always been higher than the proportion for whites, this gap is narrowing. Among women who are sexually experienced by the conclusion of their teen years, sixteen was the average age at which intercourse was initiated (Alan Guttmacher Institute 1981). These figures suggest that teenage sexuality is more of the rule than the exception, that it is becoming increasingly common, and that the possibility of teenage pregnancy for women is therefore greater than many realize.

The Role of Contraception

The increased exposure to pregnancy must of course be viewed in relation to contraceptive use, considering both the regularity of contraceptive use and the effectiveness of the methods chosen. Although contraceptive use did increase during the past decade, the trend toward the use of more effective methods—especially the pill—was reversed during the last few years. Although nearly 700,000 pregnancies are averted each year by contraceptive use, more than 300,000 pregnancies could have been averted if young women who did not want to become pregnant used some method of contraception consistently (Alan Guttmacher Institute 1981).

About half of teenage women use no method of contraception at first intercourse. More than 25 percent of sexually active teenagers report that they have never used any method to protect themselves from pregnancy. Only one in three report that they had always practiced contraception. Among the methods of contraception teenagers use when they do attempt to protect themselves from pregnancy, the pill, the condom, and withdrawal are the three favored methods (Alan Guttmacher Institute 1981).

Studies have brought to light a variety of reasons why people have premarital intercourse without adequate contraceptive protection (Lehfeldt 1971; Sandberg and Jacobs 1972; Shah, Zelnik, and Kantner 1975). Among them are ignorance of which contraceptive methods are effective and where to get them; rejection of a method prescribed by a physician because the patient thinks it unsafe; objection to contraception on religious or moral grounds; denial that contraception works; irresponsibility; immaturity; willingness to take risks; availability of abortion; rebellion against society or parents; hostility toward the other sex; equation of love with self-sacrifice; a belief that intercourse is sinful and pregnancy is the punishment; a feeling that pregnancy is a gift of love; the belief that sex is for procreation only; unwillingness to deny oneself or to delay intercourse; a desire of the female to become pregnant; the feeling that "it can't or won't happen to me;" the belief that intercourse is a demonstration of love; the assumption that the girl was too young to become pregnant; and the belief that intercourse was too infrequent or occurred at the wrong time of the month.

Additionally, many young women feel that it is awkward, presumptuous, or unromantic to be contraceptively protected. Many young men and women report that sexual intercourse is something that is supposed to happen "naturally" in a romantic context. Some females are reluctant, when asked to have coitus, to be in a position to reply, "Why yes, I was hoping you would ask, and therefore, I was fitted for a diaphragm yesterday," or "Sure—and I'm OK as far as the pill is concerned. I began taking it last month since I expected that our relationship would come to this."

Teenagers often feel also that the romance is taken out of the situation if they have anticipated it or prepared for it. Moreover, a woman does not want to appear as though she were expecting to have coitus, even though she was.

In future years, it will be increasingly important for parents and persons working with teenagers to pay attention to education about contraception and motivation for contraceptive use. The widespread lack of contraceptive use among teenagers comes at a time in history when the most effective methods of protection ever known to exist are readily available, when state laws restricting the distribution of contraception to minors have finally been eliminated (Paul, Pilpel, and Wechsler 1976), when there are family planning clinics and other health services within driving or commuting distance for virtually all American teenagers, and when knowledge about contraception is at an all-time high. In view of this reality, it is truly depressing how many unplanned and undesired pregnancies occur that could be avoided.

Factors Influencing Sexual Involvement

In recent years there has been a controversy about whether sex education in the public schools encourages teenage sexual behavior. This policy-related question is part of a larger one social scientists have also been interested in recently: What is the process that eventually leads to premarital sexual intercourse? Do parents play a part? Do the mass media have an influence? Do magazines, X-rated movies, or pornography play a part? What about pressures from friends or dating partners? There are now some research data to help answer these questions (Spanier, 1973, 1976).

Data on sexual socialization obtained during interviews with a national sample of about 1,200 college students were grouped into three categories:

1. **Formal sex education**—sex education taught within school classrooms, for example in health, biology, physical education, or family relations classes.

2. **Informal sex education**—sex information obtained from family members, peer groups, or other sources. Examples of informal sex education are a girl who has seen an older man expose himself, two children who are "playing doctor," an adolescent who discovers that touching his or her genitals is pleasurable, a mother telling her daughter about contraception, and a high school student who reads a *Playboy* magazine.

3. **Dating experiences**—frequency of dates, degree of closeness to persons dated, total amount of dating experience, and pressures and influences associated with dating.

The findings of the study showed that of all three types of influence, dating experiences were the most influential in explaining the nature and extent of adolescent sexual behavior. Persons who had a greater dating frequency, were more emotionally involved with the partners they dated, and those who had the most extensive dating history had the most active sex lives. Informal sex education experiences were not as strongly related to a person's sexual behavior, and formal sex education was least related of all.

These findings suggested the context of the person's involvement at the present time is the most influential factor. What the person was taught when growing up does not seem to be as important as what is happening in that person's life at the moment. For example, parents who were very strict and conservative about sexual matters and taught their children accordingly did not have as great an influence as the pressures from a current dating partner. Religiosity at the time of study was more important than religiosity while growing up.

Attendance in sex education classes did not seem to influence sexual behavior one way or another, regardless of when the course was taken, what kind of class it was, who taught it, and whether coitus or birth control was specifically mentioned. (This finding should allay the fears of some persons critical of sex education.) Exposure to erotic materials was related to greater sexual activity, but probably exposure to erotic materials and sexual behavior are correlated, but not causally related. In other words, they both seem to be an increasingly likely occurrence, but one cannot be attributed as the cause of the other. This research suggests, then, that the pressures and influences an individual faces in a given relationship can be powerful enough to outweigh all other teaching to the contrary.

EXTENT OF TEENAGE PREGNANCY AND PARENTHOOD

During the 1970s, the number of pregnancies increased among teenagers, despite the increased and more consistent use of contraceptives. In other words, the rate of pregnancy has been increasing more slowly than the rate of sexual activity. However, with the larger numbers of teenagers not using contraception at first intercourse, and many being protected only intermittently thereafter, the total exposure to pregnancy — and the actual numbers of pregnancies to teens — has continued to increase. *There are now more than one million pregnancies each year involving teenage women*, most involving unmarried teens (Alan Guttmacher Institute 1981).

A startling statistic is that one-fifth of teenage premarital pregnancies occur within one month after initiation of coitus, and half occur within six months. Eight in ten of these premarital pregnancies are unintended, as are two-thirds of the teenage births. Teenagers represent nearly half of all out-of-wedlock births and nearly one-third of all abortions. If the current pattern continues through the 1980s, we anticipate that four out of ten girls now in the midteens will be pregnant before they reach the age of twenty, and about two in ten will give birth. For every one hundred such girls, about fifteen can be expected to have an abortion before they reach twenty (Alan Guttmacher Institute 1981).

Some teenage females do not feel that the risk of pregnancy is very great for them. But it is evident how mistaken this belief is. Fifty-eight percent of sexually active teenagers who have never used contraception had already been pregnant at least once by the date of the survey. Forty-two percent of the sometimes users had been pregnant. And even 11 percent of those always using contraception had been pregnant. The lowest pregnancy rates — about 6 percent — were for females who had always used an effective medical method, such as birth control pills. Another analysis of teenage pregnancy considered females below the age of fifteen. Jaffee and Dryfoos (1976) estimated that 30,000 young girls under age fifteen become pregnant each year in the United States.

What do American teenagers do when faced with a pregnancy? One recent analysis of teenage pregnancy, including both married and unmarried teens (Alan Guttmacher Institute 1981) found that the largest share of the pregnancies, 38 percent, ended in abortion. Twenty-two percent resulted in out-of-wedlock births, 17 percent were postmaritally conceived births, 10 percent were legitimated births premaritally conceived (the woman married following the pregnancy but delivered the child after the wedding), and 13 percent of the pregnancies were miscarriages. There are now more than 1.5 million abortions each year in the United States, with about one-third of them performed for teenage women.

There are some significant racial differences in how the outcome of a pregnancy is managed. Whites are about four times as likely as blacks to marry after discovering that they are pregnant. Data on abortion among blacks are not as reliable as that available for whites, but Zelnik and Kantner (1978c) estimate that blacks are much more likely to carry a premarital pregnancy to term, while whites are much more likely to have an abortion. About five out of every six black teenage females who report ever being pregnant state that they continued the pregnancy and had the child. Considering this tendency to continue a pregnancy and their lesser likelihood of marriage following a pregnancy, we can easily understand why young black females have an illegitimacy rate substantially higher than that of whites.

Young women giving birth to a baby can either keep the child or give it up for adoption. Approximately 18 percent of babies born to unmarried white adolescents are given up for adoption, and an additional 6 percent live with other relatives or friends of the mother (Zelnik & Kantner, 1978a,b). Thus, more than three-fourths of illegitimate white babies are not given up for adoption. This may account for the relative scarcity of white babies available for adoption in a period when many married couples are becoming increasingly willing to adopt children (Baldwin 1976). Only 6 percent of the infants born to unmarried teenage black females live with anyone other than their mothers. Thus, black females are even less likely to give their children up for adoption.

Only a minority of teenage women now marry as a result of an unexpected pregnancy. If the female was engaged when the pregnancy started and her fiance is the father of the child, the situation is as favorable as it could be under the circumstances. If she marries a man whom she would not otherwise marry, the marriage gets an unfavorable start. If she marries a man she knows is not the father of the child and does not tell him she is pregnant, in some states the man has grounds for annulment or divorce, should that fact become known after the wedding. At best, such a procedure is a serious form of misrepresentation. A woman may, and in some cases does, marry a man who accepts the child even knowing that he is not the father.

If a couple have intercourse when they are not ready to marry, will they be more ready if a pregnancy leads them to marry earlier? Evidence suggests that marriages entered in order to camouflage a premarital pregnancy may be more unstable that would otherwise be expected. The divorce rate is more than twice as high for those marriages in which childbirth occurs before the wedding. The difference in divorce rates is not as great, however, when conception, but not childbirth, occurred before marriage (Grabill 1976).

The actual teenage birthrate in the United States is among the world's highest. It is, for example, more than twice the birth rate in Sweden, Spain, and France. It is more than three times the rate in the Soviet Union, and seventeen times as great as the birthrate for teens in Japan. Several European countries, such as Czechoslovakia and Hungary, do have higher birthrates amongst teenagers (Alan Guttmacher Institute 1981). In Figure 12.1 the increasing number of illegitimate births over the past twenty-five years is plotted in graphic form.

About 600,000 U.S. births each year involved unmarried women, and most of these women are teenagers (National Center for Health Statistics 1981b). The high out-of-wedlock birthrate to teenagers has continued to grow during the past decade, although the increase can be attributed primarily to whites. Out-of-wedlock birthrates among blacks actually declined during the past decade, although teenage blacks are still much more likely than teenage whites to become pregnant and to have a child. Considering all teenage mothers and their children, there are now about 1.3 million children living with 1.1 million teenage women. More than half of these children have mothers who are not married. Two-thirds of the children were born to mothers aged seventeen or younger (Alan Guttmacher Institute 1981).

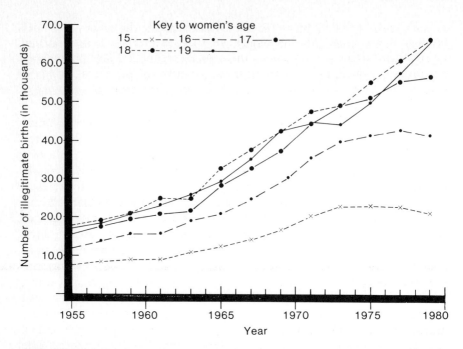

Figure 12.1 *Number of illegitimate live births to teenage women by age of woman, 1955–1979.*

Source: National Center for Health Statistics, *Monthly Vital Statistics Reports,* "Advance Report: Final Natality Statistics" (various nos.).

CONSEQUENCES OF TEENAGE PARENTHOOD

For the family of a pregnant teenager, the experience of teenage parenthood is often a social embarrassment as well as an economic strain. Parents who had considered their child-rearing years to be coming to an end may find themselves with the responsibility of supporting, if not caring for, a child born to their teenager. Needless to say, the life courses of these parents change dramatically as a consequence of their offsprings' premature entry to parenthood. Conflicts between teenage parents and their own parents are likely to increase, especially since many teenage mothers are forced to live at home. Invariably, difficulties arise regarding how the child is to be reared and who is responsible for its well-being.

It is important to note, however, that the meaning and implications of a teenage pregnancy varies depending upon the family in question. In some households, and particularly in some subcultures, reactions are likely to be less extreme if only because such life course events are not totally unexpected given the community context in which they take place. In a suburban, middle-class white home, on the other hand, a teenage pregnancy is far more likely to be viewed as a disruptive event.

For the child being born, and the teenager, the risks of teenage pregnancy are great. In this section of this chapter we review current knowledge of the consequences of teenage pregnancy and parenthood. Specifically, we focus upon medical risk to both the mother's and child's health, educational and economic impact upon the teenager, and the effect of early childbearing on parenting.

Medical Consequences

For both mother and child, teenage pregnancy represents a medical risk. In the case of mothers, teenage pregnancy is more likely to be the cause of several obstetrical complications that can create serious problems for the infant. Young mothers, for example, have been found to be more toxemic and have more cases of pre-eclampsia and iron-deficiency anemia (Crider 1976). Moreover, they appear more susceptible to urinary tract infections, prolonged labor, and death during childbirth (Magrab and Danielson-Murphy no date). In fact, in 1977–1978, the maternal death rate among mothers under age fifteen was 18 per 100,000 live births—two and one-half times the rate for mothers aged twenty to twenty-four (Alan Guttmacher Institute 1981).

Probably as a consequence of these and related disorders, babies born to girls seventeen or younger face greater health hazards than do those born to older mothers. These hazards can be conceptually distinguished by differentiating morbidity (damage) and mortality (death). Available evidence indicates that babies born to teenage mothers are more likely to die before their first birthday. In 1974, the infant mortality rate of children born to white mothers under fifteen years of age was about 44 per 1,000 infants, whereas for children of mothers aged fifteen to nineteen, the corresponding figure was 31 per 1,000, and for mothers aged twenty to twenty-four, the figure was 19 per 1,000 (Stickle 1974). In other studies published around this same time, the mortality rate of offspring of teenage parents has been reported to be 28 percent to 200 percent greater than that of children whose mothers are twenty to thirty-four years of age (Nortman 1974). In 1981, the Alan Guttmacher Institute reported data from New York State indicating that between 1974 and 1978, babies born to teenage mothers were almost twice as likely to die as those born to mothers in their twenties. In fact, infant mortality rate of teenage mothers exceeded that of mothers in their forties, another group known to be at risk for newborn complications.

On the basis of these data, it is clear not only that offspring of teenage mothers are at greater risk of death in their first year, but also that the younger the mother is at conception and birth, the greater the likelihood of the child's early death (Nye 1976). Unfortunately, the same relationship is true with respect to infant morbidity. In part because teenage mothers have not yet achieved their full biological maturity and also because of their less than optimal diets and poorer prenatal care, babies born to teenage mothers are more likely to be born with birth defects creating potentially lifelong detrimental consequences.

The most well-studied morbidity problem of offspring of teenage mothers is prematurity and low birthweight (Nye 1976). In 1973, the rate of prematurity for mothers aged fifteen to nineteen was 10.3 percent, whereas that for mothers older than nineteen was 7.6 percent (Crider 1976). Statistics from more recent years show much the same pattern. In 1975, for example, the rate of prematurity was 19.5 percent for mothers less than fifteen years of age, 9 percent for nineteen-year-old mothers and 7.1 percent for mothers aged twenty to twenty-four (McAnarney 1978; Stickle and Ma 1975). In 1977, Cooper (1977) reported that while adolescent pregnancies account for 20 percent of all births they are responsible for 26 percent of all low birthweight deliveries. Finally, the most recent data (for 1978) reveal that mothers fifteen and younger are twice as likely to bear a premature or low birthweight infant than are those aged twenty to twenty-four, and that among all teenagers the risk of such births is 39 percent higher. As with all other problems, risk declines with the age of the mother, but even mothers aged nineteen have rates of high-risk births 27 percent greater than those who delay childbearing until their early twenties (Alan Guttmacher Institute 1981).

As noted in Chapter 7, prematurity is an important diagnostic indicator of other problems that children are likely to have. Thus, in the same way that children born to young mothers are at increased risk for prematurity, they also are at risk for other developmental problems, including cerebral palsy, epilepsy, mental retardation, birth defects, deafness, and blindness (Crider 1976). We should note that, to the extent that prematurity and birth complications play a causal role in increasing the risk of such developmental disabilities, the negative consequences of teenage pregnancy are preventable. Recent research and intervention programs demonstrate that by assuring that pregnant teenage adolescents begin prenatal care early in pregnancy and maintain an adequate diet, rate of prematurity and other associated problems can be reduced (Osofsky and Osofsky 1970; Perkins et al. 1978).

In actuality, the problematic biological and developmental consequences associated with prematurity and, therefore, with adolescent pregnancy do not seem directly attributable to these causal agents per se. Available evidence indicates that prematurity is a risk factor primarily when linked to economic deprivation. That is, primarily when children are at dual risk—born prematurely and raised in an economically stressed family environment, the developmental disabilities are related to high risk birth (Sameroff and Chandler 1975). As we have already noted, unfortunately in most cases, teenage parents are likely to be at economic risk, thereby increasing the risk associated with their offspring's biological status.

Maternal Educational Attainment

The number of years of school one completes during childhood and adolescence is one of the best predictors of many individual life outcomes, including income, occupation, fertility, and unemployment. As most people are aware, the more education that one acquires, the more income they are likely to earn, the higher status occupations they are likely to find themselves in, and the fewer children they are likely to bear. Clearly, educational attainment is an important characteristic of one's life course.

Researchers have repeatedly found that teenage pregnancy exerts one of its most devastating impacts upon the years of education a woman receives. In general, women who bear children during adolescence tend to complete fewer years of schooling than their peers who become mothers later in life (Card and Wise 1978; Furstenburg 1976; Moore and Waite 1977). In 1967, nearly six of every ten women who bore their first child at age sixteen or younger had completed eight or fewer years of schooling (Bacon 1969). In a more recent study, Furstenburg (1976) found that teenagers who bore children while still in high school were significantly more likely to leave school without graduating than were their classmates who were not pregnant. Moreover, these same girls were much less likely to achieve their previously anticipated education goals, for example, receiving a high school diploma or going to college.

The most comprehensive study to date of the association between teenage pregnancy and limited schooling was conducted by Moore and Waite (1977) who gathered data on teenage mothers between 1968 and 1978. Importantly, in trying to specify cause and effect relationships, information on family origin was gathered and taken into account. Results revealed that by twenty-four years of age, the age at which a woman had her first child was an important predictor of years of schooling—even after taking into account potentially confounding factors such as number of siblings in the mother's family and her social class. More specifically, girls who had their first child at age fifteen or younger averaged 2.8 fewer years of education by the time they were twenty-four than did those who were childless into their mid-twenties. For women bearing their first child between sixteen and seventeen years, educational loss amounted to 1.4 years on the average. Interestingly, the effect of teenage pregnancy on schooling was less pronounced in the case of blacks, and Moore and Waite (1977) speculate that because the black community is more accepting of teenage parenthood, it is more likely to provide the necessary support required to enable mothers to remain in school. Nevertheless, for blacks and whites alike, every additional year that passed without children was found to be associated with increased years of schooling.

A major question asked by Moore and Waite (1977) involved the possibility of catching up for early childbearers. Results of analyses revealed that teenage mothers do not catch up to later childbearers in terms of their schooling. In fact, from ages eighteen to twenty-four the education gap between early and late childbearers actually widens. Thus, early childbearing is more than a temporary setback in one's educational career. And for mothers under nineteen years of age and still in high school, it appears to be the cause of school dropout.

Why should teenage pregnancy exert such a negative impact upon schooling? As Moore and Waite (1977, p. 225) succinctly conclude:

> The negative impact of early childbearing on a woman's educational attainment is probably due to the difficulty and cost of arranging child care and running a household (if a woman heads her own household or is married), to the necessity of earning a living, and, not least, to the pressures she encounters from family and friends to devote herself to child care.

To this list it is important to add the practices and policies of school systems. Until recently, many schools encouraged pregnant teenagers to terminate their education by leaving school. In recent years, this practice has been revised, with many schools developing programs specifically geared toward the needs of the teenage mother. We expect that such essential support systems, which often provide child care in the school setting itself so that teenage mothers can attend classes, will lessen the detrimental effect that teenage parenthood has on the teenager's individual development and eventual life course.

Income, Occupation, and Family Size

The association between individual and family earnings and teenage parenthood cannot be understood until the broader social context of this experience is appreciated. As already stated, women who bear their first child in adolescence tend to terminate their schooling earlier than age mates who delay childbearing. Since education and income are positively related, one would expect teenage parenthood to predict poor financial status. We shall soon see that this is indeed the case.

But education alone is not responsible for the poor financial status of families of women bearing children in their teenage years. Related to poor education, and probably a consequence of it, is the poorer employment status of both men and women who become parents as teenagers (Moore 1978; Nye and Berardo 1973). In a longitudinal study based upon an original survey of some 375,000 high school students first studied in 1980, Card and Wise (1978) found that, over the long term, young mothers suffer more than young fathers. By the time they were twenty-nine years of age, teenage mothers had less prestigious jobs and were less satisfied with their jobs than classmates who did not get pregnant in high school. Eleven years after high school it was found that adolescent childbearers (both mothers and fathers) were significantly more likely to have blue collar jobs and significantly less likely to be professionals.

Also important to understanding the teenage parenthood-income relationship is the subsequent fertility and, thus, family size of women who have their first baby during adolescence. Not only do early childbearers become parents before their peers, they also go on to have more offspring (Moore 1978). This fact is documented in two national surveys (Moore 1978). In one it was found that by age twenty-four, women who began childbearing at fifteen or younger had an average of three children, whereas those who did not become pregnant for the first time until after nineteen had significantly fewer. In another study aimed at obtaining a picture of family size once childbearing is completed, it was found that among women aged thirty-five to fifty-two in 1976, those having their first child at or prior to age seventeen bore over five children each, on the average, whereas women who were at least twenty at the time of first child averaged close to three children. We should recognize that not only does a larger family size make it more difficult for a mother to work, but it also requires that whatever resources she or her spouse (or both) earn must be shared among a larger number of persons. Moreover, a teenage mother is more likely to be the sole earner in the family—either because she has not married or because her marriage has ended. As noted in Chapter 2, teenage marriages are significantly more likely to end in divorce.

All these forces coalesce to produce a situation in which early fertility and low income covary with one another. In one national survey, Moore (1978) found that young women were better off at age twenty-seven by $153 (in 1976 dollars) for each year that they had postponed the birth of their first child. Moreover, the probability of these mothers being in poverty fell an average of 1.6 percent per year of delay.

Not only do lower incomes pose difficulties for a teenage mother and her family, but available evidence also indicates that they play a burden on the society at large. More specifically, the greater poverty experienced by early childbearers translates into higher welfare costs for the government. An analysis conducted for the U.S. House of Representatives Select Committee on Population (Moore 1978) revealed that federal and state governments provided more than $4.5 billion in 1975 through Aid to Families with Dependent Children (AFDC) to families with a mother who had her first child while still a teenager. This figure represented almost one half of the total amount expended in welfare payments through AFDC!

Parenting

"Children rearing children," that is one way in which some have characterized teenage parenthood. Even the most experienced parents have little doubt that parenting is a time-consuming and energy-depleting activity. For teenage parents, still in the process of growing up themselves, the task of parenthood complicates two distinct developmental imperatives—the teenager's own growth and that of the child.

Unfortunately, very little work has been done examining the parenting of teenagers. The findings of an early, uncontrolled study of high school marriages suggested that teenage parents have unrealistic expectations regarding what their babies can do and when they will achieve basic developmental landmarks, like sitting up, rolling over, walking, and talking (DeLissovoy, 1973). The results of a more recent investigation tend to substantiate the conclusion that teenage parents have little appreciation of child development (Epstein 1979); though upon first analysis they seem to contradict DeLissovoy's (1973) results.

Whereas DeLissovoy's (1973) found that teenage parents expect "too much, too soon" from their infants, Epstein (1979) reported, in an investigation of ninety-eight teenage parents between fourteen and nineteen (the average age equaled sixteen and a half) years of age, that pregnant teenagers expect "too little, too late" from their newborn babies. Prenatal evaluations assessing maternal knowledge of when babies achieve specific developmental landmarks indicated that teenage mothers frequently scored developmental accomplishments as occurring later than they in fact do, and infrequently scoring developmental accomplishments as occurring earlier than they do. Most importantly, the inaccuracies the teenagers displayed were most likely to involve areas of mental development. Specifically, mothers tended to regard babies prior to eight months as creatures of physical needs and growth without corresponding mental activity. In sum, the teenagers tended to view the baby as a mere eater-eliminator-sleeper rather than a social being capable of interacting with others and processing information about the world around him.

On the basis of these two studies, there seem to be strong grounds to expect dysfunctional, or at least nonoptimal, patterns of parenting. In certain cases such dysfunctional caregiving may stem from attributing too little to the child, whereas in other cases exactly the opposite might happen. Note that the consequences of each misattribution are problematic. If expectations are too high, then the frustration of dealing with a child whose behavior is regarded as "incompetent," or worse, "disobedient" could easily lead to parent-child conflict. Expecting too little, in contrast, could easily result in failing to provide stimulation for and encouragement of developmental processes that would otherwise support later development.

Support for the view that such distortions in viewing the child could actually undermine parental functioning comes from recent work on mother-infant interactions. Both Field (1982) and Brown and Bakeman (1977) have observed teenage mothers interacting with their infants and found these mothers frequently insensitive to the subtle behavioral cues their offspring provide. Thus, some teenage mothers tend to overload the arousal systems of infants who are often premature, thereby fostering brief and disruptive interactive exchanges. Recall that it is the presence of just such insensitivity that has been linked repeatedly with less than optimal infant development.

Recent work indicates that parenting patterns of teenage mothers such as those just noted are not inevitable. Analysis of mother-infant interaction patterns in a study of women thirteen to thirty-nine years old revealed no differences as a function of maternal age (McLaughlin et al. 1979). This striking failure to discern an influence of adolescent status on parenting, the researchers surmise, was a function of the intervention program available to the mothers in this study. More specifically, the teenage parents in this work were participating in a comprehensive child care project that provided prenatal care, prenatal education, labor and delivery care, and both medical and educational-psychological support following the baby's birth. Moreover, it was designed to overcome some of the effects poverty is known to have on child health and development. On the basis of McLaughlin et al.'s (1979) study of parenting, it appears that the extensive support involvement in the project provided had a positive impact, diverting some of the negative effects usually associated with teenage pregnancy and parenthood.

CONCLUSION

The fact that a female is biologically capable of bearing a child prior to graduation from high school, and even during the early years of junior high school, does not mean that she is ready for the responsibilities that parenthood entails. Nevertheless, as we have seen, increasing numbers of children are having children.

In earlier epochs, such youthful childbearing and childrearing probably did not represent the problem it does currently. With extended families available in tribal and even preindustrial societies to provide child care assistance, and with early childbearing a cultural norm, becoming pregnant as a teenager was consistent with cultural practices. In contemporary American society, however, where children are not expected until after graduation from high school and in the context of marriage, becoming pregnant during the teen years remains out-of-synch with current cultural practices. Such poor timing of parenting undoubtedly increases the risk to mother and child alike, above and beyond any medical risk associated with limited reproductive maturity. This observation once again underlines the need to consider context, in this case the broader cultural context, in understanding the child in the family. Whereas teenage parenthood might once have been the norm, today it remains the exception, even though the rate of such pregnancies is on the increase.

Conclusions

13

C hildren are active and interactive organisms from the moment of their birth, if not before. They affect their family, as well as being affected by it, and thus foster many of the changes in structure and function that characterize family life. In this book we have attempted to describe key features of these reciprocal relations between infant, child, and adolescent development and changes in the family. Our goal has been to illustrate the benefit of studying child-family relations with a perspective that emphasizes the life-span and ecological bases of these relations. As such, preceding chapters have indicated the following:

1. By influencing those who influence them, children are "producers" of their own development;

2. The family is composed of people who have several roles; for example, parents are also spouses and often workers outside the home. The child's influence will involve these other roles. For instance, children may affect their own development by influencing the marital relations of their parents; this, in turn, affects the parents' caregiving behaviors. In addition, parents' role in the work place can have an impact upon spousal or caregiving roles;

3. As a consequence of reciprocal, life-span-enduring relations between children and their families, there is a potential for change, for plasticity, across life on the parts of both children and their families. Because of the embeddedness of children and families, one can alter undesired child developments by influencing the family and, in turn, one can modify family life by affecting child development;

4. Therefore, considerable reason exists to be optimistic about the ability to intervene to enhance the human condition. Let us consider these implications for intervention in somewhat more detail.

IMPLICATIONS FOR INTERVENTION

The implications of a life-span, ecological orientation for interventions aimed at enhancing child-family relations are quite important. As noted in the opening chapters and throughout this volume, the presence of plasticity provides a rationale for attempting intervention, and the reciprocal relations between children and families enables one to approach a target of intervention from multiple levels. That is, a problem in child development may be dealt with by directly treating the child or it may be dealt with by altering the family and family-child interactions. In fact, because of the embeddedness of child and family in a broader ecology, one may effect changes in either child, family, or child-family interaction by focusing one's efforts at the community or societal levels. For instance, child abusive family interactions may be dealt with by intervening with a particular family directly, by altering the nature of the social supports in the community surrounding the family, or by changing the laws governing the ability of societal institutions to intercede in such family situations.

Additional implications for intervention derive, of course, from the life-span developmental nature of child-family relations. A developmental perspective suggests preventative interventions: with knowledge of children's and parents' expected developmental trajectories, one can avoid undesired behaviors by acting to eliminate their bases *before* they, in fact, occur. For example, one can prevent some of the misperceptions by adolescents and parents of each other, misperceptions that, as we have seen, lead adolescents to believe they are more different from their parents than they actually are and parents to believe they are less different from their children than they actually are (Lerner and Knapp 1975). Such prevention can be accomplished by explaining to parents and adolescents the respective developmental bases of their perceptions (i.e., adolescents need to establish an identity and parents need to feel generative), and having the family members jointly discuss their respective needs and decide themselves on ways that both generation's interests can be met.

Of course, a life-span perspective potentially extends the scope of intervention efforts beyond the specific life courses of any one family. Every family develops within a specific historical epoch. The characteristics of the historical moment influence the life-span development of all family members (Elder 1974) and, in turn, the nature of family life that is thereby shaped can influence future families. That is, children typically develop into adults having their own children, and thus their own childhood developments can influence those of their children; there is intergenerational transmission. The presence of such transmission presents yet another route to preventative intervention. For example, infants born to mothers who drink excessive amounts of alcohol during pregnancy develop a disorder labeled Fetal Alcohol Syndrome (FAS); these infants often are hyperactive, show mild mental retardation, and have physical anomalies. One might prevent the birth of FAS-affected babies by intervening with women who are "at risk" for becoming mothers because they drink excessively before the women become pregnant, indeed before they become fertile. Women alcoholics often come from low socioeconomic backgrounds or from backgrounds where poor nutrition is the norm. Nutritional education, provision of social support during childhood and adolescence, and birth control counseling and education are all strategies that may be employed with a female years before she becomes pregnant. By altering the dietary habits and prenatal "chemical environment"—essentially, by intervening when the potential mother is still "plastic"—there is the possibility of breaking the cycle of unhealthy intergenerational transmission and preventing the birth of FAS-affected infants.

We should note, however, that a life-span, ecological perspective also draws attention to potential problems that may arise as a consequence of intervention efforts. A key problem relates to the issues of direct and indirect intervention effects and of planned and unplanned consequences. If a child's plasticity both derives from and contributes to the multiple levels of context within which a child interacts, then one must anticipate that actualizing the potential for plasticity at any one level will influence changes among other variables, both at that level and at other levels. From this perspective, one should always expect that any direct and/or intended effect of one's intervention will have indirect, and often, unintended consequences (Willems 1973).

Such a recognition leads to two points. First, interventions should not be initiated without some conceptual or theoretical analysis of the potential indirect and unintended consequences. For instance, change in a spouse's assertiveness may be the direct, intended effect of a cognitive-behavior therapist's efforts. However, the changed assertiveness might lead to a lessening of marital quality and, in addition, to a divorce, and thus to an impact on the child. Such indirect effects might have been unintended by the therapist and undesired by either therapist or client. Thus, our view is that one must think quite seriously about the potential "ripple" effects of one's intervention efforts. Clearly, an ecological, life-span perspective, like the one we have been using, would be of use in this regard. This perspective would sensitize one to the general possibility of, and perhaps some specific instances of, indirect effects of one's intervention efforts. Such reflection will be useful in several ways, a major one of which is that undesirable indirect effects may be anticipated; if so, then the issue of cost-benefit ratios can be engaged before intervention begins: What will the benefit of an intervention be? What will be the likely cost? Do the potential benefits outweigh the potential costs? If the answer is yes, intervention may proceed.

Of course, the fact that undesired effects may arise from one's intervention efforts raises the point that plasticity is a double-edged sword. While plasticity permits interventions to be planned in order to enhance the target person's life condition, indirect effects may adversely alter either the condition or the context. Moreover, this problem is complicated by recognizing that as a consequence of people being reciprocally related to their multilevel contexts, a failure to intervene, to alter the context of life, is itself an intervention (i.e., it keeps the context on a trajectory it might have been taken off of if one had acted). Thus, one must assess the cost-benefit ratio not only of one's actions, but also of one's abstaining from acting.

RESEARCH METHODOLOGY ISSUES

The potentials and problems of a life-span, ecological perspective are not limited to intervention possibilities. There are pertinent issues with respect to research as well. Throughout this book we have indicated the substantial conceptual and empirical benefits associated with adopting a life-span, ecological approach to the study of child-family relations. Here, however, we should point out that this approach has not been adopted generally by behavioral and social scientists—indeed it was not until the 1970s that major interest arose in the application of such an approach to the study of child-family relations (Hartup 1978; Lerner, Hultsch, and Dixon in press)—and one reason for this lack of use is that there are several issues of research methodology that remain to be addressed.

For instance, one reason that there has been relatively little consideration of reciprocal child-family interactions is that data collection and data analytic strategies capable of dealing with the circular relations involved have not been adequate (cf. Lewis and Lee-Painter 1974). This problem is the major obstacle in exploring child-family reciprocities. Lerner and Spanier (1978) note that no existing method of data collection or technique of analysis is totally adequate. Of course, the theories that will nurture the empirical inventions once they are born have not been present long enough to advance our thinking greatly. As a consequence, we can now do no more than suggest the dimensions of future methods and analysis techniques that will have to be devised.

In regard to method, we will have to establish procedures to record reciprocal interchanges at all possible levels of analysis. We will also have to devise observational techniques capable of recording the molecular, moment-by-moment reciprocities involved in infant-mother interactions. Additionally, we will need procedures capable of providing an index of the molar reciprocities involved, for instance, an intergenerational transmission of influence (Bengtson and Troll 1978). Moreover, we will need to observe still more elusive interchanges, as between sociocultural change and individual ontogeny, and to understand simultaneously the reciprocal aspects of several, if not all, levels in each research effort.

These methodological issues might seem to preclude the exploration of reciprocal child-family interaction. However, we believe that because of the demonstrated theoretical and empirical need to study these interfaces, research consistent with a reciprocal model must indeed proceed. Although we must keep the limitations of such research in mind rather than ask only those questions we can adequately answer, let us address issues at the "cutting edge" of conceptual advancements. Only thus may we hope to stimulate methodological development.

A NOTE OF OPTIMISM

We have stressed that a life-span and human ecological-based conception of reciprocal relations between children and their families leads to a multilevel, and hence multidisciplinary, approach to human development, to a focus on the potential for plasticity across life, and to an appreciation of the role of the individual as an active producer of his or her own development.

In addition, we have pointed to some of the key intervention and methodological issues that remain to be resolved if this perspective is to be successfully used not only to study child-family relations, but also to intervene to enhance such relations. Pessimism because of the presence of these problems is not warranted, however. Every approach to human development has limitations; because there are problems to be resolved in regard to a life-span, ecological viewpoint does not single it out from other developmental paradigms.

Indeed, given that this perspective came to the fore only within the 1970s, the clearness with which the problems have been articulated (Bronfenbrenner 1977), the methodological advances that have already been made (e.g., see Nesselroade and Baltes 1979), and the several data sets that speak to the empirical use of the perspective (e.g., Baltes, Reese, and Lipsitt 1980; Brim and Kagan 1980; Bronfenbrenner 1979; Lerner and Busch-Rossnagel 1981; Lerner and Spanier 1978), are reasons for great optimism for the future. The life-span, ecological perspective represents a "different drummer" for the study of human development. Although as yet still playing relatively softly, the beat is steady, growing in intensity, and compelling. The 1980s and 1990s may see more and more scientists begin to try to dance to the music.

References

Adelson, J. What generation gap? *New York Times Magazine*, January 18, 1970.

Ainsworth, M. D. S. *Attachment: Retrospect and prospect.* Presidential address to the biennial meeting of the Society for Research in Child Development, San Francisco, March 1979.

Ainsworth, M. D. S. The development of infant-mother attachment. In B. M. Caldwell & H. N. Ricciuti (Eds.), *Review of child development research* (Vol. 3). Chicago: University of Chicago Press, 1973.

Ainsworth, M. D. S., & Bell, S. M. Some contemporary patterns of mother-infant interaction in the feeding situation. In A. Ambrose (Ed.), *Stimulation in early infancy.* New York: Academic Press, 1969.

Ainsworth, M. D. S., & Bell, S. M. Mother-infant interaction and the development of competence. In K. J. Connolly & J. Bruner (Eds.), *The growth of competence.* New York: Academic Press, 1974.

Ainsworth, M. D. S., Bell, S. M., & Stayton, D. J. Individual differences in strange situation behavior of one-year-olds. In H. R. Schaffer (Ed.), *The origins of human social relations.* New York: Academic Press, 1971.

Ainsworth, M. D. S., Bell, S. M., & Stayton, D. J. Individual differences in the development of some attachment behaviors. *Merrill-Palmer Quarterly*, 1972, *18*, 123–143.

Ainsworth, M. D. S., Bell, S. M., & Stayton, D. J. Infant-mother attachment and social development: "Socialization" as a product of reciprocal responsiveness to signals. In M. P. M. Richards (Ed.), *The integration of a child into a social world.* London: Cambridge University Press, 1974.

Ainsworth, M., Blehar, M., Waters, E., & Wall, S. *Patterns of attachment: A psychological study of the strange situation.* Hillsdale, N.J.: Lawrence Erlbaum Associates, 1978.

Ainsworth, M., & Wittig, B. Attachment and exploratory behavior of one-year-olds in a strange situation. In B. M. Foss (Ed.), *Determinants of infant behavior* (Vol. 4). London: Methuen, 1969.

Alan Guttmacher Institute. *Teenage pregnancy: The problem that hasn't gone away.* New York: The Alan Guttmacher Institute, 1981.

Aldous, J. Family interaction patterns. *Annual Review of Sociology*, 1977, *3*, 105–135.

Almquist, E. M. Sex stereotype in occupational choice: The case for college women. *Journal of Vocational Behavior*, 1974, *5*, 13–21.

Almquist, E. M., & Angrist, S. S. Role model influences on college women's career aspirations. *Merrill-Palmer Quarterly*, 1971, *17*, 263–279.

Almquist, E. M., & Angrist, S. S. Career salience and atypicality of occupatonal choice among college women. *Journal of Marriage and the Family*, 1970, *32*, 242–249.

Alvy, K. Preventing child abuse. *American Psychologist*, 1975, *30*, 921–928.

Ambron, S. Causal models in early education research. In S. Kilmer (Ed.), *Advances in early education and child care* (Vol. 2). Greenwich, Conn.: JAI Press, 1980.

Anthony, E. J. The behavior disorders of children. In P. H. Mussen (Ed.), *Carmichael's manual of child psychology* (Vol. 2). New York: Wiley, 1970.

Anthony, J. The reaction of adults to adolescents and their behavior. In G. Caplan & S. Lebovici (Eds.), *Adolescence.* New York: Basic Books, 1969.

Antonovsky, H. F. A contribution to research in the area of the mother-child relationship. *Child Development*, 1959, *30*, 37–51.

Arend, R., Gove, F., & Sroufe, L. A. Continuity of individual adaptation from infancy to kindergarten: A predictive study of ego-resiliency and curiosity in preschoolers. *Child Development*, 1979, *50*, 950–959.

Bacon, C., & Lerner, R. M. Effects of maternal development status on the development of vocational-role perception in females. *Journal of Genetic Psychology*, 1975, *126*, 187–193.

Bacon, L. Early motherhood, accelerated role transition, and social pathologies. *Social Forces*, 1969, *52*, 333.

Bakan, D. *Slaughter of the innocents.* San Francisco: Jossey-Bass, 1971.

Baldwin, A. L., Kalhorn, J., & Breese, F. H. Patterns of parent behavior. *Psychology Monograph*, 1945, *58* (3, Serial No. 268).

Baldwin, W. Adolescent pregnancy and childbearing: Growing concerns for Americans. *Population Bulletin*, 1976, *31*, 2.

Bales, K. B. Academic achievement and the broken home. *Southern Journal of Educational Research*, 1979, *13*, 145–160.

Baltes, P. B., Reese, H. W., Lipsitt, L. P. Life-span developmental psychology. *Annual Review of Psychology*, 1980, *31*, 65–110.

Bandura, A., & Walters, R. H. *Adolescent aggression.* New York: Ronald Press, 1959.

Bandura, A. The stormy decade: Fact or fiction? *Psychology in the School*, 1964, *1*, 224–231.

Bandura, A. *Aggression: A social learning analysis.* Englewood Cliffs, N.J.: Prentice-Hall, 1973.

Bandura, A. The self system in reciprocal determinism. *American Psychologist*, 1978, *33*, 344–358.

Bane, M. J. Martial disruption and the lives of children. *Journal of Social Issues*, 1976, *32*, 103–117.

Bates, J. E., Olson, S. L., Pettit, G. S., & Bayles, K. Dimensions of individuality in the mother-infant relationship at six months of age. *Child Development*, 1982, *53*, 446–461.

Baumrind, D. Child care practices anteceding three patterns of preschool behavior. *Genetic Psychology Monographs*, 1967, *75*, 43–88

Baumrind, D. Authoritarian versus authoritative parental control. *Adolescence,* 1968, *3,* 255–272.

Baumrind, D. Current patterns of parental authority. *Developmental Psychology Monographs,* 1971, *4* (1, Pt. 2).

Baumrind, D. Socialization and instrumental competence in young children. In W. W. Hartup (Ed.), *The young child: Reviews of research* (Vol. 2). Washington, D.C.: National Association for Education of Young Children, 1972.

Baumrind, D. Current patterns of parental authority. *Developmental Psychology Monographs,* 1979, *41* (1, Pt. 2).

Bayley, N., & Schaefer, E. S. Maternal behavior and personality development: Data from the Berkeley Growth Study. *Psychiatric Research Reports,* 1960, *13,* 155–173.

Bayley, N., & Schaefer, E. S. Correlations of maternal and child behaviors with the development of mental abilities: Data from the Berkeley Growth Study. *Monographs of the Society for the Research in Child Development,* 1964, *29* (6, Serial No. 97).

Beauchamp, D. *Parenthood as crisis: An additional study.* Unpublished manuscript, University of North Dakota, 1968.

Becker, W. C. Consequences of different kinds of parental discipline. In M. L. Hoffman & L. W. Hoffman (Eds.), *Review of Child Development Research* (Vol. 1). New York: Russell Sage, 1964.

Becker, W. W., Peterson, D. R., Lurie, A., Schoemaker, D. J., & Hellmer, K. Relations of factors derived from parent interviews rating to behavior problems of five-year-olds. *Child Development,* 1962, *33,* 509–535.

Beckwith, L. Relationships between attributes of mothers and their infants' IQ scores. *Child Development,* 1971, *72,* 1083–1097.

Beckwith, L., Cohen, S. E., Kopp, C. B., Parmelee, A. H., & Marcy, T. G. Caregiver-infant interaction and early cognitive development in preterm infants. *Child Development,* 1976, *47,* 579–587.

Bell, R. Q. The effect on the family of a limitation in coping ability in the child: A research approach and finding. *Merrill-Palmer Quarterly,* 1964, *10,* 129–142.

Bell, R. Q. A reinterpretation of the direction of affects in studies of socialization. *Psychological Review,* 1968, *75,* 81–95.

Bell, R. Q. Stimulus control of parent or caretaker behavior by offspring. *Developmental Psychology,* 1971, *4,* 63–72.

Bell, R. Q., & Harper, L. V. *Child effects on adults.* Hillsdale, N.J.: Lawrence Erlbaum, 1977.

Bell, S. *Cognitive development and mother-child interaction in the first three years of life.* Unpublished paper, Johns Hopkins University, 1978.

Bell, S. M., & Ainsworth, M. D. S. Infant crying and maternal responsiveness. *Child Development,* 1972, *43,* 1171–1190.

Belsky, J. A theoretical analysis of child abuse remediation strategies. *Journal of Clinical Child Psychology,* 1978, *7,* 113–117. (a)

Belsky, J. Three theoretical models of child abuse: A critical review. *International Journal of Child Abuse and Neglect,* 1978, *2,* 37–49. (b)

Belsky, J. *The interrelation of parenting, spousal interaction, and infant competence: A suggestive analysis:* Paper presented at the biennial meeting of the Society for Research in Child Behavior, March 1979. (a)

Belsky, J. The interrelation of parental and spousal behavior during infancy in traditional nuclear families: An exploratory analysis. *Journal of Marriage and the Family,* 1979, *41,* 62–68. (b)

Belsky, J. A family analysis of parental influence on infant exploratory competence. In F. Pedersen (Ed.), *The father-infant relationship: Observational studies in a family context.* New York: Praeger Special Studies, 1980.

Belsky, J. Early human experience: A family perspective. *Developmental Psychology*, 1981, *17*, 3–23.

Belsky, J., Garduque, L., & Hrncir, L. Assessing free play, elicited play and executive capacity in infant exploration: Relations to home environment and attachment. *Developmental Psychology*, 1984, in press.

Belsky, J., Gilstrap, B., & Rovine, M. Stability and change in mother-infant and father-infant interaction in a family setting: One-to-three-to-nine months. *Child Development*, 1984, in press.

Belsky, J., Goode, M. K., & Most, R. K. Maternal stimulation and infant exploratory competence: Cross-sectional, correlational, and experimental analyses. *Child Development*, 1980, *51*, 1163–1178.

Belsky, J., Robins, E., & Gamble, W. The determinants of parenting: Toward a contextual theory. In M. Lewis & L. Rosenblum (Eds.), *Beyond the dyad: Social connections.* New York: Plenum, 1984.

Belsky, J., Rovine, M., & Taylor, D. Origins of individual differences in infant-mother attachment: Maternal and infant contributions. *Child Development*, 1984, *55*, in press.

Belsky, J., & Steinberg, L. P. The effects of day care: A critical review. *Child Development*, 1978, *49*, 920–949.

Belsky, J., Steinberg, L., & Walker, A. The ecology of day care. In M. Lamb (Ed.), *Childbearing in nontraditional families.* Hillsdale, N.J.: Lawrence Erlbaum, 1982.

Belsky, J., & Tolan, W. The infant as producer of his development: An ecological analysis. In R. Lerner & N. Busch-Rossnagel (Eds.), *The child as producer of its own development: A life-span perspective.* New York: Academic Press, 1981.

Belsky, J., Walker, A., & Anderson, P. *Comments on HEW day care regulations.* Unpublished paper, Pennsylvania State University, September 1979.

Bengston, V. L., & Kuypers, J. A. Generational differences and the developmental stake. *Aging and Human Development*, 1971, *2*, 249–260.

Bengston, V. L., & Troll, Y. Youth and their parents: Feedback and intergenerational influence in socialization. In R. M. Lerner & G. B. Spanier (Eds.), *Child influences on marital and family interaction: A life-span perspective.* New York: Academic Press, 1978.

Bennett, V. C., & Bardon, J. I. The effects of a school program on teenage mothers and their children. *American Journal of Orthopsychiatry*, 1977, *47*(4), 671.

Bernard, I. *The future of motherhood.* New York: Penguin Books, 1974.

Bernstein, B. Social class and linguistic development: A theory of social learning. In A. Halsey, J. Floud, & C. Anderson (Eds.), *Education, economy, and society.* Glencoe, Ill.: Free Press, 1961.

Berscheid, E., & Walster, E. Physical attractiveness. In L. Berkowitz (Ed.), *Advances in experimental social psychology* (Vol. 7). New York: Academic Press, 1974.

Bijou, S. *Child development: The basic stage of early childhood.* Englewood Cliffs, N.J.: Prentice-Hall, 1976.

Biller, H. Paternal sex-role factors in cognitive and academic functioning. In J. Cole & R. Dienstbier (Eds.), *Nebraska symposium on motivation.* Lincoln: University of Nebraska Press, 1974.

Biller, H. B. Father dominance and sex-role in kindergarten boys. *Developmental Psychology*, 1969, *1*, 87–94.

Biller, H. B. Father absence and the personality development of the male child. *Developmental Psychology*, 1970, *2*, 181–201.

Birch, H., & Gussow, J. *Disadvantaged children: Health, nutrition and school failure*, N.Y.: Grune and Stratton, 1970.

Birnbaum, J. Life patterns and self-esteem in gifted family oriented and career committed women. In M. T. S. Mednick, S. S. Tangri, & L. W. Hoffman (Eds.), *Women and achievement*. New York: Wiley, 1975.

Birnbaum, J. A. *Life patterns, personality style, and self-esteem in gifted family-oriented and career-oriented women*. Unpublished doctoral dissertation, University of Michigan, 1971.

Blanchard, M., & Main, M. Avoidance of the attachment figure and social-emotional adjustment in day care infants. *Developmental Psychology*, 1979, *15*, 445–446.

Blehar, M. Anxious attachment and defensive reactions associated with day care. *Child Development*, 1974, *45*, 683–692.

Blehar, M. C., Ainsworth, M. D., & Main, M. *Mother-infant interaction relevant to close bodily contact: A longitudinal study*. Unpublished manuscript, Johns Hopkins University 1978.

Blehar, M. C., Lieberman, A. F., & Ainsworth, M. D. S. Early face-to-face interaction and its relation to later infant-mother attachment. *Child Development*, 1977, *48* 182–194.

Block, J. Issues, problems, and pitfalls in assessing sex differences: A critical review of the psychology of sex differences. *Merrill-Palmer Quarterly*, 1976, *22*, 283–308.

Block, J. Assimilation, accommodation, and the dynamics of personality development. *Child Development*, 1982, *53*, 281–294.

Block, J. H. Conceptions of sex role: Some cross-cultural and longitudinal perspectives. *American Psychologist*, 1973, *28*, 512–529.

Block, J. H. Another look at sex differentiation in the socialization behaviors of mothers and fathers. In J. Sherman & F. Denmark (Eds.), *Psychology of women: Future of research*. New York: Psychological Dimensions, 1982.

Block, J., Block, J. H., & Harrington, D. M. Some misgivings about the Matching Familiar Figures Test as a measure of reflection-impulsivity. *Developmental Psychology*, 1974, *10*, 611–632.

Blood, R. O., & Hamblin, R. L. The effect of the wife's employment on the family power structure. *Social Forces*, 1958, *36*, 347–352.

Blumberg, M. Psychopathology of the abusing parent. *American Journal of Psychotherapy*, 1974, *28*, 21–29.

Blumberg, M. L. Treatment of the abused child and child abuser. *American Journal of Psychotherapy*, 1977, *31*, 204–215.

Bossard, J. H. S. (Ed.). Toward family stability. *American Academy of Political Social Science*, 1950, *272*, 1.

Bowlby, J. *Maternal care and mental health*. Geneva: World Health Organization, 1951.

Bradley, R., & Caldwell, B. Early home environment and changes in mental test performance in children from six to 36 months. *Developmental Psychology*, 1976, *12*, 93–97. (a)

Bradley, R., & Caldwell, B. The relation of infants' home environments to mental test performance at 54 months: A follow-up study. *Child Development*, 1976, *47*, 1172–1174. (b)

Braun-Luckey, E., & Koym-Bain, J. Children: A factor in marital satisfaction. *Journal of Marriage and the Family*, 1970, *43*.

Brim, O. G., & Kagan, J. *Constancy and change in human development*. Cambridge, Mass.: Harvard University Press, 1980.

Brittain, C. V. Adolescent choices and parent-peer cross pressures. *American Sociological Review*, 1963, 28, 385–391.

Bronfenbrenner, U. Toward an experimental ecology of human development. *American Psychologist*, 1977, 32, 513–531.

Bronfenbrenner, U. *The ecology of human development*. Cambridge, Mass.: Harvard University Press, 1979.

Bronfenbrenner, U., & Crouter, A. *Work and family through time and space*. A report prepared for the Panel on Work, Family, and Community Committee on Child Development Research and Public Policy: National Academy of Sciences, National Research Council, 1980.

Bronson, W. C. Early antecedents of emotional expressiveness and reactivity control. *Child Development*, 1966, 37, 793–810.

Brookhart, J., & Hock, E. The effects of experimental context and experimental background on infants' behavior toward their mothers and a stranger. *Child Development*, 1976, 47, 333–340.

Brown, J., & Bakeman, R. *Antecedents of emotional involvement in mothers of premature and full-term infants*. Paper presented at the biennial meeting of the Society for Research in Child Development, New Orleans, March 1977.

Bumpass, L., & Sweet, J. A. Differentials in marital instability. *American Sociological Review*, 1972, 37, 754–756.

Burchinal, L. B. Personality characteristics of children. In F. I. Nye & L. W. Hoffman (Eds.), *The employed mother in America*. Chicago: Rand McNally, 1963.

Burchinal, L. G. Adolescent role deprivation and high school age marriage. *Marriage and Family Living*, 1959, 21, 378–384.

Burchinal, L. G. Characteristics of adolescents from unbroken, broken, and reconstituted families. *Journal of Marriage and the Family*, 1964, 26, 44–51.

Bureau of the Census. Number, timing and duration of marriages and divorces in the United States. *Current Population Reports*, Series P-20, No. 297. Suitland, Md.: Government Printing Office, 1976.

Bureau of the Census. Perspectives on American fertility. *Current Population Reports*, Series P-23, No. 70. Suitland, Md.: Government Printing Office, 1978.

Bureau of the Census. Marital status and living arrangements. *Current Population Reports*, Series P-20, No. 349. Suitland, Md.: Government Printing Office, 1980.

Burgess, E. W. Predictive methods and family stability. *American Academy of Political Social Science*, 1950, 272, 47.

Burgess, R., & Conger, R. Family interaction in abusive, neglectful and normal families. *Child Development*, 1978, 49, 1163–1173.

Caffey, J. Multiple fractures in the long bones of children suffering from chronic subdural hematoma. *American Journal of Roentgenology, Radium Therapy, and Nuclear Medicine*, 1946, 56, 163–173.

Cain, L., Kelly, D., & Shannon, D. Parents' perceptions of the psychological and social impact of home monitoring. *Pediatrics*, 1980, 66, 37–40.

Call, J. Psychological problems of the cerebral palsied child, his parents and siblings as revealed by dynamically oriented small group discussions with parents. *Cerebral Palsy Review*, 1958, September–October.

Caplan, G. *Support systems and community mental health*. New York: Behavioral Publications, 1976.

Capute, A. J., & Palmer, F. B. A pediatric overview of the spectrum of developmental disabilities. *Developmental and Behavioral Pediatrics*, 1980, *1*, 66–69.

Card, J. J., & Wise, L. L. Teenage mothers and teenage fathers: The impact of early childbearing on the parents' personal and professional lives. *Family Planning Perspective*, 1978, *10*, 199.

Carew, J. *Observation study of caregivers and children in day care homes: Preliminary results from home observations.* Paper presented at biennial meeting of the Society for Research in Child Development, San Francisco, April 1979.

Carew, J. V. *Observed intellectual competence and tested intelligence: Their roots in the young child's transactions with his environment.* Unpublished manuscript, Harvard University, 1975.

Carew, J. V. Experience and the development of intelligence in young children at home and in day care. *Monographs of the Society for Research in Child Development*, 1980, *45* (6–7, Serial No. 187).

Carter, H., & Glick, P. *Marriage and divorce: A social and economic study, revised.* Cambridge, Mass.: Harvard University Press, 1976.

Caudill, W., & Weinstein, H. Maternal care and infant behavior in Japan and America. *Psychiatry*, 1969, *32*, 12–43.

Chand, I. P., Crider, D. M., & Willets, F. K. Parent-youth disagreement as perceived by youth: A longitudinal study. *Youth and Society*, 1975, *6*, 365–375.

Chess, S., & Thomas, A. Infant bonding: Mystique and reality. *American Journal of Orthopsychiatry*, 1982, *52*, 213–222.

Chibucos, T., & Kail, P. Longitudinal examination of father-infant interaction and infant-father attachment. *Merrill-Palmer Quarterly*, 1981, *27*, 81–96.

Chwast, J. Sociopathic behavior in children. In B. B. Wolman (Ed.), *Manual of child psychopathology*. New York: McGraw Hill, 1972.

Clark, J. *The incidence of child abuse and neglect in the population at the Utah State University Industrial School.* Unpublished master's thesis, Utah State University, 1976.

Clarke-Stewart, K. A. Interactions between mothers and their young children: Characteristics and consequences. *Monographs of the Society for Research in Child Development*, 1973, *38* (6–7, Serial No. 153).

Clarke-Stewart, K. A. A review of research and some propositions for policy. *Child care in the family*. New York: Academic Press, 1977.

Clarke-Stewart, K. A. And daddy makes three: The father's impact on the mother and young child. *Child Development*, 1978, *44*, 466–478. (a)

Clarke-Stewart, K. A. Popular primers for parents. *American Psychologist*, 1978, *33*, 359–369. (b)

Clarke-Stewart, K. A. *Assessing social development.* Paper presented at biennial meeting of the Society for Research in Child Development, San Francisco, March 1979.

Clarke-Stewart, K. A. Observation and experiment: Complementary strategies for studying day care and social development. In S. Kilmer (Ed.), *Advances in early education and day care*. Greenwich, Conn.: JAI Press, 1980.

Clarke, A. M., & Clarke, A. D. B. (Eds.). *Early experience: Myth and evidence.* New York: Free Press, 1976.

Cochran, M. A comparison of group day and family child-rearing patterns in Sweden. *Child Development*, 1977, *48*, 707–720.

Cochran, M., & Brassard, J. Child development and personal social networks. *Child Development*, 1979, *50*, 601–616.

Cohen, S., & Beckwith, L. *Maternal language input in infancy.* Paper presented at meeting of American Psychological Association, Chicago, 1975.

Cohen, S. E. Maternal employment and mother-child interaction. *Merrill-Palmer Quarterly*, 1978, *24*, 189–197.

Cohen, S. E., Beckwith, L., & Parmelee, A. H. Receptive language development in preterm children as related to caregiver-child interaction. *Pediatrics*, 1978, *61*, 16–20.

Cohen, S., & Sussman, A. *The incidence of child abuse in the United States.* Unpublished manuscript, University of Delaware, 1975.

Colletta, N. D. *The influence of support systems on the maternal behavior of young mothers.* Paper presented at biennial meeting of the Society for Research in Child Development, Boston, Mass., April 1981.

Conger, R., Burgess, R., & Barrett, C. Child abuse related to life change and perceptions of illness: Some preliminary findings. *Family Coordinator*, 1979, *28*, 73–73.

Cook, N. *Marital and infant factors in the emerging parent-infant relationship.* Paper presented at meeting of the American Psychological Association, New York City, September 1979.

Cooper, T. Present HEW policies in primary prevention. *Preventative Medicine*, 1977, *6*, 198.

Coopersmith, S. *The antecedents of self-esteem.* San Francisco: Freeman, 1967.

Costanzo, P. R., & Shaw, M. E. Conformity as a function of age level. *Child Development*, 1966, *37*, 967–975.

Cowen, C., Cowen, P., Coie, L., & Coie, J. Becoming a family: The impact of a first child's birth on the couple's relationship. In L. Newman & W. Miller (Eds.), *The first child and family formation.* Chapel Hill, N.C.: Carolina Population Center, 1976.

Crandall, P., Preston, A., & Rabson, A. Maternal reactions and the development of independence and achievement behavior in young children. *Child Development*, 1960, *31*, 243–251.

Crandall, V. J., Dewey, R., Katkovsky, W., & Preston, A. Parent's attitudes and behaviors and grade school children's academic achievements. *Journal of Genetic Psychology*, 1964, *104*, 53–66.

Crandall, V. J., Orleans, S., Preston, A., & Rabson, A. The development of compliance in young children. *Child Development*, 1958, *29*, 429–443.

Crescimbeni, J. Broken homes do affect academic achievement. *Child and Family*, 1965, *4*, 24–28.

Crider, E. A. *School-age pregnancy, childbearing, and childrearing: A research review.* Unpublished manuscript submitted to Bureau of Elementary & Secondary Education, U.S. Office of Education, 1976.

Crnic, K. A., Greenberg, M. T., Ragozin, A. S., Robinson, N. M., & Basham, R. *The effects of stress and social support on maternal attitudes and the mother-infant relationship.* Paper presented at biennial meeting of the Society for Research in Child Development, Boston, April 1981.

Crockenberg, S. Infant irritability, mother responsiveness, and social support influences on the security of infant-mother attachment. *Child Development*, 1981, *52*, 857–865.

Crouter, A., Belsky, J., & Spanier, G. The family context of child development: Maternal employment and divorce. In G. Whitehurst (Ed.), *Annals of child development.* Greenwich, Conn.: JAI Press, 1983.

Cummings, E. M. Caregiver stability and day care. *Developmental Psychology*, 1980, *16*, 31–37.

Curtis, G. Violence breeds violence. *American Journal of Psychiatry*, 1963, *120*, 386–387.

Cutright, P. Timing the first birth: Does it matter? *Journal of Marriage and the Family,* 1973, *35,* 585.

Davis, K. The American family in relation to demographic change. In C. F. Westoff, & R. Park (Eds.), *Demographic and social aspects of population growth* (Vol. 1). U. S. Commission on Population Growth and the American Future Research Reports. Suitland, Md.: Government Printing Office, 1972.

Dejong, G., & R. *Childlessness: A demographic path analysis of changes among married women.* Paper presented at the annual meeting of the Southern Sociological Society, Washington, D.C., 1975.

DeLissovoy, V. High school marriages: A longitudinal study. *Journal of Marriage and the Family,* 1973, *35,* 245–255.

Denhoff, E. Current status of infant stimulation or enrichment programs for children with developmental disabilities. *Pediatrics,* 1981, *67,* 32–37.

Deutsch, I. The quality of post parental life. *Journal of Marriage and the Family,* 1964, *26,* 52–60.

Deutsch, M., & Brown, B. Social influences in negro-white intelligence differences. *Journal of Social Issues,* 1964, *20,* 24–35.

Dickie, J. R., VanGent, E., Hoogerwerf, K., Martinez, I., & Dieterman, L. *Mother-father-infant triad: Who affects whose satisfaction.* Paper presented at biennial meeting of the Society for Research in Child Development, Boston, Mass., April 1981.

Dielman, T., Barton, K., & Cattell, R. Relationships among family attitudes and child rearing practices. *Journal of Genetic Psychology,* 1977, *130,* 105–112.

Dion, K. Children's physical attractiveness and sex as determinants of adult punitiveness. *Developmental Psychology,* 1974, *10,* 772–778.

Donovan, W., Leavitt, L., & Balling, J. *Physiologic correlates of mother-infant interaction.* Paper presented at biennial meeting of the Society for Research in Child Development, Denver, March 1975.

Douvan, E. Employment and the adolescent. In F. I. Nye & L. W. Hoffman (Eds.), *The employed mother in America.* Chicago: Rand McNally, 1963.

Douvan, E., & Adelson, J. *The adolescent experience.* New York: Wiley, 1966.

Doyle, A. Infant development in day care. *Developmental Psychology,* 1975, *11,* 655–656.

Doyle, A., & Somers, K. *The effects of group and family day care on infant attachment.* Unpublished manuscript. Concordia University, Montreal, 1977.

Drake, C. T., & McDougall, D. Effects of the absence of a father and other male models on the development of boys' sex roles. *Developmental Psychology,* 1977, *13,* 537–538.

Dubnoff, S. J., Veroff, J., & Kulka, R. A. *Adjustment to work: 1957–1976.* Paper presented to the American Psychological Association, Toronto, August 1978.

Dunn, J. F. Individual differences in temperament. In M. Rutter (Ed.), *The scientific foundations of developmental psychiatry.* London: Heinemann Medical Books, 1980.

Duvall, E. *Family Development* (4th ed.). Philadelphia: Lippincott, 1971.

Duvall, E. B. *Conceptions of mother roles by five- and six-year-old children of working and non-working mothers.* Unpublished doctoral dissertation, Florida State University, 1955.

Dyer, E. Parenthood as crisis: A restudy. *Marriage and Family Living,* 1963, *25,* 488–496.

Easterbrooks, M. & Goldberg, W. Toddler development in the family; Impact of father involvement and parenting characteristics. *Child Development,* 1983, in press.

Easterbrooks, M. & Lamb, M. The relationship between quality of infant-mother attachment and infant competence in initial encounters with peers. *Child Development*, 1979, *50*, 380–387.

Egeland, B., & Brunnquell, D. An at-risk approach to the study of child abuse: Some preliminary findings. *Journal of the American Academy of Child Psychiatry*, 1979, *18*, 219–235.

Egeland, B., & Sroufe, A. Developmental sequelae of maltreatment in infancy. In R. Rizley & D. Cinchetti (Eds.), *New directions for child development*. San Francisco: Jossey-Bass, 1981.

Elardo, R., Bardley, R., & Caldwell, B. The relation of infants' home environments to mental test performance from six to thirty-six months: A longitudinal analysis. *Child Development*, 1975, *46*, 71–76.

Elder, G. H. *Children and the Great Depression*. Chicago: University of Chicago Press, 1974.

Elder, G. H., & Rockwell, R. C. Economic depression and postwar opportunity in men's lives: A study of life patterns and mental health. In R. G. Simmons (Ed.), *Research in community and mental health* (Vol. 1). Greenwich, Conn.: JAI Press 1979.

Elkind, D. Egocentrism in adolescence. *Child Development*, 1967, *38*, 1025–1034.

Elmer, E. *Children in jeopardy*. Pittsburgh, Pa.: University of Pittsburgh Press, 1967.

Elmer, E., & Gregg, G. Developmental characteristics of abused children. *Pediatrics*, 1967, *40*, 596–602.

Emlen, A. *Family day care for children under three*. Paper presented at the International Symposium on the Ecology of Care and Education of Children Under Three, February 1977.

Emmerich, W. Young children's discrimination of parent and child roles. *Child Development*, 1959, *30*, 403–419.

Emmerich, W. Personality development and concepts of structure. *Child Development*, 1968, *39*, 671–690.

Engel, M., & Keane, W. *Black mothers and their infant sons: Antecedents, correlates, and predictors of cognitive development in the second and sixth year of life*. Paper presented at biennial meeting of the Society for Research in Child Development, Denver, 1975.

Epstein, A. S. *Pregnant teenagers' knowledge of infant development*. Paper presented at biennial meeting of the Society for Research in Child Development, San Francisco, March 1979.

Erikson, E. *Childhood and society*. New York: Norton, 1950.

Erikson, E. Identity and the life cycle. *Psychological Issues*, 1959, *1*, 18–164.

Erikson, E. *Childhood and society* (2nd. ed.). New York: Norton, 1963.

Erikson, E. H. *Identity, youth, and crisis*. New York: Norton, 1968.

Eshleman, J. R. Mental Health and marital integration in young marriages. *Journal of Marriage and the Family*, 1965, *27*, 255–262.

Etaugh, C. Effects of maternal employment on children: A review of recent research. *Merrill-Palmer Quarterly*, 1974, *20*, 71–98.

Fagot, B. I. The influence of sex of child on parental relations to toddler children. *Child Development*, 1978, *49*, 459–465.

Farahoff, A., Kennell, J., & Klaus, M. Follow-up of low birth weight infants: The predictive value of maternal visiting patterns. *Pediatrics*, 1972, *49*, 287–290.

Farley, J. Maternal employment and child behavior. *Cornell Journal of Social Relations*, 1968, *3*, 58–71.

Farran, D., & Ramey, C. Infant day care and attachment behaviors toward mothers and teachers. *Child Development*, 1977, *48*, 1112–1116.

Farel, A. M. Effects of preferred maternal roles, maternal employment and socio-demographic status on school adjustment and competence. *Child Development*, 1980, *51*, 1179–1186.

Feiring, C., & Lewis, M. The child as a member of the family system. *Behavioral Science*, 1978, *23*, 225–233.

Feiring, C., & Taylor, J. *The influence of the infant and secondary behavior: Toward a social systems view of infant attachment.* Unpublished manuscript, University of Pittsburgh, 1977.

Feldman, H. Changes in marriages and parenthood: A methodological design. In A. Michel (Ed.), *Family issues of employed women in Europe and America.* Leiden, The Netherlands: Brull, 1971.

Feldman, H., & Rogoff, M. *Correlates of changes in marital satisfaction with the birth of the first child.* Paper presented at the meeting of the American Psychological Association, San Francisco, September 1968.

Feldman, S., Nash, S., & Aschenbrenner, B. *Antecedents of family.* Unpublished manuscript, Stanford University, 1982.

Feldman, S. S., Biringer, Z. C., & Nash, S. C. Fluctuations of sex related self-attributions as a function of stage of family life cycle. *Developmental Psychology*, 1981, *17*, 24–35.

Feshbach, N. D., & Feshbach, S. Children's aggression. In W. W. Hartup (Ed.), *The young child: Review of research* (Vol. 2). Washington, D.C.: National Association for the Education of Young Children, 1972.

Feshbach, S. Aggression. In P. H. Mussen (Ed.), *Carmichael's manual of child psychology* (3rd ed.). New York: Wiley, 1970.

Field, T. Self, teacher, toy and peer-directed behaviors of handicapped preschool children. In T. M. Freed, S. Goldberg, D. Stern, & A. M. Sostek (Eds.), *High risk infants and children: Adult and peer interaction.* New York: Academic Press, 1980.

Field, T. Affective displays in high-risk infants in early interaction. In T. Field & A. Fogel (Eds.), *Emotion and interactions.* Hillsdale, N.J.: Lawrence Erlbaum, 1982.

Finkelstein, N. W., & Ramey, C. T. Learning to control the environment in infancy. *Child Development*, 1977, *48*, 806–819.

Fisher, H. E. Of human bonding. *The Sciences*, 1982, *22*, 18–23.

Floyd, Jr., H. H., & South, D. R. Dilemma of youth: The choice of parents or peers as a frame of reference for behavior. *Journal of Marriage and the Family*, 1972, *34*, 627–634.

Fontana, U. The diagnosis of the maltreatment syndrome in children. *Pediatrics*, 1973, *51*, 780–782.

Fosburg, S. *Design of the National Day Care Home Study.* Paper presented at the annual meeting of the American Educational Research Association, Boston, April 1980.

Fraiberg, S. *Every child's birthright: In defense of mothering.* New York: Basic Books, 1977.

Frankel, E. Characteristics of working and non-working mothers among intellectually gifted and low achievers. *Personnel and Guidance Journal*, 1964, *42*, 776–780.

Freud, A. Adolescence as a developmental disturbance. In G. Caplan & S. Lebovici (Eds.), *Adolescence.* New York: Basic Books, 1969.

Frey, K. S., & Slaby, R. G. *Differential teaching methods used with girls and boys of moderate and high achievement levels.* Paper presented at the biennial meeting of the Society for Research in Child Development, San Francisco, March 1979.

Friedrich, W., & Boriskin, J. The role of the child in abuse: A review of the literature. *American Journal of Orthopsychiatry*, 1976, *7*, 306–313.

Frisch, H. L. Sex stereotypes in adult-infant play. *Child Development*, 1977, *48*, 1671–1675.

Frodi, A., Lamb, M., Leavitt, C., Donovan, W., Neff, C., & Sherry, D. Fathers' and mothers' responses to the faces and cries of normal and premature infants. *Developmental Psychology*, 1978, *14*, 490–498.

Frodi, A. M., Lamb, M. E., Hwang, C. P., & Frodi, M. *Characteristics of maternal and paternal behavior in traditional and nontraditional Swedish families.* Paper presented at the International Conference on Infant Studies, Austin, Texas, March 1982.

Furstenberg, F., & Nord, C. *The life course of children of divorce: Marital disruption and parental contact.* Paper presented at the annual meeting of the Population Association of America, San Diego, 1982.

Furstenberg, F., Nord, C., Peterson, J., & Zill, N. The life course of children of divorce: Marital disruption and parental contact. *American Sociological Review*, 1983, in press.

Furstenberg, Jr., F. F. The social consequences of teenage parenthood. *Family Planning Perspectives*, 1976, *8*, 148. (a)

Furstenberg, Jr., F. F. *Unplanned parenthood: The social consequences of teenage childbearing.* New York: Free Press, 1976. (b).

Gaensbauer, T. J., Mrazek, D., & Harmon, R. J. Affective behavior patterns in abused and/or neglected infants. In N. Frude (Ed.), *The understanding and prevention of child abuse: Psychological approaches.* London: Concord Press, 1981.

Gaensbauer, T. J., & Sands, K. Distorted affective communication in abused/ neglected infants and their potential impact on caretakers. *Journal of the American Academy of Child Psychiatry*, 1979, *18*, 236–250.

Galdston, R. Preventing the abuse of little children: The Parent's Center Project for the study and prevention of child abuse. *American Journal of Orthopsychiatry*, 1975, *45*, 372–381.

Gallatin, J. E. *Adolescence and individuality.* New York: Harper & Row, 1975.

Garbarino, J. The human ecology of child maltreatment: A conceptual model for research. *Journal of Marriage and the Family*, 1977, *39*, 721–736.

Gath, A. *Down's syndrome and the family: The early years.* New York: Academic Press, 1978.

Gelles, R. Child abuse as psychopathology: A sociological critique and reformulation. *American Journal of Orthopsychiatry*, 1973, *43*, 611–621.

Gelles, R. The social construction of child abuse. *American Journal of Orthopsychiatry*, 1975, *45*, 363–371.

Gelles, R. Demythologizing child abuse. *The Family Coordinator*, 1976, *25*, 135–141.

Gelles, R. Violence toward children in the United States. *American Journal of Orthopsychiatry*, 1978, *48*, 580–592.

George, C., & Main, M. Social interactions of young abused children: Approach, avoidance and aggression. *Child Development*, 1979, *50*, 306–318.

George, C., & Main, M. Abused children: Their rejection of peers and caregivers. In T. Field (Ed.), *High risk infants and children: Adult and peer interactions.* New York: Academic Press, 1980.

George, E. I., & Thomas, M. A comparative study of children of employed mothers and unemployed mothers. *Psychological Studies*, 1967, *12*, 32–38.

Gibson, H. Early delinquency in relation to broken homes. *Journal of Abnormal Psychology*, 1969, *74*, 33–41.

Gil, D. *Violence against children: Physical child abuse in the United States.* Cambridge, Mass.: Harvard University Press, 1970.

Gil, D. Violence against children. *Journal of Marriage and the Family,* 1971, *33,* 639–648.

Gil, D. Primary prevention of child abuse: A philosophical and political issue. *Journal of Pediatric Psychology,* 1976, *1,* 54–57.

Gil, D. Child abuse: Levels of manifestation, causal dimensions, and primary prevention. *Victimology,* 1977, *2,* 186–194.

Glenn, N. D., & McLanahan, S. Children and marital happiness: A further specification of the relationship. *Journal of Marriage and the Family,* 1982, *44,* 63–72.

Glick, P. C., & Norton, A. J. Number, timing and duration of marriages and divorces in the United States: June, 1975. U. S. Bureau of the Census, *Current Population Reports,* Series P-20, No. 297, Government Printing Office, 1976.

Glick, P. C., & Norton, A. J. Marrying, divorcing, and living together in the U.S. today. *Population Bulletin,* 1979, *32,* Whole No. 5.

Glick, P. C., & Spanier, G. B. Married and unmarried cohabitation in the United States. *Journal of Marriage and the Family,* 1980, *41,* 19.

Goetting, A. Divorce outcome research: Issues and perspectives. *Journal of Family Issues,* 1981, *2,* 350–375.

Gold, D., & Andres, D. Comparisons of adolescent children with employed and unemployed mothers. *Merrill-Palmer Quarterly,* 1978, *24,* 243–254. (a)

Gold, D., & Andres, D. Developmental comparisons between ten-year-old children with employed and unemployed mothers. *Child Development,* 1978, *49,* 75–84. (b)

Gold, D., & Andres, D. Relations between maternal employment and development of nursery school children. *Canadian Journal of Behavioral Science,* 1978, *10,* 116–229. (c)

Gold, D., Andres, D., & Glorieux, J. The development of Francophone nursery-school children with employed and nonemployed mothers. *Canadian Journal of Behavioral Science,* 1979, *11,* 169–173.

Goldberg, R. J. *Maternal time use and preschool performance.* Paper presented to the Society for Research in Child Development, New Orleans, March 1977.

Goldberg, S. Prematurity: Effects on parent-infant interaction. *Journal of Pediatric Psychology,* 1978, *3,* 137–144.

Goldberg, S. F., & Lewis, M. Play behavior in the year old infant: Early sex differences. *Child Development,* 1969, *40,* 21–31.

Goldberg, W. A. *Marital quality and child-mother child-father attachments.* Paper presented at the Third International Conference on Infant Studies, Austin, Texas, March 1982.

Golden, M., Rosenbluth, L., Grossi, M. L., Policave, H. J., Freeman, Jr., H., & Brownlee, M. *The New York City Infant Day Care Study: A comparative study of licensed group and family day care programs and the effects of these programs on children and their families.* New York City, N.Y.: Medical and Health Research Association of New York City, Inc., 1978.

Goldfarb, W. The effects of early institutional care on adolescent personality. *Journal of Experimental Education,* 1943, *12,* 106–129.

Goldman, R. J., & Goldman, J. How children perceive the origin of babies and the role of mothers and fathers in procreation: A cross-national study. *Child Development,* 1982, *53,* 491–504.

Goode, M. K. *Maternal stimulation strategies and infant exploratory/play be-*

havior. Unpublished master's thesis, The Pennsylvania State University, 1980.

Goode, W. J. *After divorce.* Glencoe, Ill.: Free Press, 1956.

Goode, W. J. *World revolution and family patterns.* New York: Free Press, 1963.

Gottfried, A. W., & Gottfried, A. E., Home environment and mental development in young children. In A. W. Gottfried (Ed.), *Home environment and early mental development: Longitudinal research.* New York: Academic Press, 1984.

Gould, S. J. *Ontogeny and phylogeny.* Cambridge, Mass.: Harvard University Press, Belknap Press, 1977.

Grabill, W. H. Premarital fertility. U. S. Bureau of the Census, *Current Population Reports*, Series P-23, No. 63. Suitland, Md.: Government Printing Office, August 1976.

Green, A. A psychodynamic approach to the study and treatment of child abusing parents. *Journal of Child Psychiatry*, 1976, *15*, 414.

Green, A. H. Psychopathology of abused children. *Journal of the American Academy of Child Psychiatry*, 1978, *17*, 92–103.

Grossman, K., & Grossman, K. E. *Maternal sensitivity to infant's signals during the first year related to the year olds' behavior in Ainsworth's Strange Situation: A sample of Northern German families.* Paper presented at the International Conference on Infant Studies, Austin, Texas, March 1982.

Grossman, K., Grossman, K. E., Huber, F., & Wartner, V. German children's behavior towards their mothers at 12 months and their fathers at 18 months in Ainsworth's Strange Situation. *International Journal of Behavioral Development*, 1981, *4*, 157–182.

Gunnarson, L. *Children in day care and family care in Sweden: A follow-up.* Bulletin No. 21, Department of Educational Research, University of Gothenburg, 1978.

Gutman, D. Parenthood: A key to the comparative sway of the life cycle. In N. Datan & L. Ginsberg (Eds.), *Life-span developmental psychology: Normative life crisis.* New York: Academic Press, 1975.

Hall, A., & Weiner, S. *The supply of day care services in Denver and Seattle.* Menlo Park, Calif.: Stanford Research Institute, Center for the Study of Welfare Policy, 1977.

Hall, G. S. *Adolescence.* New York: Appleton, 1904.

Hardy-Brown, K., Plomin, R., & DeFries, J. C. Genetic and environmental influences on the rate of communicative development in the first year of life. *Developmental Psychology*, 1981, *17*, 704–717.

Harlow, H. F., & Harlow, M. K. Social deprivation in monkeys. *Scientific American*, 1962, *207*, 137–146.

Harlow, H. F., & Zimmerman, R. R. Affectional responses in the infant monkey. *Science*, 1959, *130*, 421–432.

Hartup, W. W. Perspectives on child and family interaction: Past, present, and future. In R. M. Lerner & G. B. Spanier (Eds.), *Child influences on marital and family interaction: A life-span perspective.* New York: Academic Press, 1978.

Hawkins, P., Wilcox, M., Gillis, G., Porter, A., & Carew, J. *Observation study of caregivers and children in day care homes.* Paper presented at the biennial meeting of the Society for Research in Child Development, San Francisco, March 1979.

Heilbrun, A., Harrell, S., & Gillard, B. Perceived identification of late adolescents and level of adjustment: The importance of parent-model attributes, ordinal position, and sex of child. *Journal of Genetic Psychology*, 1965, *107*, 49–59.

Helson, R. Women mathematicians and the creative personality. *Journal of Consulting and Clinical Psychology*, 1971, *36*, 210–220.

Hensseler, S., & Borduin, C. Satisfied working mothers and their preschool sons. *Journal of Family Issues*, 1981, *2*, 322–335.

Herrenkohl, R. C., & Herrenkohl, E. C. Some antecedents and developmental consequences of mild maltreatment. In R. Rizley, & D. Cinchitti (Eds.), *New directions for child development*. San Francisco: Jossey-Bass, 1981.

Herzog, E., & Sudia, C. E. Children in fatherless families. In B. M. Caldwell & H. N. Riccuti (Eds.), *Review of child development research* (Vol. 3). Chicago: University of Chicago Press, 1973.

Hess, R., & Shipman, V. Early experiences and the socialization of cognitive modes in children. *Child Development*, 1965, *36*, 868–886.

Hess, R. D. Maternal behavior and children's school achievement. In E. Grotberg (Ed.), *Critical issues in research related to disadvantaged children*. Princeton, N.J.: Educational Testing Service, 1969.

Hess, R. D., & Camera, K. A. Post-divorce family relationships as mediating factors in the consequences of divorce for children. *Journal of Social Issues*, 1979, *35*, 79–96.

Hess, R. D., & Shipman, V. C. Cognitive elements in maternal behavior. In J. P. Hill (Ed.), *Minnesota symposia on child psychology* (Vol. 1). Minneapolis: University of Minnesota Press, 1967.

Hetherington, E. M. Effects of paternal absence on sex-typed behaviors in Negro and White preadolescent males. *Journal of Personality and Social Psychology*, 1966, *4*, 87–91.

Hetherington, E. M. Effects of paternal absence on personality development in adolescent daughters. *Developmental Psychology*, 1972, *7* 313–326.

Hetherington, E. M. Divorce: A child's perspective. *American Psychologist*, 1979, *34*, 851.

Hetherington, E. M. Children and divorce. In R. Henderson (Ed.), *Parent-child interaction: Theory, research and prospect*. New York: Academic Press, 1980.

Hetherington, E. M., Cox, M., & Cox, R. The development of children in mother headed families. In H. Hoffman & D. Reiss (Eds.), *The American family: Dying or developing*. New York: Plenum, 1978.

Hetherington, E. M., & Deur, J. The effects of father absence on child development. *Young Children*, 1971, *26*, 233–248.

Hildebrandt, K., & Fitzgerald, H. Facial feature determinants of perceived infant attractiveness. *Infant Behavior and Development*, 1979, *2*, 329–340.

Hill, C. R. Private demand for child care: Implications for public policy. *Evaluation Quarterly*, 1978, *2*, 523–545.

Hill, C. R., & Stafford, F. P. *Prenatal care of children: Time diary estimates of quantity, predictability, and variety*. Unpublished manuscript, Institute of Social Research, University of Michigan, 1978.

Hobbs, D. Parenthood as crisis: A third study. *Journal of Marriage and the Family*, 1965, *27*, 677–689.

Hobbs, D. Transition to parenthood: A replication and an extension. *Journal of Marriage and the Family*, 1968, *30*, 413–417.

Hobbs, D., & Cole, S. Transition to parenthood: A decade replication. *Journal of Marriage and the Family*, 1976, *38*, 723–731.

Hobbs, D., & Wimbish, J. Transition to parenthood by black couples. *Journal of Marriage and the Family*, 1977, *39*, 677–689.

Hock, E. *Alternative approaches to child rearing and their effects on the mother-*

infant relationship (Final report). Washington, D.C.: Department of HEW, Office of Child Development, Grant No. OCD-490, 1976.

Hofferth, S. Day care in the next decade: 1980–1990. *Journal of Marriage and the Family*, 1979, 644–658.

Hoffman, L. Changes in family roles, socialization, and sex differences. *American Psychologist*, 1977, *32*, 644–658.

Hoffman, L. W. Effects on children: Summary and discussion. In F. I. Nye & L. W. Hoffman (Eds.), *The employed mother in America*. Chicago: Rand McNally, 1963. (a)

Hoffman, L. W. Mother's enjoyment of work and effects on the child. In F. I. Nye & L. W. Hoffman (Eds.), *The employed mother in America*. Chicago: Rand McNally, 1963. (b)

Hoffman, L. W. Parental power relations and the division of household tasks. In F. I. Nye & L. W. Hoffman (Eds.), *The employed mother in America*. Chicago: Rand McNally, 1963. (c)

Hoffman, L. W. Effects of maternal employment on the child: A review of the research. *Developmental Psychology*, 1974, *10*, 204–228.

Hoffman, L. W. Maternal employment: 1979. *American Psychologist*, 1979, *34*, 859–865.

Hoffman, M. L. Power assertion by the parent and it's impact on the child. *Child Development*, 1960, *31*, 129–143.

Hoffman, M. L. Moral development. In P. H. Mussen (Ed.), *Carmichael's manual of child psychology* (Vol. 2). New York: Wiley, 1970.

Hoffman, M. L. Sex differences in oral internalization and values. *Journal of Personality and Social Psychology*, 1975, *32*, 720–729.

Hoffman, M. L. Empathy, its development and prosocial implications. In H. E. Howe, Jr. (Ed.), *Nebraska Symposium on Motivation, 1977*. Lincoln: University of Nebraska Press, 1978.

Hogan, R., Johnson, J. A., & Emler, N. P. A socioanalytic theory of moral development. *New Directions for Child Development*, 1978, *2*, 1–18.

Holmstrom, L. L. *The two career family*. Unpublished manuscript, Radcliffe College, 1972.

Honzik, M. P. Environmental correlates of mental growth: Prediction from the family setting at 21 months. *Child Development*, 1967, *38*, 337–364.

Houseknecht, S. K., & Spanier, G. B. Marital disruption and higher education among women in the United States. *Sociology Quarterly*, 1980, *21*, 375.

Huston-Stein, A., & Higgins-Trenk, A. Development of females from childhood through adulthood: Career and feminine orientations. In P. B. Baltes (Ed.), *Life-span development and behavior* (Vol. 1). New York: Academic Press, 1978.

Howard, J. The influence of children's developmental dysfunction on marital quality and family interaction. In R. M. Lerner & G. B. Spanier (Eds.), *Child influences on marital and family interaction: A life-span perspective*. New York: Academic Press, 1978.

Hurley, J. Parental malevolence and children's intelligence. *Journal of Consulting and Clinical Psychology*, 1967, *31*, 199–204.

Jacob, T. Patterns of family conflict and dominance as a function of age and social class. *Developmental Psychology*, 1974, *10*, 1–12.

Jaffee, F. S., & Dryfoos, J. G. Fertility control services for adolescents: Access and utilization. *Family Planning Perspectives*, 1976, *8*, 167–175.

Jayarante, S. Child abusers as parents and children: A review. *Social Work*, 1977, *22*, 5–9.

Jenkins, J. J. Remember that old theory of memory? Well forget it. *American Psychologist*, 1974, *29*, 785–795.

Joffe, L. S. *The quality of mother-infant attachment and its relationship to compliance with maternal commands and prohibitions.* Paper presented at meeting of the Society for Research in Child Development, Boston, April 1981.

Johnson, B., & Morse, H. A. Injured children and their parents. *Children*, 1968, *15*, 147–152.

Johanson, D. C., & Edey, M. A. *Lucy: The beginnings of humankind.* New York: Simon and Schuster, 1981.

Johnson, S., & Lobitz, G. The personal and marital adjustment of parents as related to observed child deviance and parenting behaviors. *Journal of Abnormal Child Psychology*, 1974, *2*, 193–207.

Jordon, B., Radin, N., & Epstein, A. Paternal behavior and intellectual functioning in preschool boys and girls. *Developmental Psychology*, 1975, *11*, 407–408.

Kacerguis, M. A., & Adams, G. R. Erikson stage resolution: The relationship between identity and intimacy. *Journal of Youth and Adolescence*, 1980, *9*, 117–126.

Kach, J., & McGhee, P. Adjustment to early parenthood: The role of accuracy of pre-parenthood expectations. *Journal of Family Issues*, 1982, *3*, 375–388.

Kagan, J. Reflection-impulsivity: The generality and dynamics of conceptual tempo. *Journal of Abnormal Psychology*, 1966, *71*, 17–29.

Kagan, J. Resistance and continuity in psychological development. In A. M. Clark & A. D. B. Clarke (Eds.), *Early experience: Myth and evidence.* New York: Free Press, 1976.

Kagan, J., Kearsley, R., & Zelazo, P. *The effects of infant day care on psychological development.* Paper presented at meeting of the American Association for the Advancement of Science, Boston, February 1976.

Kagan, J., Kearsley, R., & Zelazo, P. *Infancy: Its place in human development.* Cambridge, Mass.: Harvard University Press, 1978.

Kagan, J., & Klein, R. E. Cross-cultural perspectives on early development. *American Psychologist*, 1973, *28*, 947–961.

Kagan, J., & Moss, H. A. *Birth to maturity: A study in psychological development.* New York: Wiley, 1962.

Kandel, D. B., & Lesser, G. S. Parental and peer influences on educational plans of adolescents. *American Sociological Review*, 1969, *34*, 213–223.

Kandel, D. B., & Lesser, G. S. *Youth in two worlds.* San Francisco: Jossey-Bass, 1972.

Katz, I. Socialization of academic motivation in minority group children. In D. Levine (Ed.), *Nebraska Symposium on Motivation.* Lincoln: University of Nebraska Press, 1967.

Keidel, K. C. Maternal employment and ninth grade achievement in Bismarck, North Dakota. *Family Coordinator*, 1970, *19*, 95–97.

Kelly, J. *Children and parents in the midst of divorce: Major factors contributing to differential response.* Paper presented at the National Institute of Mental Health Divorce Conference, Bethesda, Md., 1978.

Kelly, J. A., & Worrell, L. The joint and differential perceived contribution of parents to adolescents' cognitive functioning. *Developmental Psychology*, 1977, *13*, 282–283.

Kelly, R. K. The premarital sexual revolution: Comments on research. *Family Coordinator*, 1972, *21*, 334–336.

Kempe, C. A practical approach to the protection of the abused child and rehabilitation of the abusing parent. *Pediatrics*, 1973, *51*, 804.

Kempe, C., Silverman, E., Steele, B., Droegemueller, W., & Silver, H. The battered-child syndrome. *Journal of the American Medical Association*, 1962, *181*, 17.

Kempe, R. S., & Kempe, C. H. *Child abuse*. Cambridge, Mass.: Harvard University Press, 1978.

Kemper, T., & Reichler, M. Marital satisfaction and conjugal power as determinants of intensity and frequency of rewards and punishments administered by parents. *Journal of Genetic Psychology*, 1976, *129*, 221–234.

Kennedy, W., Van de Riet, V., & White, J. A normative sample of intelligence and achievement of negro elementary school children in southeastern United States. *Monographs of the Society for Research in Child Development*, 1963, *28*, No. 6.

Kermoian, R. *Type and quality of care: Mediating factors in the effects of day care on infant responses to brief separation*. Paper presented at the International Conference on Infant Studies, New Haven, May 1980.

Kimmel, D., & Van der Veen, F. Factors of marital adjustment in Locke's Marital Adjustment Test. *Journal of Marriage and the Family*, 1974, *36*, 57–63.

Kogan, K. L. Interaction systems between preschool handicapped or developmentally delayed children and their parents. In T. M. Field, S. Goldberg, S. Stern, & A. M. Sostek (Eds.), *High-risk infants and children: Adult and peer interaction*. New York: Academic Press, 1980.

Kogan, K. L., Tyler, N., & Turner, P. The process of interpersonal adaptation between mothers and their cerebral palsied children. *Developmental Medicine and Child Neurology*, 1974, *16*, 518–527.

Komarovsky, M. *Blue-collar marriage*. New York: Random House, 1962.

Korbin, J. *Very few cases: Child abuse in the People's Republic of China*. Paper presented at the meeting of the American Anthropological Association, Los Angeles, November 1978.

Korn, S. J. *Temperament, vulnerability, and behavior*. Paper presented at the Louisville Temperament Conference, Louisville, Ky, September 1978.

Kotelchuck, M. *The nature of the child's tie to his father*. Unpublished doctoral dissertation, Harvard University, 1972.

Kurdek, L., & Berg, B. Correlates of children's adjustment to their parent's divorces. In L. Kurdek (Ed.), *Children and divorce*. New Directions for Child Development, No. 19. San Francisco: Jossey-Bass, March 1983.

Kurdek, L., Blisk, D., & Siesky, A. Correlates of children's long-term adjustment to their parents' divorce. *Developmental Psychology*, 1981, *17*, 565–579.

Kurdek, L. W. An integrative perspective on children's divorce adjustment. *American Psychologist*, 1981, *36*, 856–865.

Lally, R. *The family development research program: Progress report*. Unpublished paper, Syracuse University, 1973.

Lamb, M. Fathers and child development: An integrative overview. In M. Lamb (Ed.), *The role of the father in child development* (2nd ed.). New York: Wiley, 1981. (a)

Lamb, M. The development of father-infant relationships. In M. Lamb (Ed.), *The role of the father in child development* (2nd ed.). New York: Wiley, 1981. (b)

Lamb, M. E. Fathers: Forgotten contributors to child development. *Human Development*, 1975, 245–266.

Lamb, M. E. Effects of stress and cohort on mother- and father-infant interaction. *Developmental Psychology*, 1976, *12*, 435–443.

Lamb, M. E. Influences of the child on marital quality and family interaction during the prenatal, perinatal, and infancy periods. In R. M. Lerner & G. B. Spanier (Eds.), *Child influences on marital and family interaction: A life-span perspective*. New York: Academic Press, 1978.

Lamb, M. E. Maternal employment and child development: A review. In M. E.

Lamb (Ed.), *Nontraditional families: Parenting and childrearing.* Hillsdale, N.J.: Lawrence Erlbaum, 1982.

Lamb, M., Hwang, C., Frodi, A., & Frodi, M. Security of mother- and father-infant attachment and its relation to sociability with strangers in traditional and nontraditional Swedish families. *Infant Behavior and Development,* 1982, *5,* 355–368.

Lamb, M. E., Owen, M., & Chase-Lansdale, L. The father-daughter relationship: Past, present and future. In C. Kopp (Ed.), *Becoming female: Perspectives on development.* New York: Plenum, 1979.

Lamb, M. E., Owen, M. T., & Chase-Lansdale, P. L. The working mother in the intact family: A process model. In R. R. Abidin (Ed.), *Parent education and intervention handbook.* Springfield, Ill.: C. C. Thomas, 1980.

Lancaster, J. B., & Whitten, P. Family matter. *The Sciences,* 1980, *20,* 10–15.

Langhorst, B., & Fogel, A. *Cross validation of microanalytic approaches to quantifying maternal behavior in the context of face-to-face interaction.* Paper presented at the International Conference on Infant Studies, Austin, Texas, March 1982.

Larson, L. E. The influence of parents and peers during adolescence: The situation hypothesis revisited. *Journal of Marriage and the Family,* 1972, *34,* 67–74.

Lasch, C. *The culture of narcissism.* New York: Norton, 1978.

LaVoie, J. C. Ego identity formation in middle adolescence. *Journal of Youth and Adolescence,* 1976, *5,* 371–385.

Lay, M., & Meyer, W. *Teacher/child behaviors in an open environment day care program.* Unpublished manuscript, Syracuse University Children's Center, 1973.

LeCorgne, L. C., & Laosa, L. M. Father absence in low-income Mexican-American families: Children's social adjustment and conceptual differentiation of sex-role attributes. *Developmental Psychology,* 1976, *12,* 439–448.

Lefkowitz, M. M., Walder, L. O., & Eron, L. D. Punishment, identification, and aggression. *Merrill-Palmer Quarterly,* 1963, *9,* 159–174.

Lehfeldt, H. Psychology of contraceptive failure. *Medical Aspects of Human Sexuality,* 1971, *5,* 68–77.

Leifer, A. D., Leiderman, P. H., Barnett, C. R., & Williams, J. A. Effects of mother-infant separation on maternal attachment behavior. *Child Development,* 1972, *43,* 1203–1218.

Lein, L. Male participation in home life: Impact of social supports and breadwinner responsibility on the allocation of tasks. *The Family Coordinator,* 1979, 489–495.

LeMasters, E. Parenthood as crisis. *Marriage and Family Living,* 1957, *9,* 352–355.

Lerner, J. V. The role of temperament in psychosocial adaptation in early adolescents: A test of a "goodness of fit" model. *Journal of Genetic Psychology,* in press.

Lerner, R. M. Showdown at generation gap: Attitudes of adolescents and their parents toward contemporary issues. In H. D. Thornburg (Ed.), *Contemporary adolescence* (2nd ed.). Belmont, Ca.: Brooks/Cole, 1975.

Lerner, R. M., & Busch-Rossnagel, N. Individuals as producers of their development: Conceptual and empirical bases. In R. M. Lerner & N. Busch-Rossnagel (Eds.), *Individuals as producers of their own development: A life-span perspective.* New York: Academic Press, 1981.

Lerner, R. M., Hultsch, D. F., & Dixon, R. A. Contextualism and the character of developmental psychology in the 1970s. *Annals of the New York Academy of Sciences,* in press.

Lerner, R. M., Karson, M., Meisels, M., & Knapp, J. R. Actual and perceived attitudes of late adolescents and their parents. *Journal of Youth and Adolescence*, 1975, *4*, 17–36.

Lerner, R. M., & Knapp, J. R. Actual and perceived intrafamilial attitudes of late adolescents and their parents. *Journal of Youth and Adolescence*, 1975, *4*, 17–36.

Lerner, R. M., Schroeder, C., Rewitzer, M., & Weinstock, A. Attitudes of high school students and their parents toward contemporary issues. *Psychological Reports*, 1972, *31*, 255–258.

Lerner, R. M., Skinner, E. A., & Sorell, G. J. Methodological implications of contextual dialectic theories of development. *Human Development*, 1980, *23*, 225–235.

Lerner, R., & Spanier, G. *Child influences on marital quality: A life-span perspective.* New York: Academic Press, 1978.

Lerner, R. M., & Spanier, G. B. *Adolescent development: A life-span perspective.* New York: McGraw-Hill, 1980.

Levin, M. L., Van Loon, F., & Spitler, H. *Marital disruption and cognitive development and achievement in children and youth.* Paper delivered at the annual meeting of the Southern Sociological Society, New Orleans, La., 1978.

Levy, R. On getting angry in the Society Islands. In W. Caudill & T. Lin (Eds.), Mental health research in Asia and the Pacific. Honolulu, Hawaii: East-West Center Press, 1969.

Lewis, M., & Ban, P. *Stability of attachment behavior: A transformational analysis.* Paper presented at the Symposium on Attachment: Studies in Stability and Change, at meeting of the Society for Research in Child Development, Minneapolis, April 1971.

Lewis, M., & Goldberg, S. Perceptual-cognitive development in infancy: A generalized expectancy model as a function of the mother-infant interaction. *Merrill-Palmer Quarterly*, 1969, *15*, 81–100.

Lewis, M., & Lee-Painter, S. An interactional approach to the mother-infant dyad. In M. Lewis & L. A. Rosenblum (Eds.), *The effect of the infant on its caregiver.* New York: Wiley, 1974.

Lewis, M., & Weinraub, M. The father's role in the child's social network. In M. Lamb (Ed.), *The role of the father in child development.* New York: Wiley, 1976.

Lewis, R., & Spanier, G. B. Marital quality, marital stability, and social exchange. In I. F. Nye (Ed.), *Family relationships: Rewards and costs.* Beverly Hills, Ca.: Sage, 1982.

Lewis, R. A., & Spanier, G. B. Theorizing about the quality and stability of marriage. In W. Burr, R. Hite, I. Nye, & I. Reiss (Eds.), *Contemporary theories about the family.* Glencoe, Ill.: Free Press, 1979.

Lewontin, R. C., & Levins, R. Evolution. *Encyclopedia V: Divine-Fame.* Turin, Italy: Einauchi, 1978.

Lieberman, A. F. Preschoolers' competence with a peer: Influence of attachment and social experience. *Child Development*, 1977, *48*, 1277–1287.

Light, R. Abused and neglected children in America: A study of alternative policies. *Harvard Educational Review*, 1973, *43*, 556–598.

Londerville, S., & Main, M. Security, compliance and maternal training methods in the second year of life. *Developmental Psychology*, 1982, *17*, 289–299.

Long, B. H., Henderson, E. H., & Platt, L. Self-other orientations of Israeli adolescents reared in kibbutzim moshavin. *Developmental Psychology*, 1973, *8*, 300–308.

Longfellow, C. Divorce in context: Its impact on children. In G. Levinger & O. Moles (Eds.), *Divorce and separation.* New York: Basic Books, 1979.

Lovejoy, C. O. The origin of man. *Science,* 1981, *211,* 341–350.

Luckey, E. B., & Bain, J. K. Children: A factor in marital satisfaction. *Journal of Marriage and the Family,* 1970, *32,* 621–626.

Maccoby, E. *Social development: Psychological growth and the parent-child relationship.* New York: Harcourt, Brace, Jovanovich, 1980.

Maccoby, E. E., & Masters, J. C. Attachment and dependency. In P. H. Mussen (Ed.), *Carmichael's manual of child psychology* (3rd ed.). New York: Wiley, 1970.

Macrae, J. W., & Herbert-Jackson, E. Are behavioral effects of infant day care programs specific? *Developmental Psychology,* 1975, *12,* 269–270.

Magrab, P. R., & Danielson-Murphy, J. *Adolescent pregnancy: A review.* Unpublished manuscript, Georgetown University, Child Development Center, no date.

Main, M. *Explanation, play and level of cognitive functioning as related to child-mother attachment.* Unpublished doctoral dissertation, Johns Hopkins University, 1973.

Main, M., & Weston, D. Security of attachment to mother and father: Related to conflict behavior and the readiness to establish new relationships. *Child Development,* 1981, *57,* 932–940.

Martin, B. Parent-child relations. In F. D. Horowitz (Ed.), *Review of child development research* (Vol. 4), 1975.

Martin, B. *Abnormal psychology: Clinical and scientific perspectives.* New York: Holt, Rinehart & Winston, 1981.

Martin, H. P. Which children get abused: High risk factors in the child. In H. P. Martin (Ed.), *The abused child: A multidisciplinary approach to developmental issues and treatment.* Cambridge, Mass.: Ballinger, 1976.

Martin, H. P., & Breezley, P. Personality of abused children. In H. P. Martin (Ed.), *The abused child: A multidisciplinary approach to developmental issues and treatment.* Cambridge, Mass.: Ballinger, 1976.

Martin, J. The fetal alcohol syndrome: Recent findings. *Alcohol Health and Research World,* 1977, *1,* 8.

Martin, J. A. A longitudinal study of the consequences of early mother-infant interaction: A microanalytic approach. *Monographs of the Society for Research in Child Development,* 1981, *46* (3,Serial No. 190).

Martin, J., Maccoby, E., & Jacklin, C. N. Mothers' responsiveness to interactive bidding and nonbidding in boys and girls. *Child Development,* 1981, *52,* 1064–1067.

Martinson, F. M. Ego deficiency as a factor in marriage. *American Sociological Review,* 1955, *20,* 161–164.

Martinson, F. M. Ego deficiency as a factor in marriage — a male sample. *Marriage and Family,* 1959, *21,* 48–52.

Masters, R. D. Jean-Jacques is alive and well: Rousseau and contemporary sociobiology. *Daedalus,* 1978, *107,* 93–105.

Matas, L., Arend, R., & Sroufe, L. Continuity in adaptation in the second year: The relationship between quality of attachment and later competence. *Child Development,* 1978, *49,* 547–556.

Matteson, R. Adolescent self-esteem, family communication, and marital satisfaction. *Journal of Psychology,* 1974, *86,* 35–47.

McAllister, R., Butter, E., & Lei, T. Patterns of social interaction among families of behaviorally retarded children. *Journal of Marriage and the Family,* 1973, *35,* 93–100.

McAnarney, E. R. Adolescent pregnancy — A national priority. *American Journal of Diseases of Children,* 1978, *132,* 125.

McCall, R. B. Exploratory manipulation and play in the human infant. *Monographs of the Society for Research in Child Development*, 1974, *39* (No. 155).

McCartney, K., Scarr, S., Phillips, D., Grajik, S., & Schwartz, C. J. Environmental differences among day care centers and their effects on children's development. In E. F. Zigler & E. W. Gordon (Eds.), *Day care scientific and social policy issues*. Boston: Auburn House, 1982.

McCord, J., McCord, W., & Thurber, E. Effects of maternal employment on lower-class boys. *Journal of Abnormal and Social Psychology*, 1963, *67*, 177–182.

McCrae, J. W., & Herbert-Jackson, E. Are behavioral effects of infant day care programs specific? *Developmental Psychology*, 1975, *12*, 269–270.

McCutcheon, B., & Calhoun, K. Social and emotional adjustment of infants and toddlers to a day care setting. *American Journal of Orthopsychiatry*, 1976, *46*, 104–108.

McLaughlin, F. J., Sandler, H. M., Sherrod, K., Vietze, P. M., & O'Conner, S. Social-psychological characteristics of adolescent mothers and behavioral characteristics of their first-born infants. *Journal of Population*, 1979, *2*, 69–73.

Meyerowitz, J., & Feldman, H. Transition to parenthood. *Psychiatric Research Report*, 1966, *20*, 78–84.

Miller, B. A multivariate developmental model of marital satisfaction. *Journal of Marriage and the Family*, 1976, *38*, 643–658.

Miller, B., & Sollie, P. Normal stresses during the transition to parenthood. *Family Relations*, 1980, *29*, 459–465.

Minde, K., et al. *Mother-child relationships in the premature nursery: An observational study*. Unpublished manuscript, Department of Psychiatry, Hospital for Sick Children, Toronto, Canada, 1977.

Minde, K., Marton, P., Manning, D., & Hines, B. Some determinants of mother-infant interaction in the premature nursery. *Journal of the American Academy of Child Psychiatry*, 1980, *19*, 1–21.

Mischel, W. On the future of personality measurement. *American Psychologist*, 1977, *32*, 246–254.

Moore, K. A. Teenage childbirth and welfare dependency. *Family Planning Perspectives*, 1978, *10*, 233–235. (a)

Moore, K. A. *The social and economic consequences of teenage childbearing*. Paper presented at the Conference on Young Women and Employment. The Women's Bureau and Office of Youth Programs, Department of Labor, Washington, D.C., May 1, 1978. (b)

Moore, K. A., & Caldwell, S. B. The effect of government policies on out-of-wedlock sex and pregnancy. *Family Planning Perspective*, 1979, *9*, 164–225.

Moore, K. A., & Waite, L. J. Early childbearing and educational attainment. *Family Planning Perspective*, 1977, *9*, 220.

Moore, T. Children of full-time and part-time mothers. *International Journal of Social Psychiatry*, Special Congress Issue 2, 1964, 1–10.

Moore, T. Exclusive early mothering and its alternatives: The outcome of adolescence. *Scandinavian Journal of Psychology*, 1975, *16*, 255–272.

Morrow, W. R., & Wilson, R. C. Family relations of bright, high achieving and under achieving high school boys. *Child Development*, 1961, *32*, 501–510.

Moskowitz, D., Schwarz, J., & Corsini, D. Initiating day care at three years of age: Effects on attachment. *Child Development*, 1977, *48*, 1271–1276.

Moss, H. A., & Kagan, J. Maternal influences on early development. *Psychological Reports*, 1958, *4*, 655–661.

Mueller, C., & Pope, H. Marital instability: A study of its transmission between generations. *Journal of Marriage and the Family*, 1977, *39*, 83–93.

Mussen, P., & Distler, L. Masculinity identification and father-son relationships. *Journal of Abnormal and Social Psychology,* 1959, *59,* 350–356.

Mussen, P., & Parker, A. Mother nurturance and girls' incidental imitative learning. *Journal of Personality and Social Psychology,* 1965, *2,* 94–97.

Mussen, P., & Rutherford, E. Parent-child relations in relation to young children's sex role preferences. *Child Development,* 1963, *34,* 589–607.

Mussen, P. H., Harris, S., Rutherford, E., & Keasey, C. B. Honesty and altruism among preadolescents. *Developmental Psychology,* 1970, *3,* 169–194.

Myers, B. J. Early intervention using Brazelton training with middle-class mothers and fathers of newborns. *Child Development,* 1982, *53,* 462–471.

National Center for Health Statistics. Births, marriages, divorces and deaths for 1977. Provisional statistics. *Monthly Vital Statistics Report, 26,* 1978.

National Center for Health Statistics. National estimates of marriage dissolution and survivorship: United States. Series 3, No. 19. U. S. Department of Health and Human Services, November 1980.

National Center for Health Statistics. *Monthly Vital Statistics Report.* Annual summary of births, deaths, marriages, and divorces: United States, 1980. September 17, 1981, *29*(13). (a)

National Center for Health Statistics. *Monthly Vital Statistics Report.* Advance report of final natality statistics, 1979. September 29, 1981, *30*(6), Supplement 2. (b)

National Center for Health Statistics. *Monthly Vital Statistics Report.* Advance report of final divorce statistics, 1979. May 29, 1981, *30*(2), Supplement. (c)

National Center for Health Statistics. *Monthly Vital Statistics Report.* Births, marriages, divorce and deaths for 1981. Vol. 30, No. 12, March 18, 1982. (a)

National Center for Health Statistics. *Monthly Vital Statistics Report.* Trends in first birth to older mothers: 1970–1979. Vol. 31, No. 3, Supplement 2, May 27, 1982. (b)

Neal, J. Children's understanding of their parents' divorce. In L. Kurdek (Ed.), Children and divorce. New Directions for Child Development, No. 19. San Francisco: Jossey-Bass, March 1983.

Nelson, D. D. A study of school achievement among adolescent children with working and nonworking mothers. *Journal of Educational Research,* 1969, *62,* 456–457.

Nelson, D. D. A study of personality adjustment among adolescent children with working and nonworking mothers. *Journal of Education Research,* 1971, *64,* 1328–1330.

Nelson, K. Structure and strategy in learning to talk. *Monographs of the Society for Research in Child Development,* 1973, *83* (12, Serial No. 149).

Nesselroade, J. R., & Baltes, P. B. (Eds.). *Longitudinal research in the study of behavioral development.* New York: Academic Press, 1979.

Nichols, I. A., & Schaffer, C. B. *Self concept as a prediction of performance in college women.* Paper presented at the 83rd annual convention of the American Psychological Association, Chicago, September 1975.

Nock, S. L. The family life cycle: Empirical or conceptual tool. *Journal of Marriage and the Family,* 1979, *41,* 15–26.

Noller, P. Sex difference in the socialization of affectionate expression. *Developmental Psychology,* 1978, *14,* 317–319.

Norman-Jackson, J. Family interactions, language development, and primary reading achievement of black children in families of low income. *Child Development,* 1982, *53,* 349–358.

Nortman, D. Parental age as a factor in pregnancy outcome and child development. *Reports on Population/Family Planning,* 1974, XVI, 32.

Nye, F. I. School-age parenthood: Consequences for babies, mothers, fathers, grandparents and others. Cooperative Extension Service Bulletin 667, Washington State University, Pullman, Wash., 1976.

Nye, F. I., & Berardo, F. M. *The family: Its structure and interaction.* New York: Macmillan, 1973.

Nye, F. I., Perry, J. B., & Ogles, R. H. Anxiety and anti-social behavior in preschool children. In F. I. Nye & L. W. Hoffman (Eds.), *The employed mother in America.* Chicago: Rand McNally, 1963.

Nye, I. Child adjustment in broken and in unhappy unbroken homes. *Marriage and Family Living,* 1957, *19,* 365–361.

O'Connor, S., Altemeier, W., Sherrod, K., Sandler, H., & Vietze, P. *Prospective study of non-organic failure to thrive.* Paper presented at the meeting of the Society for Research in Child Development, San Francisco, March 1979.

O'Donnel, W. J. Adolescent self-esteem related to feelings toward parents and friends. *Journal of Youth and Adolescence,* 1976, *5,* 179–185.

Office of Assistant for Planning and Evaluation. *The appropriateness of the Federal Interagency Day Care Requirements (FIDCR): Report on findings and recommendations.* Washington, D.C.: U. S. Department of Health, Education, & Welfare, June 1978.

O'Leary, K., & Emery, R. Marital discord and child behavior problems. In M. Levine & P. Satz (Eds.), *Developmental variation and dysfunction.* New York: Academic Press, 1983.

Olweus, D. Familial and temperamental determinants of aggressive behavior in adolescent boys: A causal analysis. *Developmental Psychology,* 1980, *16,* 644–660.

O'Neill, . *Divorce in the Progressive Era.* New Haven: Yale University Press, 1967.

Orlofsky, J. L., Marcia, J. E., & Lesser, I. M. Ego identity states and the intimacy versus isolation crisis of young adulthood. *Journal of Personality and Social Psychology,* 1973, *27,* 211–219.

Osofsky, J. D., & O'Connell, E. J. Parent-child interaction: Daughters' effects upon mothers' and fathers' behaviors. *Developmental Psychology,* 1972, *7,* 157–168.

Osofsky, J. J., & Osofsky, J. D. Adolescents as mothers. *American Journal of Orthopsychiatry,* 1970, *40,* 825.

Owen, M. T., Chase-Lansdale, P. L., & Lamb, M. E. *Mothers' and fathers' attitudes, maternal employment, and the security of infant-parent attachment.* Unpublished manuscript, University of Michigan, 1981.

Parke, F. Perspectives in father-infant interaction. In J. Osofsky (Ed.), *Handbook of infancy.* New York: Wiley, 1978.

Parke, R. Rules, roles and resistance to deviation in children: Explorations in punishment, discipline and self-control. In A. Pick (Ed.), *Minnesota Symposium on child psychology* (Vol. 8). Minneapolis: University of Minnesota Press, 1974.

Parke, R., & Collmer, C. Child abuse: An interdisciplinary review. In E. M. Hetherington (Ed.), *Review of child development research* (Vol. 5). Chicago: University of Chicago Press, 1975.

Parke, R., Power, T., & Gottman, J. Conceptualizing and quantifying influence patterns in the family triad. In M. Lamb, S. Suomi, & G. Stephenson (Eds.), *Social interaction analysis: Methodological issues.* Madison: University of Wisconsin Press, 1979.

Parsons, J. E., Adler, T. F., & Keczala, C. M. Socialization of achievement attitudes and beliefs: Parental influences. *Child Development,* 1982, *53,* 310–320.

Pastor, D. C. The quality of mother-infant attachment and its relationship to toddler's initial sociability with peers. *Developmental Psychology*, 1981, *17*, 326–335.

Patterson, G. Mothers: The unacknowledged victims. In T. H. Stevens & R. V. Matthews (Eds.), *Mother-child, father-child relations.* Washington, D.C.: National Association for the Education of Young Children, 1978.

Patterson, G., Littman, . & Bricker, W. Assertive behavior in children: Toward a theory of aggression. *Monographs of the Society of Research in Child Development*, 1967, *32*, (5, Serial No. 113).

Patterson, G. R. The aggressive child: Victim and architect of a coercive system. In E. J. Mash, L. Hamerlynck, & L. Handy (Eds.), *Behavior modification and families: Theory and research.* New York: Brunner/Mazel, 1976.

Patterson, G., & Cobb, J. A dyadic analysis of aggressive behavior. In J. Hills (Ed.), *Minnesota Symposium on child psychology* (Vol. 5). Minneapolis: University of Minnesota Press, 1971.

Paul, E. W., Pilpel, H. F., & Wechsler, N. F. Pregnancy, teenagers, and the law, 1976. *Family Planning Perspectives*, 1978, *8*, 16–21.

Payne, D. E., & Mussen, P. H. Parent-child relations and father identification among adolescent boys. *Journal of Abnormal and Social Psychology*, 1956, *52*, 358–362.

Pederssen, A., & colleagues. *Variation in infant experience associated with alternative family roles.* National Institute of Child Health & Human Development. Paper presented at the International Conference on Infant Studies, New Haven, April 1980.

Pedersen, F. *Mother, father and infant as an interactive system.* Paper presented at the annual convention of the American Psychological Association, Chicago, September 1975.

Pedersen, F., Anderson, B., & Cain, L. *An approach to understanding linkages between the parent-infant and spouse relationships.* Paper presented at the biennial meeting of the Society for Research in Child Development, New Orleans, March 1977.

Pedersen, F., Anderson, B., & Cain, L. *Parent-infant interaction observed in a family setting at age five months.* Paper presented at the biennial meeting of the Society for Research in Child Development, San Francisco, March 1979.

Pedersen, F., & Robson, K. Father participation in infancy. *American Journal of Orthopsychiatry*, 1969, *39*, 466–472.

Pedersen, F., Rubenstein, J., & Yarrow, L. Infant development in father-absent families. *Journal of Genetic Psychology*, 1979, *135*, 51–61.

Perkins, R. P., Nakashima, I. I., Mullin, J., Dubansky, L. S., & Chin, M. L. Intensive care in adolescent pregnancy. *Obstetrics and Gynecology*, 1978, *52*, 179.

Petrinovich, L. Probabilistic functionalism: A conception of research method. *American Psychologist*, 1979, *34*, 373–390.

Piaget, J. *The psychology of intelligence.* New York: International Universities Press, 1950.

Piaget, J. The intellectual development of the adolescent. In G. Caplan & S. Lebovici (Eds.). *Adolescence: Psychosocial perspective.* New York: Basic Books, 1969.

Piaget, J. Piaget's theory. In P. H. Mussen (Ed.), *Carmichael's manual of child psychology* (Vol. 1). New York: John Wiley, 1970.

Piaget, J. Intellectual evolution from adolescence to adulthood. *Human Development*, 1972, *15*, 1–12.

Plateris, A. A. Divorces: Analysis of changes, U.S., 1969, Department of Health, Education & Welfare. *Vital and Health Statistics*, Publications No. (HSM) 73–1900. Rockville, Md., 1973.

Pleck, J. H. Men's family work: Three perspectives and some new data. *Family Coordinator*, 1979, *28*, 481–488.

Pleck, J. H., & Rustad, M. *Husbands' and wives' time in family work and paid work in the 1975–76 study of time use.* Unpublished manuscript, Wellesley College, 1980.

Polansky, N., Hally, C., & Polansky, N. *Profile of neglect.* Washington, D.C.: U. S. Department of Health, Education, & Welfare, 1975.

Porter, R., & Laney, M. Attachment theory and the concept of inclusive fitness. *Merrill-Palmer Quarterly*, 1980, *26*, 35–52.

Portnoy, F., & Simmons, C. Day care and attachment. *Child Development*, 1978, *49*, 239–242.

Prescott, E. *A comparison of three types of day care and nursery school-home care.* Paper presented at the biennial meeting of the Society for Research in Child Development, Philadelphia, March 1973.

Price, G. *Factors influencing reciprocity in early mother-infant interaction.* Paper presented at the biennial meeting of the Society for Research in Child Development, New Orleans, March 1977.

Radbill, S. A history of child abuse and infanticide. In R. Helfer & C. Kempe (Eds.), *The battered child* (2nd ed.). Chicago: University of Chicago Press, 1974.

Radin, N. Maternal warmth, achievement motivation and cognitive functioning in lower-class preschool children. *Child Development*, 1971, *42*, 1560–1565.

Radin, N. Father-child interaction and the intellectual functioning of four-year-old boys. *Developmental Psychology*, 1972, 353–361.

Radin, N. Observed paternal behaviors as antecedents of intellectual functioning in young boys. *Developmental Psychology*, 1973, *8*, 369–376.

Radin, N. The role of the father in cognitive, academic and intellectual development. In M. Lamb (Ed.), *The role of the father in child development.* New York: Wiley, 1976.

Radin, N. The role of the father in cognitive, academic, and intellectual development. In M. Lamb (Ed.) *The role of the father in child development.* New York: Wiley, 1981.

Radin, N., & Epstein, A. Observed paternal behavior and the intellectual functioning of preschool boys and girls. Paper presented to the Society for Research in Child Development, Denver, April 1975.

Ralph, J. B., Thomas, A., Chess, S., & Korn, S. J. The influence of nursery school on social interactions. *Journal of Orthopsychiatry*, 1964, *39*, 144–152.

Ramey, C., Dorval, B., & Baker-Ward, W. L. Group day care and socially disadvantaged families: Effects on the child and the family. In S. Kilmer (Ed.), *Advances in early education and day care.* Greenwich, Conn.: JAI Press, 1981.

Ramey, C., MacPhee, D., & Yeats, K. Preventing development retardation: A general systems model. In L. Bond & J. Joffe (Eds.), *Primary Prevention of Psychopathology* (Vol. 6). *Facilitating infant and early childhood development,* Hanover, N.H.: University Press of New England, 1982.

Ramey, C. T., & Finkelstein, N. W. Contingent stimulation and infant competence. *Journal of Pediatric Psychology*, 1978, *3*, 89–96.

Raschke, H. J., & Raschke, V. J. Family conflict and children's self-concepts: A comparison of intact and single parent families. *Journal of Marriage and the Family*, 1979, (May), 367–374.

Rebelsky, F. First discussant's comments: Cross-cultural studies of mother-infant interaction: Description and consequences. *Human Development*, 1972, *15*, 128–130.

Rees, A. N., & Palmer, F. H. Factors related to change in mental performance. *Developmental Psychology Monograph*, 1976, *3*, (2, Part 2).

Rehberg, R. A., & Westby, D. L. Parental encouragement, occupation, education and family size: Artifactual or independent determinants of adolescent educational expectations? *Social Forces*, 1967, *45*, 262–274.

Reichle, J. E., Longhurst, T. M., & Stepanich, L. Verbal interaction in mother-child dyads. *Developmental Psychology*, 1976, *12*, 273–277.

Reidy, T. J. The aggressive characteristics of abused and neglected children. *Journal of Clinical Psychology*, 1977, *33*, 1140–1145.

Repp, A. C., Deitz, D. E. D., Boles, S. M., Deitz, S. M., & Repp, C. F. Differences among common methods for calculating interobserver agreement. *Journal of Applied Behavior Analysis*, 1976, *9*, 109–113.

Ricciuti, H. Fear and development of social attachments in the first year of life. In M. Lewis & L. A. Rosenblum (Eds.), *The origins of human behavior: Fear.* New York: Wiley, 1974.

Ricks, M. The origins of individual differences in quality of attachment to the mother: Infant, maternal and familial variables. Paper presented at the International Conference of Infant Studies, Austin, Texas, March 1982.

Riegel, K. F. Toward a dialectical theory of development. *Human Development*, 1975, *18*, 50–64.

Riegel, K. F. The dialectics of human development. *American Psychologist*, 1976, *31*, 689–700. (a)

Riegel, K. F. From traits and equilibrium toward developmental dialectics. In W. J. Arnold & J. K. Cole (Eds.), *Nebraska symposium on motivation.* Lincoln: University of Nebraska Press, 1976. (b)

Rigsby, L. C., & McDill, E. L. Adolescent peer influence processes: Conceptualization and measurement. *Social Science Research*, 1972, *37*, 189–207.

Riksen-Walraven, J. M. Effects of caregiver behavior on habituation rate and self-efficacy in infants. *International Journal of Behavioral Development*, 1978, 105–130.

Roberts, F., & Miller, B. *Infant behavior effects on the transition to parenthood: A mini-theory.* Paper presented at the Preconference Theory and Methodology Workshop of the National Council on Family Relations, Washington, D.C., October 1978.

Roberts, G. C., Block, J. H., & Block, J. *Continuity and change in parents' child rearing practices.* Paper presented at the meetings of the Society for Research in Child Development, Boston, Mass., April 1981.

Robertson, A. Day care and children's responsiveness to adults. In E. Zigler & E. Gordon (Eds.), *Day care: Scientific and social policy issues.* Boston, Mass.: Auburn House, 1982.

Rohner, R. Parental acceptance-rejection and personality: A universalistic approach to behavioral science. In R. Brislin et al. (Eds.), *Cross-cultural perspectives on learning.* New York: Halsted Press, 1975.

Rollins, B., & Gannon, K. Marital satisfaction over the family life cycle: A reevaluation. *Journal of Marriage and the Family*, 1974, *36*, 271–282.

Rollins, B., & Feldman, H. Marital satisfaction over the family life cycle. *Journal of Marriage and the Family*, 1968, *30*, 26–39.

Rollins, B., & Gallinger, R. The developing child and marital satisfaction. In R. Lerner & G. Spanier (Eds.), *Child influences on marital interaction: A life-span perspective.* New York: Academic Press, 1979.

Rollins, B. C., & Galligan, R. The developing child and marital satisfaction of parents. In R. M. Lerner & G. B. Spanier (Eds.), *Child influences on marital and family interaction: A life-span perspective.* New York: Academic Press, 1978.

Romer, N., & Cherry, D. *Developmental effects of preschool and school age maternal employment on children's sex role concepts.* Unpublished manuscript, Brooklyn College, 1978.

Roopnarine, J., & Lamb, M. Peer and parent-child interaction before and after enrollment in nursery school. *Journal of Applied Developmental Psychology,* 1980, *1,* 77–81.

Rosen, B. C., & D'Andrade, R. The psychological origins of achievement motivation. *Sociometry,* 1959, *22,* 185–218.

Ross, G., Kagan, J., Zelazo, P., & Kotelchuck, M. Separation protest in infants and home and laboratory. *Developmental Psychology,* 1975, *11,* 256–257.

Rouman, J. School children's problems as related to parental factors. *Journal of Educational Research,* 1956, *50,* 105–112.

Rubenstein, J. Maternal attentiveness and subsequent exploratory behavior in the infant. *Child Development,* 1967, *38,* 1089–1100.

Rubenstein, J. L., & Howes, C. Caregiving and infant behavior in day care and in homes. *Developmental Psychology,* 1979, *15,* 1–24.

Rubin, J. Z., Provenzano, F. J., & Luria, Z. The eye of the beholder: Parents' views on sex of newborns. *American Journal of Orthopsychiatry,* 1974, *44,* 512–519.

Ruddy, M., & Bornstein, M. Cognitive correlates of infant attention and maternal stimulation over the first year of life. *Child Development,* 1982, *53,* 183–188.

Ruopp, R. R., & Travers, J. Janus-faced day care: Perspectives on quality and cost. In E. F. Zigler & E. W. Gordon (Eds.), *Day care: Scientific and social policy issues.* Boston: Auburn House, 1982.

Russell, C. Transition to parenthood: Problems and gratifications. *Journal of Marriage and the Family,* 1974, *36,* 294–301.

Rutter, M. Parent-child separation: Psychological effects on the children. *Journal of Child Psychology and Psychiatry,* 1971, *13,* 233–260.

Rutter, M. Protective factors in children's responses to stress and disadvantage. In M. W. Kent & J. E. Rolf (Eds.), *Primary prevention of psychopathology* (Vol. 3). *Promoting social competence and coping in children.* Hanover, N.H.: University Press of New England, 1979.

Ryder, N. B., & Westoff, C. F. Wanted and unwanted fertility in the United States: 1965–1970. In C. F. Westoff & R. Parke, Jr. (Eds.), *Demographic and social aspects of population growth* (Vol. 1). Commission on Population Growth and the American Future, Government Printing Office, 1972.

Ryder, R. Longitudinal data relating marital satisfaction and having a child. *Journal of Marriage and the Family,* 1973, *35,* 604–607.

Sahlins, M. D. The use and abuse of biology. In A. L. Caplan (Ed.), *The sociobiology debate.* New York: Harper and Row, 1978.

Sameroff, A. Transactional models of early social relations. *Human Development,* 1975, *18,* 65–79.

Sameroff, A. J., & Chandler, M. J. Reproduction risk and the continuum of caretaking causality. In S. Scarr-Schapatek & G. Siegal (Eds.), *Review of child development research* (Vol. 4). Chicago: University of Chicago Press, 1975.

Sandberg, E. C., & Jacobs, R. I. Psychology of the misuse and rejection of contraception. *Medical Aspects of Human Sexuality,* 1972, *6,* 34–70.

Sanford, N. Developmental status of the entering freshman. In N. Sanford (Ed.), *The American college.* New York: Wiley, 1962.

Santrock, J. & Warshak, R. Father custody and social development in boys and girls. *Journal of Social Issues,* 1979, *35,* 112–125.

Santrock, J., Warshak, R., & Elliot, G. Social development and parent-child interaction in father-custody and stepmother families. In M. Lamb (Ed.), *Nontraditional families.* Hillsdale, N.J.: Lawrence Erlbaum, 1982.

Santrock, J. W. Influence of onset and type of paternal absence on the first four Eriksonian developmental crisis. *Developmental Psychology,* 1970, *3,* 273–274.

Santrock, J. W. Relation of type and onset of father-absence of cognitive development. *Child Development,* 1972, *43,* 455–469.

Santrock, J. W., Warshak, R., Lindbergh, C., & Meadows, L. Children's and parent's observed social behavior in stepfather families. *Child Development,* 1982, *53,* 472–480.

Sarbin, T. B. Contextualism: A world view for modern psychology. In J. K. Cole (Ed.), *Nebraska Symposium on Motivation, 1976.* Lincoln, Nebr.: University of Nebraska Press, 1977.

Scarr-Salapatek, S. An evolutionary perspective on infant intelligence: Species patterns and individual variations. In M. Lewis (Ed.), *Origins of intelligence.* New York: Plenum, 1976.

Schneirla, T. C. The concept of development in comparative psychology. In D. B. Harris (Ed.), *The concept of development.* Minneapolis: University of Minnesota Press, 1957.

Schwarz, J., et al. Infant day care: Behavioral effect at preschool age. *Developmental Psychology,* 1974, *10,* 502–506.

Schwarz, J. C., Scarr, S. W., Caparulo, B., Furrow, D., McCartney, K., Billington, R., Phillips, D., & Hindy, C. *Center, sitter, and home day care before age two: A report on the first Bermuda infant care study.* Paper presented at the American Psychological Association Annual Convention in Los Angeles, August 1981.

Sears, R. R. Relation of early socialization experience to self-concepts and gender role in middle childhood. *Child Development,* 1970, *41,* 267–290.

Sears, R. R., Maccoby, E. E., & Levin, H. *Patterns of child rearing.* New York: Harper & Row, 1957.

Shah, F., Zelnick, M., & Kantner, J. F. Unprotected intercourse among unwed teenagers. *Family Planning Perspectives,* 1975, *7,* 39–43.

Shaw, M. E., & White, D. L. The relationship between child-parent identification and academic under-achievement. *Journal of Clinical Psychology,* 1965, *21,* 10–13.

Shelton, J. D. Very young adolescent women in Georgia: Has abortion or contraception lowered their fertility. *American Journal of Public Health,* 1977, *67,* 616.

Shelton, L. G., & Gladstone, T. *Childbearing in adolescence.* Paper presented at the American Orthopsychiatric Association, Washington, D.C., April 4, 1979.

Shere, M. Social-emotional factors with families of twins with cerebral palsy. *Exceptional Children,* 1955, *22,* 197–199.

Shinn, M. Father absence and children's cognitive development. *Psychology Bulletin,* 1977, *85,* 295–324.

Sibbison, V. H. The influence of maternal role perceptions on attitudes toward and utilization of early child care services. In D. Peters (Ed.), *A summary of the Pennsylvania Day Care study.* University Park: The Pennsylvania State University, 1973.

Sidell, R. *Women and child care in China.* New York: Hill & Wang, 1972.

Siegel, A. E., Stolz, L. M., Hitchcock, E. A., & Adamson, J. Dependence and independence in children. In F. I. Nye & L. W. Hoffman (Eds.), *The employed mother in America.* Chicago: Rand McNally, 1963.

Smith, T. E. Push versus pull: Intrafamily versus peer-group variables as possible determinants of adolescent orientations towards parents. *Youth and Society*, 1976, *8*, 5–26.

Sollie, D. L., & Miller, B. C. The transition to parenthood as a critical time for building family strengths. In N. Stinnett, B. Chesser, J. Defain, & P. Kraul (Eds.), *Family strengths: Positive models of family life*. Lincoln: University of Nebraska Press, 1980.

Solomon, D. The generality of children's achievement-related behavior. *Journal of Genetic Psychology*, 1969, *114*, 109–125.

Solomon, J. *Marital intimacy and parent-infant relationships*. Unpublished doctoral dissertation. University of California, Berkeley, 1982.

Spanier, G. B. *Sexual socialization and premarital sexual behavior: An empirical investigation of the impact of formal and informal sex education*. Unpublished doctoral dissertation, Northwestern University, 1973.

Spanier, G. B. Measuring dyadic adjustment: New scales for assessing the quality of marriage and similar dyads. *Journal of Marriage and the Family*, 1976, *38*, 15–28.

Spanier, G. B., & Casto, R. F. Adjustment to separation and divorce: A qualitative analysis. In G. Levinger & O. Moles (Eds.), *Divorce and separation: Context, causes, and consequences*. New York: Basic Books, 1979.

Spanier, G. B., & Glick, P. C. Marital instability in the United States: Some correlates and recent changes. *Family Relations*, 1981, *31*, 329–338.

Spanier, G. B., Lewis, R. A., & Cole, C. L. Marital adjustment over the family life cycle: The issue of curvilinearity. *Journal of Marriage and the Family*, 1975, *37*, 263–275.

Spanier, G. B., Sauer, W., & Larzelere, R. An empirical evaluation of the family life cycle. *Journal of Marriage and the Family*, 1979, *41*, 27–38.

Spelke, E., Zelazo, P., Kagan, J., & Kotelchuck, M. Father interaction and separation protest. *Developmental Psychology*, 1973, *9*, 83–90.

Spinetta, J., & Rigler, D. The child-abusing parent: A psychological review. *Psychological Bulletin*, 1972, *77*, 296–304.

Spitz, R. A. Hospitalism: An inquiry into the genesis of psychiatric conditions in early childhood. *Psychoanalytic Study of the Child*, 1945, *1*, 53–74.

Sroufe, C. The coherence of individual development. *American Psychologist*, 1979, *34*, 834–841.

Stallings, J., & Porter, A. *National day care home study: Observation component*. Draft final report of the Day Care Division, Administration for Children, Youth, & Families, DHEW, April 1980.

Stayton, D. J., & Ainsworth, M. D. S. Individual differences in infant responses to brief, everyday separations as related to other infant and maternal behavior. *Developmental Psychology*, 1973, *9*, 226–235.

Stayton, D. J., Ainsworth, M. D. S., & Main, M. B. The development of separation behavior in the first year of life: Protest following and greeting. *Developmental Psychology*, 1973, *9*, 213–225.

Stayton, D. J., Hogan, R., & Ainsworth, M. D. S. Infant obedience and maternal behavior: The origins of socialization reconsidered. *Child Development*, 1971, *42*, 1057–1069.

Steele, B. F., & Pollack, D. A. A psychiatric study of parents who abuse infants and small children. In R. E. Heller & C. H. Kempe (Eds.), *The battered child*. Chicago: University of Chicago Press, 1968.

Stein, A. H. The effects of maternal employment and educational attainment on the sex-typed attributes of college females. *Social Behavior and Personality*, 1973, *1*, 111–114.

Steinberg, L. Transformation in family relations at puberty. *Developmental Psychology*, 1981, *17*, 833–840.

Steinberg, L. D., Greenberger, E., Garduque, L., Ruggiero, M., & Vauz, A. Effects of working on adolescent development. *Developmental Psychology*, 1982, *18*, 385–395.

Steinberg, L. D., & Hill, I. P. Patterns of family interactions as a function of age, the onset of puberty, and formal thinking. *Developmental Psychology*, 1978, *14*, 683–684.

Steinmetz, S. The use of force for resolving family conflict: The training ground for abuse. *Family Coordinator*, 1977. *26*, 19–26.

Stickle, G. *Perinatal health challenge to medicine and society*. White Plains, N.Y.; The National Foundation/March of Dimes, 1974.

Stickle, G., & Ma, P. Pregnancy in adolescence: Scope of the problem. *Contemporary Ob/Gyn*, 1975, *5*, 85.

Stone, L., Smith, H., & Murphy, B. *The competent infant: Research and commentary*. New York: Basic Books, 1973.

Straus, M. Cultural and social organizational influences on violence between family members. In R. Prince & D. Barrier (Eds.), *Configurations: Biological and cultural factors in sexuality and family life*. Lexington, Mass.: Lexington Books, 1974.

Strauss, M. A. Family patterns and child abuse in a nationally representative American sample. *Child abuse and neglect*, 1979, *3*, 213–225.

Strauss, M. A., Gelles, R. J., & Steinmetz, S. K. *Behind closed doors: Violence in the American family*. New York: Anchor Press, 1980.

Stuckey, M., McGhee, P., & Bell, N. Parent-child interaction: The influence of maternal employment. *Developmental Psychology*, 1982, *4*, 635–644.

Super, C. M., & Harkness, S. Figure, ground, and Gestalt: The cultural context of the active individual. In R. M. Lerner & N. A. Busch-Rossnagel (Eds.), *Individuals as producers of their development: A life-span perspective*. New York: Academic Press, 1981.

Swift, D. F. Family environment and 11 + success: Some basic predictions. *British Journal of Educational Psychology*, 1967, *37*, 10–21.

Switzky, L., Vietze, P., & Switzky, H. *Attitudinal and demographic predictors of breast-feeding and bottle-feeding behavior in mothers of six-week-old infants*. Unpublished manuscript, George Peabody College, 1974.

Tangri, S. S. *Role innovation in occupational choice. Unpublished doctoral dissertation*, University of Michigan, 1969.

Tangri, S. S. Determinants of occupational role innovation among college women. *Journal of Social Issues*, 1972, *28*, 177–200.

Thomas, A., & Chess, S. *Temperament and development*. New York: Brunner/Mazel, 1977.

Thomas, A., & Chess, S. *The dynamics of psychosocial development*. New York: Brunner/Mazel, 1980.

Thomas, A., & Chess, S. Temperament. In R. M. Lerner & N. A. Busch-Rossnagel (Eds.), *Individuals as producers of their own environment: A life-span perspective*. New York: Academic Press, 1981.

Thomas, A., Chess, S., & Birch, H. G. *Temperament and behavior disorders in children*. New York: New York University Press, 1968.

Thomas, A., Chess, S., Sillan, J., & Mendez, O. Cross-cultural study of behavior in children with special vulnerabilities to stress. In D. F. Ricks, A. Thomas, & M. Roff (Eds.), *Life history research in psychopathology*. Minneapolis: University of Minnesota Press, 1974.

Thompson, R. A., & Lamb, M. E. Individual differences in dimensions of socioemotional development in infancy. In R. Plutchik & H. Kellerman (Eds.), *Emotion: Theory, research and experience* (Vol. 2). *Emotions in early development*. New York: Academic Press, 1981.

Tobach, E., & Schneirla, T. C. The biopsychology of social behavior of animals. In R. E. Cooke & S. Levin (Eds.), *Biologic basic of pediatric practice*. New York: McGraw-Hill, 1968.

Touke, S. *Adjustment to parenthood among a select group of disadvantaged parents*. Unpublished master's thesis, Montana State University, 1974.

Travers, J. & Ruopp, R. *National Day Care Study: Preliminary Findings and Their Implications:* 31 January, 1978. Cambridge, Mass.: Alot Associates, 1978.

Tulkin, S., & Covitz, F. *Mother-infant interactions and intellectual functioning at age six*. Paper presented at the biennial meeting of the Society of Research in Child Development, Denver, April 1975.

Tulkin, S. R., & Kagan, J. Mother-child interaction in the first year of life. *Child Development*, 1972, *43*, 31–41.

Uhlenberg, B. *Crisis factors in transition of college students to parenthood*. Unpublished master's thesis, Ohio State University, 1970.

U.S. Bureau of the Census. Characteristics of American youth: 1974. *Current Population Reports*, Series P-23, No. 51, April 1975. Washington, D.C.: U.S. Government Printing Office.

U.S. Bureau of the Census. Number, timing, and duration of marriages and divorces in the United States. *Current Population Reports*, Series P-20, No. 297. Washington, D.C.: U.S. Government Printing Office, 1976.

U.S. Bureau of the Census. *Statistical abstract of the United States: 1978* (99th ed.), Washington, D.C., 1978.

U.S. Bureau of the Census, Series P-20, No. 352. Household and family characteristics: March 1979. *Current Population Reports*. Washington, D.C.: Government Printing Office, July 1980.

U.S. Bureau of the Census. *Statistical Abstract of the United States: 1981* (102nd ed.). Washington, D.C.: U.S. Government Printing Office.

U.S. Bureau of the Census. Household and family characteristics: March 1981. *Current Population Reports*, Series P.20, No. 371, Washington, D.C.: U.S. Government Printing Office, 1982.

U.S. Bureau of the Census. Fertility of American women: June 1981. *Current Population Reports*, Series P-20, No. 378. Washington, D.C.: U.S. Government Printing Office, 1983.

U.S. Department of Agriculture. *USDA Estimates of the Cost of Raising a Child: A Guide to Their Use and Interpretation*. Publication 1411, 1981.

Vaughn, B., Crichton, L., & Egeland, B. Individual differences in qualities of caregiving during the first six months of life: Antecedents in maternal and infant behavior during the newborn period. *Infant Behavior and Development*, 1982, *5*, 77–96.

Vaughn, B., Gove, F., & Egeland, B. The relationship between out-of-home care and the quality of infant-mother attachment in an economically disadvantaged population. *Child Development*, 1980, in press.

Viano, E. *Attitudes toward child abuse among American professionals*. Paper presented at the meeting of the International Society for Research on Aggression, Toronto, Canada, 1974.

Vincent, J. P., Cook-Illback, N., & Messerly, L. A social learning analysis of couples during the second postnatal month. *American Journal of Family Therapy*, 1980.

Vincent, P., Cook, N., Brady, C., Harris, G., & Messerly, L. *Learning to be a family: Struggle of the emergent triad*. Symposium presented at the biennial meeting of the Society for Research in Child Development, San Francisco, March 1979.

Wachs, T. Utilization of a Piagetian approach in the investigation of early experience effects: A research strategy and some illustrative data. *Merrill-Palmer Quarterly*, 1976, *22*, 11–30.

Wachs, T., Uzgiris, I., & Hunt, J. Cognitive development in infants of different age levels and from different environmental backgrounds: An exploratory investigation. *Merrill-Palmer Quarterly*, 1971, *17*, 283–317.

Wainwright, W. Fatherhood as a precipitant of mental illness. *American Journal of Psychiatry*, 1966, *123*, 40–44.

Waite, L. U.S. women at work. *Population Bulletin*, 1981, *36*(2).

Waite, L., & Moore, K. *Marital dissolution, early marriage, and early childbearing: Evidence from the National Longitudinal Survey of Young Women.* Paper accepted for presentation at the 1978 meetings of the American Sociological Association. Washington, D.C.: The Urban Institute, 1977.

Waldron, H., & Routh, D. The effect of the first child on the marital relationship. *Journal of Marriage and the Family*, 1981, *43*, 785–788.

Walker, K. E. How much help for working mothers? The children's role. *Home Ecology Forum*, 1970, *1*, 13–15. (a)

Walker, K. E. *Time-use patterns for household work related to homemakers employment.* Unpublished manuscript, Cornell University, 1970. (b)

Wallerstein, J., & Kelly, J. The effects of parental divorce: Experiences of preschool child. *Journal of the American Academy of Child Psychiatry*, 1975, *14*, 600–616.

Wallerstein, J. S., & Kelly, J. B. The effects of parental divorce: The adolescent experience. In J. Anthony & C. Koupernik (Eds.), *The child in his family: Children at psychiatric risk.* New York: Wiley, 1974.

Wallerstein, J. S., & Kelly, J. B. *Solving the breakup: How children and parents cope with divorce.* New York: Basic Books, 1980.

Walters, J., & Stinnett, N. Parent-child relationships: A decade review of research. *Journal of Marriage and the Family*, 1971, *33*, 70–111.

Wandersman, L. P. The adjustment of fathers to their first baby: The roles of parenting groups and marital relationships. *Birth and the Family Journal*, 1980, *30*, 155–161.

Warshak, J., & Santrock, J. The impact of divorce in father-custody and mother-custody homes: The child's perspective. In L. Kurdek (Ed.), *Children and divorce.* New Directions for Child Development, No. 19. San Francisco: Jossey-Bass, March 1983.

Washburn, S. L. (Ed.). *Social life of early men.* New York: Wenner-Gren Foundation, 1961.

Waterman, A. S., & Goldman, J. A. A longitudinal study of ego identity development at a liberal arts college. *Journal of Youth and Adolescence*, 1976, *5*, 361–370.

Waterman, A. S., & Waterman, C. K. A longitudinal study of changes in ego identity status during the freshman year at college. *Developmental Psychology*, 1971, *5*, 167–173.

Waterman, G., Geary, P., & Waterman, C. K. Longitudinal study of changes in ego identity status from the freshman to the senior year at college. *Developmental Psychology*, 1974, *10*, 387–392.

Waters, E., Vaughn, B. E., & Egeland, B. R. Individual differences in infant-mother attachment relationships at age one: Antecedents in neonatal behavior in an urban, economically disadvantaged sample. *Child Development*, 1980, *51*, 208–216.

Waters, E., Wippman, J., & Sroufe, L. A. Attachment, positive affect, and competence in the peer group: Two studies in construct validation. *Child Development,* 1979, *50,* 821–829.

Watson, J. S., & Ramey, C. T. Reactions to response contingent stimulation in early infant. *Merrill-Palmer Quarterly,* 1972, *18,* 219–227.

Weinstock, A., & Lerner, R. M. Attitudes of late adolescents and their parents toward contemporary issues. *Psychological Reports,* 1972, *30,* 239–244.

Weiss, R. S. *Marital separation: Coping with the end of marriage and the transition to being single again.* New York: Basic Books, 1975.

Westinghouse Learning Corp. & Westat Research, Inc. *Day care survey—1970: Summary report and basic analysis.* Washington, D.C.: Office of Economic Opportunity, 1971.

Whiteman, M., & Deutsch, M. Social disadvantage as related to intellective and language development. In M. Deutsch, I. Katz, & A. R. Jensen (Eds.), *Social class, race and psychological development.* New York: Holt, Rinehart & Winston, 1968.

Willems, E. P. Behavioral ecology and experimental analysis: Courtship is not enough. In J. R. Nesselroade & H. W. Reese (Eds.), *Life-span developmental psychology: Methodological issues.* New York: Academic Press, 1973.

Winch, R. *The modern family* (3rd ed.). New York: Holt, Rinehart & Winston, 1971.

Winch, R. Theorizing about the family. In R. F. Winch & G. B. Spanier (Eds.) *Selected Studies in Marriage and the Family* (4th ed.). New York: Holt, Rinehart, and Winston, 1974.

Wolf, R. M. The identification and measurement of environmental process variables related to intelligence. Unpublished doctoral dissertation, University of Chicago, 1964.

Woods, M. B. The unsupervised child of the working mother. *Developmental Psychology,* 1972, *6,* 14–25.

Yarrow, L., Goodwin, M., Manheimer, H., & Milowe, I. Infancy experiences and cognitive and personality development at ten years. In L. Stone, L. Murphy, & H. Smith (Eds.), *The competent infant.* New York: Basic Books, 1973.

Yarrow, L., Klein, R., Lomonaco, S., & Morgan, G. Cognitive and motivational development in early childhood. In B. Friedlander, G. Sterritt, & G. Kirk (Eds.), *The exceptional infant* (Vol. 3). *Assessment and intervention.* New York: Brunner/Mazel, 1975.

Yarrow, L. J., Rubenstein, J. L., & Pedersen, F. A. *Infant and environment: Early cognitive and motivational development.* New York: Halsted Press, Wiley, 1975.

Yarrow, M. R. Maternal employment and child rearing. *Children,* 1961, *8,* 223–228.

Yarrow, M. R., Scott, P., deLelver, L., & Heinig, C. Child rearing in families of working and non-working mothers. *Sociometry,* 1962, *25,* 122–140.

Young, L. *Wednesday's children: A study of child neglect and abuse.* New York: McGraw-Hill, 1964.

Zelnick, M., & Kanter, J. F. Sexual and contraceptive experience of young unmarried women in the United States, 1976 and 1971. *Family Planning Perspective,* 1977, *9,* 55.

Zelnick, M., & Kantner, J. F. Contraceptive patterns and premarital pregnancy among women aged 15–19 in 1976. *Family Planning Perspective,* 1978, *10,* 11. (a).

Zelnick, M., & Kantner, J. F. Contraceptive patterns and premarital pregnancy among women aged 15–19 in 1976. *Family Planning Perspective,* 1978, *10,* 135–142. (b)

Zelnick, M., & Kantner, J. F. Sexual activity, contraceptive use, and pregnancy among metropolitan area teenagers: 1971–1979. *Family Planning Perspective*, 1978, *12*, 230–237. (c)

Zigler, E. Supreme Court on spanking: Upholding discipline or abuse? *Society for Research in Child Development Newsletter*, Fall 1977.

Zigler, E. Controlling child abuse in America: An effort doomed to failure. In R. Bourne & E. Newberger (Eds.), *Critical perspectives on child abuse.* Lexington, Mass.: D.C. Heath, 1978.

Zigler, E., Abelson, W. D., Trickett, P. K., & Seitz, V. Is an intervention program necessary in order to improve economically disadvantaged children's IQ scores? *Child Development*, 1981, *53*, 340–348.

Zill, N. *Divorce, marital happiness, and the mental health of children: Findings from the Foundation for Child Development: National survey of children.* Paper presented at NIMH Workshop on Divorce and Children, Bethesda, Md., February 7–8, 1978.

Zur-Spiro, S., & Longfellow, C. *Support from fathers: Implications for the well-being of mothers and their children.* Paper presented at the biennial meeting of the Society for Research in Child Development, Boston, April 1981.

Zussman, J. V. Relationship of demographic factors to parental discipline techniques. *Developmental Psychology*, 1978, *14*, 685–686.

Index

SUBJECT